LONGMAN STUDY GUIDES

GCSE
Information
Technology

Roger Crawford

LONGMAN

LONGMAN STUDY GUIDES

SERIES EDITORS: **Geoff Black and Stuart Wall**

Titles available

Biology
Business Studies
Chemistry
Design and Technology
Economics
English
English Literature
French
Geography
German
Information Technology

Mathematics
Mathematics: Higher Level
Music
Physical Education
Physics
Psychology
Religious Studies
Science
Sociology
Spanish
World History

Pearson Education Limited
Edinburgh Gate, Harlow,
Essex CM20 2JE, UK
and Associated Companies throughout the world.

© Addison Wesley Longman Limited 1997

First published 1994
Second edition 1997
Second impression 1999

British Library Cataloguing-in-Publication Data
A catalogue record for this book is
available from the British Library

ISBN 0 582 30494 6

Set by 30 in 9.75/12pt Sabon
Produced by Pearson Education Asia Pte Ltd
Printed in Singapore (COS)

▷ CONTENTS

EDITORS' PREFACE

Longman Study Guides have been written by the people who set and mark the exams – the examiners. Examiners are aware that, due to lack of practice and poor preparation, some students achieve only the lowest grades: they are not able effectively to show the examiner what they know. These books give excellent advice about exam practice and preparation, and organizing a structured revision programme, all of which are essential for examination success. Remember: the examiners are looking for opportunities to *give* you marks, not take them away!

Longman Study Guides are designed to be used throughout the course. The self-contained chapters can be read in any order appropriate to the stage you have reached in your course. The examiner guides you through the essential parts of each topic, making helpful comments throughout.

We believe that this book, and the series as a whole, will help you establish and build your basic knowledge and examination technique skills. For additional help with exam practice and revision techniques, there is a companion series available called **Longman Exam Practice Kits**, which are available from all good bookshops, or direct from Addison Wesley Longman.

GEOFF BLACK AND STUART WALL

AUTHOR'S PREFACE

Throughout this book the emphasis is on understanding how Information Technology is used. The chapters are arranged in a fairly logical order but it is not necessary to study them in the sequence in which they appear. Each chapter is self-contained and can be studied independently of the other chapters. There is a glossary of jargon in Chapter 3 that should help explain unfamiliar technical words.

In writing this book I have valued the help and advice given to me both directly and indirectly. I especially thank Stuart Wall and Geoff Black for their editorial advice and assistance. I am grateful to colleagues at Rhodesway Upper School and at Queensbury School for their help and assistance while I was employed at each school. I am also grateful for the help and assistance given to me by the School of Education at the University of Huddersfield where I am now employed as a Senior Lecturer in Information Technology in Education. My wife, Jennie, has patiently tolerated the long hours I have spent at the wordprocessor. Without the support of colleagues, friends and family this book would not have been written.

ROGER CRAWFORD

This book has been written as a course companion for use throughout your GCSE course in Information Technology. The first chapter focuses on examination requirements, including details about the aims of a GCSE in Information Technology, assessment, grade descriptions, how to get the best grade and how to prepare for examinations. The second chapter gives details about the requirements of individual examining boards. You should read these first two chapters carefully as they give invaluable advice which will be useful throughout your Information Technology course.

Each of the remaining chapters, 3 to 14, deals with key topic areas covered by the examining boards. Each chapter starts with a **Getting Started** section which is an introduction to the chapter. This includes a **Topic Chart** (see below): a table which, at a glance, shows which parts of the chapter are relevant to a particular examining board's requirements. You should use this to identify whether topics in a specific chapter are covered by your examining board. The chart can also be used to check your study and revision progress over the two years. The central column details the main topics in the book, these headings can be found in the left-hand margin in the 'What you need to know' part of the chapter. To the left of the chart, the examining boards are listed and you will be able to identify whether a particular topic is part of your syllabus. Use the right-hand side of the chart to track your study and revision of each topic throughout your course.

C & G	LONDON	MEG	NDTEF	NEAB	RSA	SEG	WJEC	TOPIC		STUDY	REVISION 1	REVISION 2
✓	✓	✓	✓	✓	✓	✓	✓	Monitors				
✓	✓	✓	✓	✓	✓	✓	✓	Printers				
✓	✓						✓	Computer output on microfilm				
✓	✓	✓	✓	✓	✓	✓	✓	Graph plotters				
✓	✓	✓	✓	✓	✓	✓	✓	Speech synthesis				
✓	✓	✓	✓	✓	✓	✓	✓	Actuators				

You will see that if your syllabus has been set by the Northern Examinations and Assessment Board (NEAB) you will not need to study the topic 'Computer output on microfilm' in Chapter 6 as it is not a topic covered in the NEAB syllabus. On the Getting Started page there is also a chapter glossary giving you key words and their definitions that have been used in that particular chapter. For a general glossary of technical terms turn to page 27 in Chapter 3.

Each topic listed in the Topic Chart is then explained in the **What You Need to Know** section – the core of the chapter. To help you practice what you have just learnt, there are then a series of **Examination Questions** with answers. Do not look at the answers until you have attempted to answer the questions yourself. There is then a further question with a student's answer which is annotated with examiner comments. In some chapters the student's answer may be an example of an A grade answer, but we have also tried to show examples of weaker answers where the examiner has then pointed out faults or problems with the way the student has approached the question. These student answers should help you to see how you could improve your own answers.

At the end of each chapter there is a **Summary Box** which briefly identifies the key points about topics covered in the chapter. You should check that you know, and understand more fully, each of the key points listed.

► **ACKNOWLEDGMENTS**

The following organizations have kindly given their permission to use material they have provided for illustrations or to refer to their products.

Apple Computers UK Ltd
Amstrad plc
Barclays Bank plc
Camelot Group plc
Computer Associates plc
Digital Integration Ltd (image from Digital Integration's 'Hind' helicopter simulation, 'Hind' is a registered trade mark)
IBM UK Ltd
The Data Consultancy on behalf of the URPI Group Ltd,
Microsoft Inc.
The University of Huddersfield
Lloyds TSB Group Plc
Valiant Technology Ltd

The following GCSE examination boards have given permission for questions from their sample papers to be used at the end of each chapter. The answers given are the author's, except for Midland Examination Group questions, where answers were provided. The questions may not indicate the format and content of future examination papers.

C & G
London
MEG
NDTEF
NEAB
RSA
SEG
WJEC

Examinations and assessment

GETTING STARTED

GCSE Information Technology (IT) should be an enjoyable and worthwhile experience. To get the most out of your course and to get the best possible grade it is important to understand what will be expected of you. Chapter 2 looks in detail at the contents of the different syllabuses offered by the examining boards in England and Wales. This chapter introduces the main objectives of GCSE Information Technology and how it is examined.

Assessment is based on your performance in coursework and written examinations. You will be awarded one of grades A* to G, where A* is the highest grade.

The grade you are awarded is based on your work in coursework and the examination. This may be an underestimation of your real ability. Your performance may be improved by better preparation, planning and presentation. Work steadily and plan ahead to meet deadlines. You should start your coursework as soon as possible. Present your work in an attractive manner using IT where possible. Illustrate your work with pictures, diagrams, flowcharts, etc. Prior to the written examinations revise all your work thoroughly, condense and learn it. On the day of the written examinations make sure you are alert and well-prepared. Arrive early. During the examination, use your time effectively, write neatly and express yourself clearly. If you finish early, check your work. Never leave before the end of the examination.

GLOSSARY

Coursework	The projects you do in class that are for GCSE assessment. These will probably be done in years 10 and 11.
Grade description	Grade descriptions are general descriptions in broad terms of what a GCSE candidate of a particular grade should be able to achieve.
Syllabus	A syllabus states exactly what you should study and how your knowledge, skills and understanding will be assessed.
Written examinations	The written papers that are sat at the end of year 11.

C & G	LONDON	MEG	NDTEF	NEAB	RSA	SEG	WJEC	TOPIC	STUDY	REVISION I	REVISION 2
✓	✓	✓	✓	✓	✓	✓	✓	Aims			
✓	✓	✓	✓	✓	✓	✓	✓	Assessment objectives			
✓	✓	✓	✓	✓	✓	✓	✓	The two themes of IT			
✓	✓	✓	✓	✓	✓	✓	✓	Software			
✓	✓	✓	✓	✓	✓	✓	✓	Hardware			
✓	✓	✓	✓	✓	✓	✓	✓	Assessment			
✓	✓	✓	✓	✓	✓	✓	✓	Grade descriptions			
✓	✓	✓	✓	✓	✓	✓	✓	Getting the best grade			

WHAT YOU NEED TO KNOW

▷ **Aims**   A course in IT should encourage your interest in IT, and help you develop your skills, knowledge and understanding of IT. You should become confident and expert in using IT. You should acquire a broad understanding of a wide range of applications of IT, and understand what IT can and cannot do, and the impact of using IT.

You should have the opportunity to use IT as a problem-solving tool. The problems you solve could be drawn from a variety of contexts. These could be:

▶ at home or at school;
▶ for recreation or other applications in the community;
▶ in business, in commerce or in industry.

▷ **Assessment objectives**   You will be assessed on your ability to:

▶ apply your knowledge, skills and understanding of IT in a wide range of situations;
▶ understand how and when IT can be used;
▶ build IT systems for use by yourself and others;
▶ think critically about the effects of using IT;
▶ discuss the moral, legal, ethical, social and personal issues that arise when IT systems are used.

▷ **The two themes of IT**   You will be expected to show that your knowledge, skills and understanding cover the two themes of IT. These are described in detail in the National Curriculum subject orders for IT. They are:

▶ communicating and handling information;
▶ controlling, measuring and modelling.

All GCSE IT syllabuses cover these two themes.

▷ **Software**   You will need to be able to understand and use most of this software:

▶ a graphic user interface;
▶ a wordprocessor;
▶ graphics (paint and draw) software;
▶ desk top publishing (DTP) software;
▶ a database;
▶ a spreadsheet;
▶ modelling or simulation software;
▶ teletext or on-line information services;
▶ control software;
▶ data logging software;
▶ communications software, especially electronic mail;
▶ a programming language;
▶ computer assisted learning (CAL) software.

▷ **Hardware**   You will need to be able to understand the function and use of most of this hardware:

▶ a personal computer, e.g. a desk top computer;
▶ input devices, e.g. a keyboard;
▶ different types of memory, e.g. RAM and ROM;
▶ backing storage devices, e.g. a floppy disk;
▶ output devices, e.g. a printer;
▶ networks.

▷ **Assessment**   Assessment is based on a combination of written papers and coursework. The emphasis of assessment is always on what you can do, not on what you cannot do. You will be given marks for what you do well. It is unlikely that marks will be deducted for what you do incorrectly.

You will be entered for assessment in one of two tiers. The tier you are entered for is determined by your attainment and ability. The tiers are:

- the Foundation tier (grades C to G);
- the Higher tier (grades A* to D).

You can only be awarded the range of grades available in the tier that you are entered for.

Sixty per cent of GCSE IT assessment is based on coursework, and 40 per cent is based on written papers. The coursework will be done throughout the course, possibly as a part of the learning process. The written papers are usually taken at the end of the course.

Coursework

Coursework is likely to consist of one or more tasks, projects, design assignments, portfolios, coursework collections or case studies that demonstrate your ability to use IT. You may be required to build an IT system for yourself and others to use. If so, you will have to analyse, design, implement, test, document and evaluate it. You may do coursework that is based on your own interests, perhaps building an IT system to solve a problem you have chosen. Alternatively, you may be given a coursework task by your teacher. Coursework is almost always marked by the teachers who have supervised you doing it. The way they have to mark it is shown in the syllabus. The examination boards make sure that marking is accurate, and that standards are the same.

Written papers

You will do one or more written papers. Written papers may consist of several independent questions set in different contexts, or a series of questions linked by a theme. Written papers are marked by examiners employed by the examination boards. They make sure the marking is accurate and consistent using a detailed mark scheme. This mark scheme is published, and can be obtained from the relevant examination board. Unfortunately, the mark scheme is only available *after* you have sat the written papers!

Spelling, Punctuation and Grammar (SPaG)

You may be awarded up to five per cent more marks for accurate Spelling, Punctuation and Grammar (SPaG). The performance criteria for SPaG are given in detail in the *GCSE Mandatory Code of Practice* available from HMSO. These are:

- threshold – you are reasonably accurate, making use of a limited range of specialist terms;
- intermediate – you will usually be accurate, making use of a good range of specialist terms;
- higher - you will almost always be accurate, and use a wide range of grammatical constructions and specialist terms adeptly and with precision.

Results and appeals

The results of assessment are reported as grades from A* to G. Grade A* is the highest grade. You or your school can appeal against the grades awarded. As a result of an appeal your grade could go up. It could also go down! However, it is much more likely to stay the same as the examining boards go to great lengths to make sure the grade they give you is the one which you have earned. You can also get a report on your work, and your school can get a report on the work a class has done. Reports are usually written by the Chief Examiner.

▷ **Grade descriptions**

Grade descriptions help teachers and examiners decide what GCSE grade you should be awarded. You could use the grade descriptions to help you assess your own progress and achievements. They are indications of the knowledge, skills and understanding that a GCSE candidate working at that grade might have rather than complete descriptions.

Grade F

▶ You can demonstrate a basic knowledge and understanding of simple, familiar applications of IT.
▶ You know some basic terms and definitions.
▶ You can see when IT should be used.
▶ You can use IT to present your work, and know how using IT can change the way you organize your ideas.
▶ You can study the behaviour of computer models and simulations.
▶ You understand why it is important to be precise when collecting information.
▶ You can use IT to manipulate information and search it.
▶ You can develop, test and modify programs to control hardware devices.

Grade C

▶ You can demonstrate some knowledge and understanding of a range of applications of IT.
▶ You know what software and hardware is used to support these applications.
▶ You know basic terms and definitions, and can use them appropriately.
▶ You can see when IT should be used and know how to use it.
▶ You can build appropriate IT systems to solve a range of problems.
▶ You can develop, test and modify programs to control hardware devices, producing increasingly efficient, economical sets of instructions.
▶ You use increasingly complex computer models and simulations to test hypotheses, and know their limitations.
▶ You demonstrate a clear sense of audience when you use IT to present information.

Grade A

▶ You can demonstrate a sound knowledge and understanding of a range of applications of IT.
▶ You know what software and hardware is used to support these applications. Some of this hardware and software is beyond your everyday experiences.
▶ You have a good knowledge of terms and definitions, and can use them appropriately.
▶ You can derive general principles from an understanding of particular applications of IT and can apply these when using IT.
▶ You can build the most appropriate IT systems to solve a range of problems of varying complexity.
▶ You can evaluate software packages and complex computer models, taking into account the situation for which they were developed.
▶ You know how data can be corrupted, and are aware of its uses and abuses, and can describe how to prevent these.

▷ Getting the best grade

Coursework

Coursework is an important part of GCSE assessment. It is often 60 per cent of the total marks available.

Coursework is an excellent opportunity to show what you can do if you have plenty of time. You will have to meet deadlines in handing in coursework but you should still have enough time to work carefully and produce your best work. Don't leave things to the last minute. Start your coursework as soon as you know what is required of you. However, there is no need to do everything in the first lesson! Find out when the deadline is and plan ahead. It is possible that your teacher is planning lessons that will help you with your coursework. At some stage you will study the different aspects of IT system design, such as data files and documentation. All these topics and others may be helpful to you. Don't rush your project. Don't leave it too late. Plan ahead and work steadily.

For your coursework assessment you will have to prepare a report describing the practical work you have done. The evidence that you have done what you describe will be drawings, printed material and possibly photographs. The assessment of your work will be based on this report. To improve your marks it is important to communicate clearly what you have done. Write neatly or use a wordprocessor. Express yourself clearly. Too much detail is much better than too little. Use diagrams, flowcharts, pictures, printed output, etc. to illustrate your work. A cheerful, topical front cover will make your project look more attractive. Show the examiner clearly what you have done and emphasize your achievements.

While you are doing your coursework you have access to a wide range of resources. You can refer to any material you need to help you. You can ask other people for advice and discuss your progress with them. You may be expected to work cooperatively with other students. However, you must make sure that **you** do your project. You will be asked to sign a form by the examining board certifying that your coursework is all your own work.

If you find exams difficult and they make you nervous then coursework may be your best chance to demonstrate your skills. You must not neglect your coursework and expect to pass only on the results of the written papers. Every candidate who wishes to succeed must take coursework very seriously indeed.

Written examinations

To do well in an exam you need to pay careful attention to preparing yourself for it. You will need knowledge of the subject. You will do better if you are alert and in good health. If you follow some simple techniques in the exam you may improve your marks.

Knowledge
The purpose of exams is to test your **knowledge** and **understanding** of a subject. If you do not know your subject well then you cannot expect to do well in an exam. Preparation for the exam begins on the first day of the course. Try not to miss lessons. If you do, catch up with the work quickly. Keep all the notes you write and the work you do. Do all your homework to your best standard. Learn your work as you progress. If you have any spare time go back over the course and revise the work. Make sure you understand all the work you do. Use the library to look up topics you are unsure of. Reading another book about the same topic can often make things clearer. Improve your notes in the light of any new insights. If you have problems, ask your teacher.

You can extend your background knowledge by a variety of other activities. Talk to a friend who is also doing the course and see if you can improve your knowledge of the subject by discussing topics which interest you. Read computer magazines. Go into local shops that sell computers and ask the sales staff about the computers they are selling and what they can be used for. Go on trips to computer exhibitions. Get to know someone who works with Information Technology and talk to them about their job. Try and arrange a visit to an office or factory where information systems are used.

When you are preparing for the exams this is the time to make sure you have learnt all that is required. A useful technique for learning a large volume of material is to repeatedly **revise, condense** and **learn**. Read through your notes and all the work you have done and, as you revise your knowledge, take a brief note of all the topics studied. These brief notes should cover all the important points in enough detail to refresh your memory of them at a later date. Try and learn these brief notes. If there is still too much material to learn then condense these brief notes yet again. You should end up with condensed notes covering two or three A4 sheets which summarize the course. These can be learnt and revised frequently. You can carry them with you and revise on the bus, in the queue for the cinema, waiting for a friend or taking the dog for a walk!

Practise for the exam by doing questions from previous exam papers. Work through these carefully making sure that you understand the answers to all the questions. It is likely that similar questions will appear on the written papers that you will take.

Try to complete a paper under exam conditions in the time that was allowed for it. This will give you some idea how fast you need to work. When you take your GCSE Information Technology exam you will probably be taking other subjects which are also important to you. You will find that you are short of time. You will need to plan ahead and use your time effectively.

Alertness
However much you know, if you are not **alert** you will not do your best work. You will perform better if you are wide awake, healthy and relaxed. Make sure you get plenty of sleep in the days before the exam. You may think it is necessary to stay up late revising but if you make yourself too tired you will not learn very much. If you need to do a lot of revision start it a long time before the exam. Go to bed reasonably early and you will be more

alert and cope with the exam much better. This is particularly important the night before the exam. Don't go to a disco, party or any activity that might involve staying up late. You will regret it the following day when you are too tired to cope.

You are also likely to perform better if you are fit and healthy. A bad cold, hay fever, headaches, broken bones, sprained ankles and other maladies can distract you from your work in the exam. The best remedy is to avoid situations that could make you ill. Perhaps the days before your exam are not the time to go horse riding, skiing, sky diving, etc. Avoid accidents. If you have unavoidable medical problems, your doctor may be able to help. Lastly, make sure you go to the lavatory just before the exam. You could waste five or ten minutes of valuable exam time if you have to go to the lavatory during the exam!

Many people find that exams make them nervous. They get so nervous they make silly mistakes and are unable to do their best. Most people are affected by exam nerves to some extent. Being too nervous will probably have a bad effect on your work. On the other hand some people are so relaxed they do sloppy, careless work. Being too relaxed is as inappropriate as being too nervous. Make sure you are keen to do well but keep calm.

You can waste months of careful preparation by lack of consideration for your own needs. Look after yourself! You are likely to do your best work if you are alert. Alertness depends on good health, plenty of sleep and a calm determination to do well.

Exam techniques

Exam techniques are not magic! Using them will not make up for lack of thorough preparation or ignorance. In an exam you try to communicate your knowledge to the examiner who will mark your work. Exam techniques are common sense methods to help you communicate what you know.

Before you arrive at the exam, make sure you have any equipment you will need in the exam. You will require at least a pencil, a pencil sharpener, a rubber, a ruler and at least two pens, in case one runs out. A calculator might be useful. This equipment is essential for accurate, written communication. If you have to borrow a pen, for example, it may not suit you or it may not work properly and consequently you may work at a slower pace. It is possible that equipment may not be available to borrow and you will have to manage without it. Make sure you are well prepared so that you can get down to work quickly and are not interrupted.

The first task to do in any exam is to find out what questions you are expected to answer. Doing extra questions will not earn extra marks but if you leave questions out you will lose marks.

Next, work out how much time you can spend on each question. It is often useful to work out how much time you can devote to each mark. This is the number of **minutes per mark**. You can use this to work out how long can be spent on questions that may not be worth the same amount of marks. For example, in a two hour paper you have 120 minutes to earn perhaps 100 marks. This is 1.2 minutes per mark. You can spend 2.4 minutes on a question worth 2 marks and 6 minutes on a question worth 5 marks. Having worked out the time you can spend on a question, stick to it. This is very important. The first part of each question is usually the easiest to answer and the first few marks on any question are the easiest to obtain. After the first half of a question, marks become increasingly difficult to obtain. Try to answer all the questions. You cannot be given marks for questions you haven't answered. Higher marks will almost certainly be given for correct answers to part of all the required questions than for complete answers to only a few questions.

Always arrive on time for an exam. Never leave an exam before the end. Spend all the time allowed to you to do the exam, answering questions or checking your answers. Make sure that what you can do is correct and make a determined attempt at the more difficult questions. Marks are given for correct answers but you will not have marks deducted if you are wrong.

Make sure you read the question thoroughly. Many candidates lose marks because they read the question in a hurry and do not fully grasp what it means. They then answer the question they think they have read. You will only be awarded marks for a correct answer to the actual question set. Read questions slowly and carefully.

The examiner who marks your written paper will be looking for opportunities to give you marks. If it is impossible to read your answers because your writing is illegible you will probably lose marks. Write neatly. Set out your work clearly. Give examples and draw diagrams to illustrate your answers. Communicate clearly and in full. Make sure your spelling, punctuation and grammar are correct, and use technical terms correctly.

SUMMARY

▷ GCSE IT should help you become confident and expert in using IT. You should understand what IT can and cannot do, and the impact of using IT.

▷ You should study the two themes of IT. These are: Communicating and handling information; Controlling, measuring and modelling.

▷ You will use software for: Graphical user interfaces (GUI); wordprocessing; graphics; DTP; database; spreadsheet; modelling or simulation; teletext or on-line information services; control; data logging; electronic mail; programming language; CAL.

▷ You will use this hardware: a personal computer; input devices; memory; backing storage devices; output devices; networks.

▷ You will be assessed by written papers (40 per cent) and coursework (60 per cent). The coursework will be done throughout the course; the written papers are taken at the end of the course.

▷ You will be entered for assessment in one of two tiers. These are: the Foundation tier (grades C to G) the Higher tier (grades A* to D).

▷ Coursework consists of one or more tasks, projects, design assignments, portfolios, coursework collections or case studies.

▷ You will do one or more written papers. These may consist of several independent questions set in different contexts, or a series of questions linked by a theme.

▷ You may be awarded up to five per cent for SPaG.

▷ Grade descriptions help teachers and examiners decide what GCSE grade you should be awarded. They are indications of the knowledge, skills and understanding that a GCSE candidate working at that grade might have. You could use the grade descriptions to help you assess your own progress and achievements.

Chapter

2

The syllabuses

> ### GETTING STARTED

The GCSE syllabuses in Information Technology (IT) are all based on the National Curriculum (NC) orders for IT, and the aims and objectives for IT described in the GCSE regulations and criteria. Consequently although each syllabus is different they are all very similar.

This chapter will outline the content of the various syllabuses. It is advisable to obtain a copy of your syllabus. Syllabuses are important because they outline in detail what is to be studied. A syllabus can also be used as a checklist to make sure that you have studied or revised all the topics. All syllabuses for GCSE IT are available from the examining boards and can be obtained by contacting the subject officer at the relevant board. The addresses of the examining boards are given at the end of this chapter. The NC orders for IT are published by HMSO and are available from bookshops. The GCSE regulations and Criteria are available from the Qualifications and Curriculum Authority (QCA).

Please make use of the topic charts on the Getting Started page of each chapter in this book. This will help you to identify which topics in the chapter are covered by your syllabus. For more details on the topics you should consult the syllabus.

C & G	LONDON	MEG	NDTEF	NEAB	RSA	SEG	WJEC	TOPIC	STUDY	REVISION I	REVISION 2
✓	✓	✓	✓	✓	✓	✓	✓	The examining boards			
✓	✓	✓	✓	✓	✓	✓	✓	Full or short course?			
✓	✓	✓	✓	✓	✓	✓	✓	Content of the GCSE syllabuses			
✓	✓	✓	✓	✓	✓	✓	✓	Names and addresses of the examining boards			

WHAT YOU NEED TO KNOW

▷ **The examining boards**

The syllabuses in Information Technology are:

▶ City and Guilds of London Institute (C & G)
▶ London (EDEXCEL Foundation)
▶ Midland Examining Group (MEG)
▶ National Design and Technology Education Foundation (NDTEF)
▶ Northern Examinations and Assessment Board (NEAB)
▶ Royal Society of Arts (RSA)
▶ Southern Examining Group (SEG)
▶ Welsh Joint Education Committee (WJEC)

▷ **Full or short course?**

Each syllabus can be:

▶ GCSE IT (full course)
▶ GCSE IT (short course)

A GCSE IT (short course) is usually a part of the corresponding GCSE IT (full course). A GCSE IT (short course) may only cover the two themes of IT (see p. 2), whereas a GCSE IT (full course) will include additional material which extends your experience of IT.

A brief review of the GCSE IT syllabuses available follows.

City and Guilds of London Institute (C & G)

GCSE IT (full course)

The syllabus content is organized into six sections. These are:

▶ communicating information;
▶ handling information;
▶ modelling;
▶ measurement and control;
▶ design and development;
▶ business applications and systems analysis.

Coursework is 60 per cent of the final assessment. It consists of a portfolio that includes:

▶ at least four short IT tasks;
▶ a design assignment;
▶ a case study.

In each short IT task, you have to use IT to solve a simple problem. The problem can be given to you by your teacher. A solution to the problem should be possible using a narrow range of IT skills or processes. In the design assignment, you are expected to solve a more substantial problem that you have identified yourself by building an information system. You have to analyse, design, develop, evaluate and document the information system so that others can use it. In the case study, you do a detailed study of an information system that is used in a commercial or industrial environment.

The written papers are 40 per cent of the final assessment. You do one of two tiers:

▶ Foundation tier; one paper of 2 hours; target grades C to G;
▶ Higher tier; one paper of 2.5 hours; target grades A* to D.

Each paper has three sections. Section A has general questions; section B has questions on IT in banking; section C has questions on IT in newspapers. The applications that are the focus of sections B and C will be changed regularly. They will be based on a study document available from the board in March in the last year of the course.

GCSE IT (short course)

The syllabus content is organized into five sections. These are:

- communicating information;
- handling information;
- modelling;
- measurement and control;
- design and development.

Coursework is 60 per cent of the final assessment. It consists of a portfolio that includes:

- at least two short IT tasks;
- a design assignment.

In each short IT task, you have to use IT to solve a simple problem. The problem can be given to you by your teacher. A solution to the problem should be possible using a narrow range of IT skills or processes. In the design assignment, you are expected to solve a more substantial problem that you have identified yourself by building an information system. You have to analyse, design, develop, evaluate and document the information system so that others can use it.

The written papers are 40 per cent of the final assessment. You do one of two tiers:

- Foundation tier; one paper of 1 hour; target grades C to G;
- Higher tier; one paper of 1.5 hours; target grades A* to D.

Each paper has two sections. Section A has general questions; section B has questions on IT in banking. The application that is the focus of section B will be changed regularly. It will be based on a study document available from the board in March in the last year of the course.

London (EDEXCEL Foundation)

GCSE IT (full course)

The syllabus content is specified as 54 learning objectives.

The production of the coursework collection is the key to the learning approach of the whole syllabus. Coursework is 60 per cent of the final assessment. You do a coursework collection. This involves you in the solution of four distinct types of problem. These should be small but worthwhile problems.

Two of the types of problem must be:

- file creation and interrogation;
- creation and manipulation of spreadsheets.

You choose the remaining two types of problem from:

- data logging and control;
- wordprocessing;
- desk top publishing;
- free choice 1;
- free choice 2.

Any free choice task you do must be different from any other task you have done. These may be 'different by software' or 'different within a family of software'.

The written papers are 40 per cent of the final assessment. You are entered in one of two tiers:

- Foundation tier; one paper of 2.5 hours; target grades C to G;
- Higher tier; one paper of 2.5 hours; target grades A* to D.

The written paper is divided into two sections. Section A examines your knowledge of systems design. The framework for this section is a detailed specification of a design problem available from the board in the last year of the course. Section B includes more difficult structured questions.

GCSE IT (short course)
The syllabus content is specified as 38 learning objectives.

The production of the coursework collection is the key to the learning approach of the whole syllabus. Coursework is 60 per cent of the final assessment. You do a coursework collection. This involves you in the solution of two distinct types of problem. These should be small but worthwhile problems.

One of the types of problem must be chosen from:

▶ file creation and interrogation;
▶ creation and manipulation of spreadsheets.

You choose the remaining problem from:

▶ data logging and control;
▶ wordprocessing;
▶ desk top publishing;

The written papers are 40 per cent of the final assessment. You are entered in one of two tiers:

▶ Foundation tier; one paper of 1.25 hours; target grades C to G;
▶ Higher tier; one paper of 1.25 hours; target grades A* to D.

The written paper examines your knowledge of systems design. The framework for this section is a detailed specification of a design problem available from the board in the last year of the course.

Midland Examining Group (MEG)

GCSE IT (full course)
The syllabus content is organized into seven sections. These are:

▶ communicating information;
▶ handling;
▶ measuring;
▶ control;
▶ modelling;
▶ IT systems design;
▶ effects of using IT.

Coursework is 60 per cent of the final assessment. You do between one and three coursework tasks. At least one task must be a solution to a Systems Design problem. Each task has to cover at least two of:

▶ information handling;
▶ communicating;
▶ measuring;
▶ control;
▶ measurement.

The written papers are 40 per cent of the final assessment. You do one of two tiers:

▶ Foundation tier; two papers each of 1 hour; target grades C to G;
▶ Higher tier; two papers each of 1.25 hours; target grades A* to D.

In each tier, the first written paper covers Information Handling, Communicating, Modelling, Control, Measurement, Systems Design, and Applications and Effects. The second paper focuses on Systems Design, and Applications and Effects.

GCSE IT (short course)
The syllabus content is organized into seven sections. These are:

▶ communicating information;
▶ handling;
▶ measuring;

▶ control;
▶ modelling;
▶ IT systems design;
▶ effects of using IT.

Coursework is 60 per cent of the final assessment. You do one or two coursework tasks. Each task has to cover at least two of:

▶ information handling;
▶ communicating;
▶ measuring;
▶ control;
▶ measurement.

The written paper is 40 per cent of the final assessment. You do one of two tiers:

▶ Foundation tier; one paper of 1 hour; target grades C to G;
▶ Higher tier; one paper of 1.25 hours; target grades A* to D.

In each tier, the written paper covers Information Handling, Communicating, Modelling, Control, Measurement, Systems Design, and Applications and Effects.

National Design and Technology Education Foundation (NDTEF)

GCSE IT (full course)
The syllabus content is organized into two sections with several subsections. These are:

▶ development of systems – this includes the analysis, design, implementation and testing, evaluation, and documentation of information systems;
▶ practical activities/systems in society – this includes communicating and handling information; controlling, measuring and modelling; social, moral and ethical aspects; and hardware and software.

Coursework is 60 per cent of the final assessment. You do:

▶ a portfolio;
▶ a case study.

The portfolio records a major system design and development task that you have chosen to do. It can be supplemented by other coursework. The case study is an investigation of a control system, focusing on its use in manufacturing, production or the service industries.

The written paper is 40 per cent of the final assessment. You are entered in one of two tiers:

▶ Foundation tier; one paper of 1.5 hours; target grades C to G;
▶ Higher tier; one paper of 2 hours; target grades A* to D.

The written papers are based on a research task issued to schools one year previously.

GCSE IT (short course)
The syllabus content is organized into two sections with several subsections. These are:

▶ development of systems – this includes the analysis, design, implementation and testing, evaluation, and documentation of information systems;
▶ practical activities/systems in society – this includes communicating and handling information; controlling, measuring and modelling; social, moral and ethical aspects; and hardware and software.

Coursework is 60 per cent of the final assessment. You do:

▶ a portfolio;
▶ a case study.

The portfolio records a major system design and development task that you have chosen to do. It can be supplemented by other coursework. The case study is an investigation of a control system, focusing on its use in manufacturing, production or the service industries.

The written paper is 40 per cent of the final assessment. You are entered in one of two tiers:

▶ Foundation tier; one paper of 1 hour; target grades C to G;
▶ Higher tier; one paper of 1.5 hours; target grades A* to D.

The written papers are based on a research task issued to schools one year previously.

Northern Examinations and Assessment Board (NEAB)

GCSE IT (full course)
The syllabus content is organized into two sections each with several subsections. These are:

▶ tools, techniques and systems – this section includes awareness of the structure of information systems; hardware; software; evaluation of the suitability of information systems; the methods used to gather, store and process data; presenting information; modelling and simulation; and the system life cycle;
▶ information systems in society – this section includes communications; the Data Protection Act; copyright law and anti-hacking legislation; and the effects on society of the growth of information.

Coursework is 60 per cent of the final assessment. You do:

▶ an assignment;
▶ a project.

The assignment is set by the board. It is sent to schools at the start of the course. You have to produce a report that demonstrates your ability to design, implement, test and evaluate solutions to the set assignment using IT. The project involves you in producing a report that describes how you solved a problem using IT. This should demonstrate your IT capability. The problem can arise in any curriculum area or from any other area of interest to you.

The written papers are 40 per cent of the final assessment. You are entered in one of two tiers:

▶ Foundation tier; two papers each of 1.5 hours; target grades C to G;
▶ Higher tier; two papers each of 1.5 hours; target grades A* to D.

GCSE IT (short course)
The syllabus content is organised into two sections, each with several subsections. These are:

▶ tools, techniques and systems – this section includes awareness of the structure of information systems; hardware; software; the methods used to gather, store and process data.
▶ information systems in society – this section includes communications; the Data Protection Act; and the effects on society of the growth of information.

Coursework is 60 per cent of the final assessment. You do an assignment. The assignment is set by the board. It is sent to schools at the start of the course. You have to produce a report that demonstrates your ability to design, implement, test and evaluate solutions to the set assignment using IT.

The written papers are 40 per cent of the final assessment. You are entered in one of two tiers:

▶ Foundation tier; one paper of 1.5 hours; target grades C to G;
▶ Higher tier; one paper of 1.5 hours; target grades A* to D.

Royal Society of Arts (RSA)

GCSE IT (full course)
The syllabus content is not organized into sections but listed as a whole. It includes the applications of IT, problem solving using IT, the effectiveness and limitations of IT, selecting the IT resources appropriate to a particular task, hardware and software, the systems development cycle, methods of data capture, verification and validation. You have to study:

▶ communicating and handling information;
▶ measuring, modelling and controlling;

▶ evaluation and problem solving;
▶ applications and implications of IT.

Coursework is 60 per cent of the final assessment. You do:

▶ practical tasks;
▶ a case study.

The practical tasks include a compulsory task set by RSA. This is set in the context of a particular industry, commerce or community. You can choose other practical tasks from a list of tasks provided by RSA. You can choose your own task but you have to agree it with your teacher and get it approved by RSA. In the case study, you explore a particular information system within a business or community organization. You write about its context, how the system handles information, and the technology used. You also evaluate the information system.

The written papers are 40 per cent of the final assessment. You are entered in one of two tiers:

▶ Foundation tier; one paper of 1.5 hours; target grades C to G;
▶ Higher tier; one paper of 2.25 hours; target grades A* to D.

The written papers include some questions set in the same context as the compulsory practical coursework task set by RSA.

GCSE IT (short course)
The syllabus content is not organized into sections but listed as a whole. It includes problem solving using IT, the effectiveness and limitations of IT, selecting IT resources appropriate to a particular task, hardware and software. You also have to study:

▶ communicating and handling information;
▶ measuring, modelling and controlling;
▶ evaluation and problem solving.

Coursework is 60 per cent of the final assessment. You do several practical tasks. The practical tasks include a compulsory task set by RSA. This is set in the context of a particular industry, commerce or community. You can choose other practical tasks from a list of tasks provided by RSA. You can choose your own task but you have to agree it with your teacher and get it approved by RSA.

The written papers are 40 per cent of the final assessment. You are entered in one of two tiers:

▶ Foundation tier; one paper of 1 hour; target grades C to G;
▶ Higher tier; one paper of 1.75 hours; target grades A* to D.

The written papers include some questions set in the same context as the compulsory practical coursework task set by RSA.

Southern Examining Group (SEG)

GCSE IT (full course)
The syllabus content is organized into four sections. These can be summarized as:

▶ IT skills;
▶ hardware and software;
▶ using IT to solve problems;
▶ social, legal, ethical and moral issues.

Coursework is 60 per cent of the final assessment. You do two coursework tasks. One task is from the theme of Communicating and Handling Information and the other task is from the theme of Controlling, Measuring and Modelling. Each task consists of the specification, analysis, design, implementation, testing, documentation and evaluation of an IT system. You are assessed on the extent to which you successfully complete each stage of the task.

The written paper is 40 per cent of the final assessment. You are entered in one of two tiers:

▶ Foundation tier; one paper of 1.5 hours; target grades C to G;
▶ Higher tier; one paper of 1.5 hours; target grades A* to D.

You are expected to be familiar with a range of IT hardware, software and applications. The papers include all the material examined in the corresponding IT (short course) paper.

GCSE IT (short course)

The syllabus content is organized into four sections. These can be summarized as:

- ▶ IT skills;
- ▶ hardware and software;
- ▶ using IT to solve problems;
- ▶ social, legal, ethical and moral issues.

Coursework is 60 per cent of the final assessment. You do a coursework task. This task is from either the theme of Communicating and Handling Information, or from the theme of Controlling, Measuring and Modelling. The task consists of the specification, analysis, design, implementation, testing, documentation and evaluation of an IT system. You are assessed on the extent to which you successfully complete each stage of the task.

The written paper is 40 per cent of the final assessment. You are entered in one of two tiers:

- ▶ Foundation tier; one paper of 1 hour; target grades C to G;
- ▶ Higher tier; one paper of 1 hour; target grades A* to D.

You are expected to be familiar with a range of IT hardware, software and applications.

Welsh Joint Education Committee (WJEC)
Cyd-Bwyllgor Addysg Cymru (CBAC)

GCSE IT (full course)

The syllabus is divided into three sections, each with several subsections. These are:

- ▶ the core – this includes measurement and control, databases, data logging, spread-sheets, wordprocessing and desk top publishing;
- ▶ IT applications – this includes IT in the High Street; the electronic office; and the implications of using IT;
- ▶ tools, techniques and systems.

Coursework is 60 per cent of the final assessment. You do:

- ▶ a portfolio;
- ▶ a project.

The portfolio is based on any two of the four elements of Communicating Information, Handling Information, Controlling and Measuring, and Modelling. The project is a report on a solution to a problem which demonstrates your information systems capability. It is based on the two elements not covered in the portfolio.

The written papers are 40 per cent of the final assessment. You are entered in one of two tiers:

- ▶ Foundation tier; two papers each of 1 hour; target grades C to G;
- ▶ Higher tier; two papers each of 1.5 hours; target grades A* to D.

The first written paper covers the requirements of the Key Stage 4 programmes of study for IT. You are expected to have had experience of software for information retrieval, measurement and control, data logging, spreadsheets, wordprocessing and desk top publishing. The second paper focuses on the extension content. This includes hardware, software, and operating systems.

GCSE IT (short course)

The syllabus is divided into three sections, each with several subsections. These are:

- ▶ the core – this includes measurement and control, databases, data logging, spread-sheets, wordprocessing and desk top publishing;
- ▶ IT applications – this includes IT in the High Street; the electronic office; and the implications of using IT;
- ▶ tools, techniques and systems.

Coursework is 60 per cent of the final assessment. You do a portfolio based on any two of the four elements of Communicating Information, Handling Information, Controlling and Measuring, and Modelling.

The written paper is 40 per cent of the final assessment. You are entered in one of two tiers:

- ▶ Foundation tier; one paper of 1 hour; target grades C to G;
- ▶ Higher tier; one paper of 1.5 hours; target grades A* to D.

The written papers cover the requirements of the Key Stage 4 programmes of study for IT. You are expected to have had experience of software for information retrieval, measurement and control, data logging, spreadsheets, wordprocessing and desk top publishing.

▷ Content of the GCSE syllabuses

To guide you to the topics covered by your syllabus, you should consult the Topic Charts found on the Getting Started page of each chapter. You may need to consult your particular syllabus for a more detailed breakdown.

Remember that all syllabuses cover the Key Stage 4 Programmes of Study from the National Curriculum. If you want to be sure that you have covered all the topics for the course that you are studying you should buy a syllabus. It is important to get the syllabus that you are studying as each examining board has a different one.

Below is an example of the **Topic Charts** found in this book. You should use these to find the topics covered by your particular syllabus. The central coloum details the main topics in the book, these headings can be found in the left-hand margin in the 'What you need to know' part of the chapter. To the left of the chart, you will be able to identify whether a particular topic is part of your syllabus. Use the right-hand side of the chart to track your study and revision of each topic throughout your course.

C & G	LONDON	MEG	NDTEF	NEAB	RSA	SEG	WJEC	TOPIC	STUDY	REVISION 1	REVISION 2
✓	✓	✓	✓	✓	✓	✓	✓	Monitors			
✓	✓	✓	✓	✓	✓	✓	✓	Printers			
✓	✓						✓	Computer output on microfilm			
✓	✓	✓	✓	✓	✓	✓	✓	Graph plotters			
✓	✓	✓	✓	✓	✓	✓	✓	Speech synthesis			
✓	✓	✓	✓	✓	✓	✓	✓	Actuators			

You will see that if your syllabus has been set by the Northern Examinations and Assessment Board (NEAB) you will not need to study the topic 'Computer output on microfilm' in Chapter 6 as it is not a topic covered in the NEAB syllabus.

▷ Names and addresses

Your syllabus for Information Technology can be obtained from the Subject Officer at the relevant address listed below. Remember to specify whether you are studying the Information Technology short course or full course.

C & G
City and Guilds of London Institute
46 Britannia St
London WC1X 7RG
(0171 278 2468)

London
EDEXCEL Foundation
Stewart House
32 Russell Square
London WC1B 5DN
(0171 331 4000)

MEG
Midland Examining Group
Syndicate Buildings
1 Hills Rd
Cambridge CB1 2EU
(01223 553311)

NDTEF
National Design and Technology Education Foundation
The Old Chapel House
Pound Hill
Alresford
Hampshire
(01962 735801)

NEAB
Northern Examinations and Assessment Board
Devas Street
M15 6EX
(0161 953 1180)

RSA
Royal Society of Arts
RSA Examinations Board
Westwood Way
Coventry CV4 8HS
(01203 470033)

SEG
Southern Examining Group
Stag Hill House
Guildford GU2 5XJ
(01483 506506)

WJEC
Welsh Joint Education Committee
245 Western Avenue
Cardiff CF5 2YX
(01222 265000)

SUMMARY

▷ The syllabuses for the General Certificate of Secondary Education (GCSE) in Information Technology (IT) are:
   City Guilds of London Institute (C & G).
   London (EDEXCEL Foundation).
   Midland Examining Group (MEG).
   National Design and Technology Education Foundation (NDTEF).
   Northern Examinations and Assessment Board (NEAB).
   Royal Society of Arts (RSA).
   Southern Examining Group (SEG).
   Welsh Joint Education Committee (WJEC).

▷ All syllabuses for GCSE IT must cover the IT content of the National Curriculum (NC), and meet the aims and assessment objectives for IT given in the *GCSE Regulations and Criteria*.

▷ You can get a copy of your GCSE syllabus by contacting the subject officer for IT at the relevant examining board. The addresses of the examining boards are given above.

▷ The NC orders for IT are published by HMSO and are available from bookshops.

▷ The *GCSE Regulations and Criteria* are available from the Qualifications & Curriculum Authority (QCA).

An introduction to Information Technology

This chapter should be read if you are preparing for GCSE IT assessment with the following examining boards:

C & G	MEG	NEAB	SEG
London	NDTEF	RSA	WJEC

GETTING STARTED

This chapter introduces some important ideas and technical terms that are fundamental to an understanding of IT. The differences between data and information; hardware and software; memory and backing storage; mainframe computers and microcomputers; input and output; digital and analog; and numbers and characters are reviewed.

A complete **Glossary of technical terms** appears later in this chapter on p. 27. You may find it helpful to refer to this when you need to know what certain technical words mean. A short glossary of some of the technical terms used in each chapter also appears at the beginning of each chapter.

GLOSSARY

ASCII   The American Standard Code for Information Interchange. This is the most commonly used character code.

Program   A set of instructions used to control a computer.

Volatile   When a computer is switched off, the volatile RAM memory is cleared. This is one reason you save information on a floppy disk.

C & G	LONDON	MEG	NDTEF	NEAB	RSA	SEG	WJEC	TOPIC	STUDY	REVISION 1	REVISION 2
✓	✓	✓	✓	✓	✓	✓	✓	Information Technology			
✓	✓	✓	✓	✓	✓	✓	✓	Hardware			
✓	✓	✓	✓	✓	✓	✓	✓	Software			
✓	✓	✓	✓	✓	✓	✓	✓	Numbers and characters			
✓	✓	✓	✓	✓	✓	✓	✓	Glossary of technical terms			

> ## WHAT YOU NEED TO KNOW

> ## Information Technology

Computers process data. The data is not understood by the computer. Computers cannot tell the difference between sensible data or nonsense, unless we tell them how to. The use of computers is often referred to as **data processing**. However, because we are only interested in doing *useful* tasks with computers, we actually use them to process information, that is, data that has some meaning to us.

> **information = data + meaning**

e.g.   230575 is *data*.
If we add *meaning* it could be any of the following:
a date; a telephone number; a serial number; £230,575; etc.
It then becomes *information*.

'Information is data that has some meaning'

> Information Technology is the hardware (computers and other equipment) and software used to store, process and transmit information.

An **IT System** is the organization of human and other resources, including IT, into a coherent system for the purposeful storage, processing and transmission of information.

Information processing is a **cycle** of input, processing and output (see Fig. 3.1). We input the data we have collected, then process it. When the data has been processed, some data is output. In response to the data output we may wish to respond by inputting further data in reply. This is in turn processed and the cycle continues until we have no further data to input.

The information processing cycle may be based on a computer (see Fig. 3.2). The **Central Processing Unit** (CPU) of the computer does the actual processing of the data. Within the CPU are the **Memory**, the **Control Unit** (CU) and the **Arithmetic and Logic Unit** (ALU).

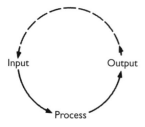

Fig. 3.1 The information processing cycle

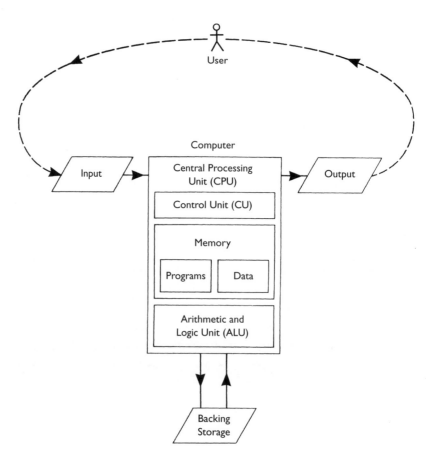

Fig. 3.2 The information processing cycle based on a computer

▶ Programs and data are stored in the memory while the programs are run and the data is processed.

　　There are two types of memory:

　　▶ **Random Access Memory** (RAM) is the *volatile* or temporary memory in which the programs and data are stored.

　　▶ **Read Only Memory** (ROM) can only be read and is not volatile. It is used to store programs permanently, for example, the Operating System.

▶ The **CU** controls the hardware so that it carries out the instructions given in the program being run. It controls the input and output of data and the transfer of data between different parts of the CPU.

▶ The **ALU** is a specialized unit within the CPU that does all the arithmetic and logic.

▶ A **program** is a set of instructions that tell a computer what to do. Programs are stored in the memory of the computer and *executed* or *run* in order to process the input data. The input data is also stored in the memory of the computer while it is processed. The processed data is then output. When the computer is switched off the programs and data in the RAM memory of the computer are 'wiped out'. To avoid losing the programs and data when we switch off, the programs and data can be saved on **backing storage**.

Example: calculating a gas bill

Suppose we want to use a computer to calculate a gas bill. We will have to do the following:

1. *Switch on* the computer.
2. *Load the program* which will do the calculation into the memory of the computer.
3. *Run* (or *execute*) the program.
4. *Input* the old and the new meter readings in response to requests from the computer.
5. *Output* the gas bill.
6. *Exit* the program
7. *Switch off* the computer.

▷ Hardware

'An important distinction between hardware and software'

Hardware is physical equipment. Hardware is hard! You can touch it and even bump into it and hurt yourself! By contrast, software refers to the programs that control the computer. It is usually invisible!

Mainframes and micros

'Note the difference between mainframe computers and microcomputers'

Computers are hardware. Computers come in different sizes. Essentially, microcomputers are small computers while mainframes are large computers.

　　Mainframe computers are many and varied. They offer a wide range of facilities and can vary dramatically in size and power. Most of them are very big in size, extremely fast in operation, have very large memories and offer access to a wide range of complex software and hardware. Mainframes are used in large companies and similar organizations, such as major banks, local authorities, etc.

　　Mainframe computers need *special environments*:

▶ in particular they need *air conditioning* to dissipate the heat generated when they are in use;

▶ *filters* are used to keep the air free from dust particles;

▶ *smoke detectors* are used to help prevent the outbreak of a serious fire;

▶ *false floors and ceilings* may be used to hide the miles of cable connecting the computer to the various peripherals;

▶ the electricity supply is often 'smoothed' to prevent power surges or 'spikes' which may damage the computer;

▶ the computer may have its own *electricity generator* for emergency use in case of a power failure.

The IBM ES/9000 is a typical mainframe computer (see Fig. 3.3).

Fig. 3.3 An IBM ES/9000 mainframe system configuration

A typical **microcomputer** is small enough to fit on an average-sized desk. Microcomputers are found in homes, offices, schools, etc. They may be 'personal computers', 'desk top', 'portable' or 'lap top' computers. In industry the standard microcomputer is the IBM Personal Computer (PC) (see Fig. 3.4).

Microcomputers usually consist of a monitor, a processor box, a hard disk, a floppy disk drive, a keyboard and a mouse. A multimedia PC will also have a CD-ROM drive and stereo speakers.

Peripherals

Peripherals are hardware devices attached to the computer. They are often essential to the successful operation of the computer. They usually have a special purpose.

The following are examples of peripherals:

Input peripherals

- keyboard,
- mouse, joystick, tracker ball
- pen, graphics pad, scanner, video digitiser, digital camera
- OCR reader, OMR reader
- light pen, laser scanner for bar codes
- stripe card reader
- Kimball tag reader
- MICR reader
- microphone
- sensors

Output peripherals
- monitor
- printer
- COM recorder
- loudspeaker
- graph plotter

Backing storage peripherals
- magnetic disk drive, using floppy disks or hard disks
- CD-ROM drive

Fig. 3.4 The IBM PC 300 personal computer. It is a typical example of a powerful desktop computer.

▷ magneto-optical disk drive
▷ magnetic tape drive, using reel to reel and cassette tapes

Digital and analog

Most computers are digital, electronic machines. Their electronic circuitry is constructed using binary logic. **Binary logic** is two-state logic. This means that only two states are possible. These two states are voltage levels of 5 V or 0 V. The 5 V level is used to represent the digit 1 and 0V is used to represent 0. The memory of the computer is simply a very large number of 1s and 0s that form patterns that are recognized by the computer. The computer is described as being **digital** because everything in its memory is represented using 1s and 0s, i.e. binary digits.

'An important distinction between digital and analog'

Data is represented using patterns of 1s and 0s. A 1 or 0 is a **binary digit** or **bit**. Bits are grouped together to form bytes. A **byte** is the number of bits used to represent one character. It is very common for computers to have 8 bits in a byte. Memory size is measured in bytes.

The *units of memory size*, in bytes, are as follows:

▷ **1 Kilobyte** or 1 Kbyte = 1024 bytes = 2^{10} bytes
▷ **1 Megabyte** or 1 Mbyte = 1024 K bytes = 2^{20} bytes
▷ **1 Gigabyte** or 1 Gbyte = 1024 M bytes = 2^{30} bytes

ADCs and DACs

Most computers and peripherals are digital but some are not. Sensors are analog devices. For example, a heat sensor produces a small voltage in response to temperature changes. This small voltage is known as an analog signal. When the analog signal is input to a digital computer it must be converted from analog to digital form. This is done using an Analog to Digital Convertor or ADC.

If a digital computer outputs to an analog device then a Digital to Analog Converter or DAC is used. This converts the digital signal from the computer to an analog form. For example, a motor may need a continuously varying voltage to control its speed. The output from the digital computer to the motor will need to be converted to an analog voltage using a DAC.

▷ **Software**

Software refers to the *programs* that control the running of the computer. Software can be held in the memory of the computer. It can also be recorded on floppy disk. Software is *not* floppy disks. It is the *programs recorded* on the floppy disks.

Software can be obtained in many ways. You can write your own, using a computer language such as BASIC or LOGO. You can buy software. Bought software is referred to as a package. Most packages have a specific purpose or application. You might buy an **applications package** to do the stock keeping in a shop, to calculate the wages for a factory or to do your budgeting at home.

'Applications packages'

'Content free packages'

Content free packages are packages which are useful in a *variety* of ways, but are used to do *similar* tasks. These packages cover application *areas* rather than specific applications. For example, content free packages are used for Wordprocessing, Databases, Spreadsheets, Graphic Design and Desk Top Publishing.

'The Operating System'

One of the most important programs that a computer runs is the **Operating System**. The Operating System is always present when a computer is being used. The Operating System controls the hardware. Applications packages and other user software run on the Operating System which, in turn, runs or controls the hardware. The Operating System helps the user do a variety of tasks associated with the day-to-day operation of the computer, such as loading and saving data.

'Utility programs'

Utility programs are used to do tasks which relate more to the successful use of the computer than to any IT systems task. For example, some utility programs are part of the Operating System. These would be used to do tasks such as copying or formatting disks. You could buy new utility programs to do the same tasks. You might chose to buy new utility programs because they are faster or more versatile than those supplied with the Operating System. Utility programs can also perform tasks that are often not done by the Operating System, such as the detection of computer viruses.

▷ **Numbers and characters**

Data can be *numbers* or *character strings*. For example, '34 High Road' is a **character string**; 45.6 is a **number**. Note that numbers can be characters as well as numbers (but not both at the same time!). The bit patterns in memory can be interpreted only if we know whether they are meant to be numbers or characters, and if we know the codes and conventions being used.

Denary or base 10 numbers

While computers use bit patterns to represent numbers, people use **denary**, i.e. **base 10** numbers. Computer number systems are constructed using the same method we use for base 10, so it is useful to analyse our own number system before looking at how the computer represents numbers. By making use of a **place value number system** we can represent any number using only the digits 0, 1, 2, . . ., 9 and no others.

This works as follows:

'The denary or base 10 number system'

10^3	10^2	10^1	10^0	:	base	
1000	100	10	1	:	place value	Available digits are
2	5	7	4	:	denary number	0, 1, 2, 3, 4, 5, 6, 7, 8, 9

This number is read as two thousand, five hundred and seventy four. We can construct other number systems using this framework.

Binary or base 2 numbers

We construct binary numbers as follows:

'The binary or base 2 number system'

2^7	2^6	2^5	2^4	2^3	2^2	2^1	2^0	:	base		Available digits
128	64	32	16	8	4	2	1	:	place value		0,1
0	1	0	1	1	1	0	1	:	binary number		

Binary numbers are constructed using only two digits, 1 and 0, making this system very easy for computers to represent in an electronic two state system. Unfortunately, this system is not so easy for people to use! We must be able to convert binary to denary and vice versa before we can begin to use the same system as the computer.

Converting binary to denary

Look again at the binary number 0101 1101 used in the example above. Each bit has a place value depending on its position in the number. These values are expressed in denary. Where there is a 1 in the binary number we add in the place value; where there is a 0 we do not add in the place value. The calculation is as follows:

128	64	32	16	8	4	2	1	:	place value
0	1	0	1	1	1	0	1	:	binary number

denary number   =   64 + 16 + 8 + 4 + 1

                 =   93

Counting in binary

It is useful to be able to count in binary. Fig. 3.5 shows the numbers from 1 to 20 in binary. Notice how the patterns of 0s and 1s are repeated in the binary count. Recognizing these patterns will help you understand how to count in binary.

Hexadecimal or base 16

Computers store numbers using the binary number system. Unfortunately, binary numbers are hard for us to remember and understand.

denary number	binary number
1	1
2	10
3	11
4	100
5	101
6	110
7	111
8	1000
9	1001
10	1010
11	1011
12	1100
13	1101
14	1110
15	1111
16	10000
17	10001
18	10010
19	10011
20	10100

Fig. 3.5 Counting from 1 to 20 in binary

For these reasons, other number systems are often used instead of binary. The most important of these is **hexadecimal** or **base 16**. This number system is constructed as follows:

'The hexadecimal or base 16 number system'

16^3	16^2	16^1	16^0	:	base
4096	256	16	1	:	place value
2	8	A	3	:	hexadecimal number

Available digits:
0, 1, 2, 3, . . . 9, A, B, C, D, E, F

In base 16 we should use the single digits 0, 1, 2, 3, 4, 5, 6, 7, 8, 9, 10, 11, 12, 13, 14, 15. However, 10, 11, 12, 13, 14, 15 expressed in decimal all contain two digits. To avoid this problem we use the digits A, B, C, D, E, F to represent the single digits 10, 11, 12, 13, 14, 15 respectively.

Converting hexadecimal to binary and denary

Any hexadecimal digit can be represented as four binary bits and four binary bits are always equivalent to a hexadecimal digit. For example:

Binary number	:	Hexadecimal digit	Binary number	:	Hexadecimal digit
0000	:	0	1000	:	8
0001	:	1	1001	:	9
0010	:	2	1010	:	A
0011	:	3	1011	:	B
0100	:	4	1100	:	C
0101	:	5	1101	:	D
0110	:	6	1110	:	E
0111	:	7	1111	:	F

To convert *hexadecimal to binary* we change each hexadecimal digit to four binary bits, e.g. A43E = 1010 0100 0011 1110.

If we have to convert *hexadecimal to denary* it is easiest first to convert the hexadecimal to binary and then convert the binary to denary as we did earlier in this chapter.

Characters

Characters are represented using codes. These codes are simply bit patterns that we agree to interpret as particular characters. They are arbitrary, although they may be quite well organized. There is no particular reason why a bit pattern should represent one character rather than another. For this reason there are several different codes used to represent characters. They have been developed by different manufacturers of computers and others for their own purposes.

ASCII

'Part of the ASCII code'

ASCII (American Standard Code for Information Interchange) is the most common code in use for representing characters. Part of this code is shown in the table below:

Character	:	Binary code	Character	:	Binary code
Space	:	010 0000	G	:	100 0111
			H	:	100 1000
0	:	011 0000	I	:	100 1001
1	:	011 0001	J	:	100 1010
2	:	011 0010	K	:	100 1011
3	:	011 0011	L	:	100 1100
4	:	011 0100	M	:	100 1101
5	:	011 0101	N	:	100 1110
6	:	011 0110	O	:	100 1111
7	:	011 0111	P	:	101 0000
8	:	011 1000	Q	:	101 0001
9	:	011 1001	R	:	101 0010
			S	:	101 0011
+	:	010 1011	T	:	101 0100
A	:	100 0001	U	:	101 0101
B	:	100 0010	V	:	101 0110
C	:	100 0011	W	:	101 0111
D	:	100 0100	X	:	101 1000
E	:	100 0101	Y	:	101 1001
F	:	100 0110	Z	:	101 1010

Notice that although ASCII code is in ascending binary number order, the code for the character 3 is not the binary number for three.

Control characters

Control characters (or control codes) are not usually displayed or printed. They are not characters that are meaningful to most people as part of a routine communication. When entered at the keyboard or sent to a peripheral they are treated as a signal to begin or end some operation. For example, there is a control code associated with pressing the <ENTER> or <RETURN> key on the keyboard; there are others that tell the printer to turn on and off features such as bold printing and underlining. Control characters are part of the character set and must have different codes from other characters.

The size of the character set

Each different character must have a different binary code associated with it. Hence the number of bits used determines the number of characters it is possible to code. The **character set** is all the characters it is possible to represent using the code. The **size** of the character set is the number of different characters represented. This cannot be more than the maximum number of different codes. The relationship between the number of bits and the maximum size of the character set is shown in the table below:

'The relation between the number of bits and the maximum size of the character set'

Number of bits	Different codes	Maximum size of the character set
1	0 1	$2 = 2^1$
2	00 01 10 11	$4 = 2^2$
3	000 001 010 011 100 101 110 111	$8 = 2^3$
4	0000 0100 1000 1100	$16 = 2^4$
	0001 0101 1001 1101	
	0010 0110 1010 1110	
	0011 0111 1011 1111	
5	....	$32 = 2^5$
6	....	$64 = 2^6$
7	....	$128 = 2^7$
8	....	$256 = 2^8$
x	....	2^x

Since ASCII is a 7 bit code, the maximum number of possible characters is 128, more than enough for most purposes!

GLOSSARY OF TECHNICAL TERMS

Actuator	The device that performs some action required by a control system, e.g. a motor.
Algorithm	A set of rules to solve a problem.
Amend	To change.
Analog data	The representation of data as a *range* of variable voltages.
Analog to Digital Converter (ADC)	A hardware device to convert analog voltage to binary numbers.
Ancestral system	The ancestral system for file backups consists of the son (the latest version), the father (the previous version) and the grandfather (the version before the previous version).
AND gate	A logic gate that sets the output high if all the inputs are high.
Applications software	Software designed to do a specific job, e.g. payroll.
Arithmetic and Logic Unit (ALU)	The part of the CPU where arithmetic and logical operations are done.
ASCII	The American Standard Code for Information Interchange.
Background mode	When printing in background mode on a standalone computer, the output is spooled to the hard disk so that the computer can be used while the printing is done.
Backing storage	A means of storing programs and data outside the computer's memory, e.g. magnetic disk or tape.
Backup	A backup of a file is another copy of it. The ancestral system is often used for backups.
Bar code	A code represented by a series of vertical black and white lines, often used to encode an identity number.
Bar code reader	A hardware device used to read a bar code. This could be a light pen or a laser scanner.
BASIC	Beginners All-purpose Symbolic Instruction Code. A high level language which is suitable for learning to write computer programs.

Batch processing	A method of processing data where the data is gathered into batches before being processed.
Binary	The base 2 number system. Allowable digits are 0 and 1.
BIT	A BInary digiT. This takes the value 1 or 0.
Block	1. A section of the screen display that has been highlighted.
	2. A group of records on magnetic tape or disk that is read or written together.
Bridge	A bridge connects two similar local area networks making them appear to be the same network to users
Browser	This is GUI software that is used to access Web servers.
Buffer	A printer buffer is extra memory, usually in the printer itself, which is used to hold output while it is waiting to be printed.
Bug	An error in a computer program.
Byte	A byte is a set of bits used to represent one character. There are normally eight bits to the byte.
Catalogue	A list of all the files on a disk. A catalogue is also known as a directory.
CD-ROM	The use of Compact Disc technology for backing storage for computers. CD-ROMs can store programs, text, sound, pictures, music and video.
Ceefax	The teletext service broadcast by the BBC.
Cell	The intersection of a row and a column in a spreadsheet.
Central Processing Unit (CPU)	The main part of the computer, where all the processing takes place. It consists of the CU, the ALU and the memory.
Character	One of the symbols that can be represented by a computer. Characters include A to Z.
Character code	A code used to represent characters, e.g. ASCII.
Character printer	A printer that prints one character at a time, e.g. a dot matrix printer.
Character set	All the characters that can be represented by a computer.
Check digit	An extra digit calculated from the original digits in a number, using a predetermined formula, and attached to the number. It can be re-calculated to check that none of the digits in the number have been altered.
COBOL	COmmon Business Orientated Language. One of the more popular high level languages used for business and commercial applications.
Computer	A computer is an automatic, information processing machine which inputs, processes and outputs data under the control of a stored program.
Computer Aided Design (CAD)	Using graphics software to help design illustrations, products, etc.
Computer Aided Manufacture (CAM)	Using a computer to control the manufacture of a product.
Computer Output on Microfilm (COM)	Output from a computer written directly onto microfilm. Output in this form is compact and does not deteriorate in storage as rapidly as printout.
Content free software	Software designed to do a range of similar tasks, e.g. a spreadsheet.
Control character	Control characters are used to control the operation of peripherals, in particular, printers. They are part of the character set and have an ASCII code but are not usually visible on the monitor screen or printout.
Control Interface	The hardware that provides the interface between a computer and a control system.
Control system	An IT system used to monitor and control robots, environmental conditions, etc.
Control total	A meaningful total calculated from a batch of source documents that is used to check that the batch is complete.
Control Unit (CU)	The part of the CPU that controls the running of programs and the input and output of data.
Corrupt data	Corrupt data is data that has been altered so that it is no longer meaningful.
Create	Set up for the first time.
Cursor	Often a rectangular block one character in size that appears on a monitor screen at the point at which the next character entered through the keyboard will be displayed. The cursor often flashes on and off to attract attention. It can be different shapes.
Cursor control keys	The 'arrow' keys used to control the movement of the cursor around the screen.

Data	Numbers or characters.
Database	A database is a collection of structured data (see files, records, fields) and the software to allow the user to easily access the data.
Data capture	Data capture is the collection of data. Data capture can be on-line, e.g. POS terminals for stock keeping, or off-line, e.g. questionnaires.
Data control clerks	The job of a data control clerk is to monitor the flow of data through a computer system.
Data logging	Data logging is the automatic collection and storage of data for processing at a later date.
Data preparation	This is the transfer of data from a source document to a computer readable medium, e.g. disk.
Data preparation clerks	Data preparation clerks work in the data preparation department.
Data processing	Computers input, process and output data. This is sometimes called 'data processing'.
Debug	To look for, find and remove bugs in a computer program.
Delete	Remove. A file is deleted from a disk when it is removed from it.
Denary	The base 10 number system. Available digits are 0 to 9.
Desk Top Publishing (DTP)	Combines graphics and wordprocessing in a format typical of a newspaper.
Digital	The representation of data as codes made up of 1s and 0s. These can be stored in the computer as 5 V and 0 V, respectively.
Direct access	A method of accessing a file where it is possible to store or retrieve data records without the need to read other data records first. Direct access is used with magnetic disks but not with magnetic tape.
Direct data entry	Data entry to the program that processes the data while it is running.
Directory	See catalogue.
Disk	Magnetic disks are a backing storage medium. Microcomputers use floppy disks or hard disks. Mainframes use disk packs that may be exchangeable or fixed.
Documentation	A written description of what a program does and how it is run. Often containing details of program design, coding and testing, and how to to use the program.
Dot matrix printer	A printer that has a print head consisting of a matrix of steel pins. Character shapes are made up from a pattern of dots.
Edit	Amend, delete or insert.
Electronic funds transfer (EFT)	A paperless method of transferring money between bank accounts using a communications network.
Electronic Funds Transfer at Point of Sale (EFTPOS)	See Electronic funds transfer and Point of sale terminal.
Electronic mail (e-mail)	A paperless method of sending mail, i.e. letters, etc., from one computer to another using a communications network.
Execute	To execute a program is to run it.
Expert system	Software that allows users to identify particular situations and gives them advice on the appropriate action to take.
Feedback	Feedback occurs when a sensor detects a situation that causes the computer to initiate action that alters the data collected by the sensor. Feedback is cyclical.
Fibre optics	The use of very thin fibre glass strands to transmit data encoded as light pulses.
Field	A field is an item of data within a record.
File	A file can be stored on backing storage. It may contain data, templates, graphics, etc. A data file used with a database is likely to contain a collection of similar and related records.
File librarian	The person responsible for the library of disks and tapes kept by a computer department.
Filename	The name of a file. This should be unique.
File server	A computer attached to a network whose main function is to enable network stations to access files stored on its hard disk.
Firewall	Security software used to prevent unauthorized access to file servers.
Flowchart	A graphical representation of the flow of data through a computer or an algorithm.
Font	A set of consistently shaped characters.
Format	Layout.

Front end processor	A small computer used to control communications between a larger mainframe computer and the terminals and other peripherals connected to it.
Gateway	A gateway connects one network to another. It converts the data passing through it so that each network can understand it. It can control access and monitor usage.
Gigabyte	1 Gigabyte is 1024 Megabytes or 2^{30} bytes.
Graphic design package	A software package that allows the user to draw on the screen, providing a range of design tools, different colours and patterns.
Graphics	Pictures or symbols which can be processed by a computer. They can be displayed on the screen, saved on disk, imported into DTP software, etc.
Graphics pad	A peripheral which allows the user to transfer drawings to the computer by drawing on paper resting on the graphics pad.
Graphic User Interface (GUI)	Another name for a WIMP (Windows, Icons, Menus, Pointers) user interface.
Graph plotter	An output peripheral that produces detailed pictures and diagrams on paper using a pen.
Hacker	An unauthorized user of a computer system who has broken into the system either by guessing a user Id (identity) and the associated password or by bypassing them.
Hard copy	Printout.
Hardware	The physical components of a computer system.
Hash total	A total calculated from a batch of source documents that is used to check that the batch is complete. The total has no meaning in itself.
Help	Instructions showing how to use software, often accessible whilst the software is running.
Hexadecimal	The base 16 number system. Allowable digits are 0 to 9 and A to F.
High level language	A problem-orientated programming language, e.g. COBOL, BASIC, Pascal, Logo.
Icon	A picture representing a command or function.
Information	Information is data that is meaningful to us.
Information Technology (IT)	The use of computer-based technology to store, process and transmit information.
Ink jet printer	A printer that prints by squirting jets of ink onto paper. The jets are arranged in a matrix. Character shapes are made up from a pattern of dots.
Input	Data supplied to a computer.
Insert	To put into. 'To insert a record' means to put a new record into a file.
Integer	Positive and negative whole numbers, e.g. 1, –6, 0, 3, 7.
Interactive processing	Interactive processing takes place when the user and the computer are in two-way communication.
Inter block gap	A gap left between two data blocks on a magnetic tape.
Interface	The interconnection between two different systems.
Internet	An international network made up of smaller networks that are interconnected.
Interrogate	See search.
Inter sector gap	A gap left between two sectors on a magnetic disk.
Intranet	The use of Internet technology to provide similar services but with access within a particular organization or group. For example, a company may run an Intranet for the information of its own employees only.
IT system	The organization of human and other resources, including IT, into a coherent system for the purposeful storage, processing and transmission of information.
Joystick	A lever used to move a pointer or other image around a monitor screen. A joystick is often used with computer games.
Key field	A field in a record used to identify the record.
Key-to-disk	A method of data preparation where data is entered at a keyboard and saved on disk.
Key-to-tape	A method of data preparation where data is entered at a keyboard and saved on tape.
Kilobyte	1024 or 2^{10} bytes.
Kimball tag	A small punched card which identifies a garment and holds details of its size, colour, price, etc.

Laptop	A portable computer that is small enough and light enough to be carried around. It has a fold-up LCD screen, and can be powered by battery or mains allowing its use in a variety of locations.
Laser printer	A page printer that works by etching a stencil of the page to be printed on an electrostatic drum, which is then transferred to the paper.
Laser scanner	A hardware device that inputs bar codes by scanning the pattern of light reflected off a bar code by a laser beam.
Light pen	A hardware device that inputs bar codes by scanning the pattern of light reflected off a bar code. It is shaped like a pen.
Liquid Crystal Display (LCD)	The technology used to provide screen displays on calculators and portable computers.
Load	To retrieve from backing storage. Load means the same as Open.
Local Area Network (LAN)	A network with permanent links between all the hardware connected to the network. It is probably located in one building.
Logic circuit	A circuit made up of individual logic gates.
Logic gate	A fundamental logic operation, e.g. AND, OR, NOT.
Logo	A high level language designed to manipulate words and sentences, and control movement.
Magnetic Ink Character Recognition (MICR)	A method of input where characters printed in magnetic ink are read directly into a computer.
Mail merge	The merging of a data file and a standard letter to produce personalized letters.
Mainframe computer	A large, fast computer, probably having a variety of peripherals, including a high capacity backing store and many terminals.
Mark sensing	An input method where pencil marks on paper are detected. Their position on the paper determines their meaning.
Master file	A data file which is used to store most of the data for a particular application. It is updated from the transaction file.
Megabyte	1 Megabyte is 1024 Kilobytes or 2^{20} bytes.
Memory	The part of the CPU that is used to store programs while they are running and data while it is being processed.
Menu	A list of tasks which can be carried out by a computer program. The user selects a task from the menu.
Merge	To combine one or more files into a single file.
Microcomputer	A small computer. Desk top computers, laptops, palmtops and PCs are all mirocomputers.
Microfilm	An output medium similar to photographic film.
Microprocessor	A single microchip containing all the elements of the CPU, except the memory.
MIDI	Musical Instrument Data Interface. The technology used to connect computers to synthesizers, drum machines and other music hardware.
Model	A representation of a real or imagined system. Computer based models can be constructed using a spreadsheet.
Modem	A MOdulator/DEModulator. Used to convert digital data output by a computer to analog signals that can be transmitted along a telephone line and vice versa.
Monitor	A screen used to display the output from a computer.
Mouse	A hand held input peripheral having buttons on top and a ball underneath. When the mouse is moved over a flat surface, a pointer on the screen moves in a corresponding direction.
Multiaccess	When many users are connected to a single computer.
Multimedia	The combination of text, sound, pictures, music and video in database type applications. Often based on CD-ROM backing storage technology.
Multiprogramming	When one computer is running more than one program at the same time, this is multiprogramming. It is likely that some of the programs will be under the control of different users from different terminals attached to a mainframe computer.
Multitasking	One user, on one computer, is apparently running more than one program at the same time.

Network	A network is a system of connecting cables. For example, networks can be used to connect computers; the telephone network connects telephone users.
Network station	A computer connected to a network.
Non-volatile memory	Non-volatile memory does not lose its contents when the power is switched off. ROM memory is non-volatile.
Notebook	A smaller version of a Laptop computer. Usually A4 size.
Off-line	Not on-line.
On-line	Connected to the computer and in communication with it.
Open	See Load.
Operating System	The Operating System is a program that makes the computer hardware more easily accessible to other programs. An Operating System is always present when a computer is used.
Operator	An operator looks after the computer while it is running, changing disks, tapes and printer paper as required.
Optical Character Recognition (OCR)	An input method that can read printed characters.
Optical Mark Recognition (OMR)	An input method that reads marks on a document. See Mark sensing.
OR gate	A logic gate that sets the output high if any of the inputs are high.
Page printer	A printer that prints a page at a time, e.g. a laser printer.
Parity	An automatic hardware check that data that has been transferred or stored has not been corrupted. An extra bit is added to make the number of bits set to 1 odd (odd parity) or even (even parity).
Pascal	A high level language named after Blaise Pascal, the French mathematician. Pascal is a structured language.
Password	A code that restricts access to a computer system. Usually associated with the User Id.
Pen	An input device used in a similar way to an ordinary pen. You press on a touch sensitive screen. It is often used with a GUI interface on a PDA.
Personal digital assistant (PDA)	A pocket-sized computer that has similar functions to a filofax. They can often read handwriting.
Peripheral	A peripheral is a hardware device that is connected to a computer system but is not part of the computer itself, e.g. a printer.
Pixel	The smallest area of a screen that can be used in building up a picture.
Pointer	An arrow or similar symbol which appears on the monitor screen. The position of the pointer is controlled by a mouse.
Point of Sale (POS) terminal	A terminal used to collect data at the point of sale. Often incorporates a laser scanner to read bar codes and a dot matrix printer to print receipts. May be on-line to a supermarket's computer system.
Port	A socket built into a computer used to link peripherals to it.
Portable	Portable programs can be run on a variety of different computers.
Printer server	A computer attached to a network whose main function is to enable network stations to use a printer that is attached to it.
Printout	The output from a printer.
Procedure	A set of instructions that performs a specific task. A procedure is a part of a computer program but it is not a complete program.
Program	A set of instructions used to control a computer. See Software.
Programmer	A computer programmer designs, codes, test and documents programs for a computer.
Programming language	A language that allows a computer user to control the computer. For example: Logo, BASIC, Pascal.
Pseudocode	A method of representing an algorithm, using words and sentences.
Pull-down menu	A feature of a WIMP (Windows, Icons, Menus, Pointers) user interface where a hidden menu can be revealed, i.e. pulled down, by pointing at its name.

Query	See search condition.
Random access	See direct access.
Random Access Memory (RAM)	Read/write memory within the computer's memory. RAM is volatile.
Range check	A check that a data value is within realistic limits.
Read Only Memory (ROM)	Memory that can only be read. ROM is non-volatile.
Real numbers	For practical purposes, real numbers are all the numbers we can use. Mathematicians sometimes use complex or imaginary numbers as well as real numbers.
Real time processing	The processing of input data that takes place so fast that when more data is input the results of the processing are already available. Real time processing occurs in real time, i.e. as it happens.
Record	A record is a collection of related fields.
Remote access	Access to a computer using a terminal or other network connection that is located a long way from the computer.
Robot	An electro-mechanical device that can be programmed to follow a sequence of commands in order to perform a specified task.
Router	A router connects one network to another. It can direct a message received from one network to its destination in another network.
Run	When software is run it is in use on a computer.
Save	To record on backing storage.
Scanner	A peripheral used to input photographs and pictures into a computer.
Scroll	The display on a monitor screen is said to scroll when, for example, it moves off the screen at the top and onto the screen at the bottom, automatically, at the same time.
Search	Look for.
Search condition	A search condition is used to determine which records are selected when searching a database. Also called a query command, a search string, etc.
Search engine	A Web server that can be used to search the Internet for information in the same way that a search condition is used to search a database.
Sensor	An input device used to sense environmental conditions.
Sequential access	Similar to serial access but the data records are stored in some order.
Serial access	A method of accessing data records. In order to access a data record in a serial access file, it is necessary to start at the beginning of the file and read all the preceding records. The records are not stored in any particular order.
Software	Computer programs and data.
Software package	A complete set of programs and documentation to enable a particular computer program to be used.
Sort	To put into order.
Source document	A document or questionnaire used for data capture. It is a written source of the data input to a computer.
Speech recognition	A method of input to a computer by speaking to it.
Speech synthesis	Sounds generated by a computer that synthesize human speech.
Spooling	A method of queueing output directed to a printer before printing it. The queue is usually saved on a hard disk.
Spreadsheet	Spreadsheets are used to calculate and display financial and other numerical information in rows and columns.
Standalone	A computer that is not communicating with any other computer is being used in stand-alone mode.
Stripe card	A plastic card containing a magnetic stripe which stores data. For example, a credit card.
Subroutine	See Procedure.
Systems analysis and design	The in-depth analysis of the software and hardware requirements of an IT system and its detailed design.

Systems analyst	A systems analyst is responsible for the progress of an IT system throughout the system's life cycle.
Systems life cycle	IT systems go through the cycle of systems investigation; feasibility study; systems analysis and design; program design, coding, testing and documentation; implementation, maintenance and evaluation.
Syntax	The set of rules which define the way an instruction in a programming language can be written.
Tapes	Magnetic tapes are a backing storage medium.
Technical documentation	Documentation written for technical specialists, e.g. computer programmers. Technical documentation contains the design of the system, program listings, testing schedules, etc.
Teletext	Text-based information accessible using a specially adapted television set, e.g. Oracle broadcast by ITV and Ceefax by the BBC.
Terminal	A network station.
Time sharing	A method of meeting the demands of a multiaccess system where many programs are required to be run apparently at the same time. Each program is given access to the CPU for a very short period of time (a time slice) in rotation.
Track	A track is the path on a magnetic tape or disk along which data is stored.
Tracker ball	A ball and buttons with the same function as a mouse. Instead of moving a mouse you turn the ball.
Transaction file	A file used to store recent data captured since the last master file update. The transaction file is used to update the master file.
Truth table	A table showing all the possible inputs to a logic gate or circuit and the corresponding outputs.
Turnaround document	A printout which has data written on it and is then used as a source document.
Turtle	A programmable robot with wheels. A turtle is used to learn how to control the movement of mobile robots on a flat surface. It is often controlled using Logo or a similar programming language.
Update	To bring up-to-date.
User documentation	Documentation written for users. User documentation should be user friendly.
User friendly	Easy for users to operate and understand.
User Id	The User Identification number that enables a computer system to recognize a user.
Utility program	A program that is used to do a task that is useful only in relation to the organization of a computer system, e.g. a virus scan.
Validation	A check that data is realistic.
Verification	A check that what is written on a source document is accurately transferred to a computer readable medium.
Videotext	A page-based information retrieval system, e.g. teletext.
Viewdata	A form of videotext that is accessed using a microcomputer and a modem via the telephone network.
Visual Display Unit (VDU)	A keyboard and screen used as a terminal.
Volatile memory	Volatile memory loses its contents when the power is switched off. RAM memory is volatile.
Wide Area Network (WAN)	A network spread over a wide area, possibly international, making use of both permanent cable connections and temporary connections, for example, using the telephone network.
Window	A rectangular subdivision of the screen. There may be more than one window on the screen at the same time.
Windows, Icons, Menus, Pointers (WIMP)	A user interface that avoids the need to remember complex, text Operating System commands by providing menus and icons that represent the commands. To select a command the user points and clicks a button on the mouse.
Wordprocessing	The preparation of letters and other documents using a computer in a manner similar to a typewriter but with additional features.

Wordwrap	A feature of a wordprocessor. When you type beyond the right hand margin, the word automatically carries over to the next line.
World Wide Web (The Web)	The Web runs across the Internet. It consists of many Web servers at locations throughout the world.
WORM (Write once read many) disk	A CD-ROM that can have data written to it by the user once only. The data can then be read many times.
Web server	A computer attached to the Web that provides information to users who access it using a browser.
WYSIWYG (What You See Is What You Get)	What is displayed on the screen is what will be printed on the printer. This phrase is particularly used in connection with wordprocessors.

 EXAMINATION QUESTIONS

▷ **Question 1**   The diagram shows a microcomputer system.

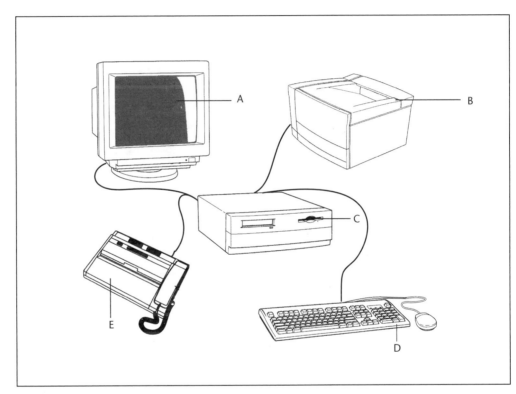

Fig. 3.6

Complete the table below using words from this list.
Communications   Main processor   Input   Output   Storage
(A word can be used more than once if necessary)

(SEG, 1993)

Label	Description
A	
B	
C	
D	
E	
F	

▷ **Question 2**

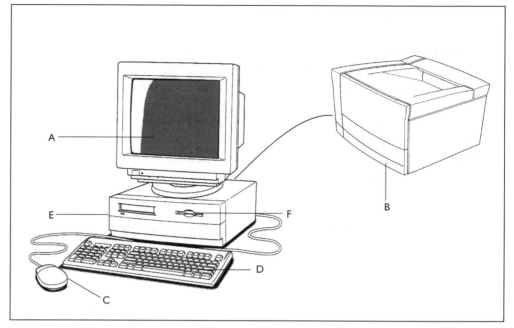

Fig. 3.7

(a) Fill in the table:

Label	Name of hardware device	Used for input, output, backing storage or processing?
A		
B		
C		
D		
E		
F		

(b) Which hardware device would you use to:
(i) type a letter?
(ii) draw a picture on the screen?
(iii) save information?
(iv) print a report?

(SEG, 1993)

▷ **Question 3**   (a) Draw and label a diagram of a computer system which will allow you to print out your work.
(b) Describe TWO things a computer is used for.

(NDTEF)

▷ **Question 4**   A pelican crossing has input, processing and output. Write the word input, output or process to describe each of the following:

Bleeper   ....
Button   ....
Red light   ....

(SEG, 1993)

▷ **Question 5**

MEGA-MICRO

Yours for only £1300. The new Mega-Micro comes with

▶   high resolution SVGA monitor
▶   540 Mbyte hard disk
▶   3.5 inch floppy disk drive
▶   32 Mbyte RAM
▶   MS-DOS Operating System
▶   Windows

Integrated wordprocessing, spreadsheet, database and graphics software and an ink jet printer.

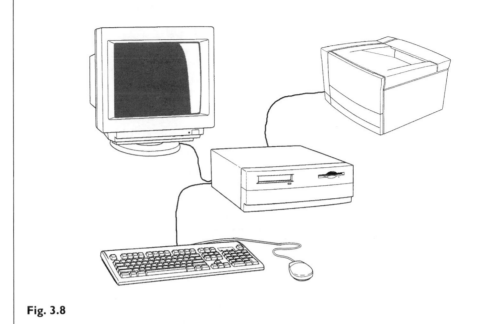

Fig. 3.8

Look at the above advertisement for a microcomputer.
(a)   Name the hardware units shown.
(b)   Explain what is meant by
    (i)   RAM
    (ii)   an Operating System

(City and Guilds)

▷ **Question 6**   Ring TWO items of software.

OMR form   spreadsheet   weather station   Operating System   printed paper   Kimball tag
(MEG)

▷ **Question 7**   From the list write down TWO items of hardware.
    documentation
    floppy disk
    mouse
    printer
    wordprocessor

(SEG, 1993)

▷ **Question 8**   A letter is stored on a computer disk and needs editing. Show which order you would carry out the following instructions by entering a number between 1 and 4 in each pair of brackets.

     edit and insert corrections   ( )
     load the data file   ( )
     print a copy   ( )
     load and run the software   ( )

(City and Guilds)

▷ **Question 9**   A local council is planning to build a new road. It will use information technology at many stages of the planning. Some of the systems available to it are:

     CAD (Computer Aided Design)
     Data logging
     Database
     DTP (Desk top publishing)
     Spreadsheet
     Word processing

Choose from the list above the most sensible system for each job below. Write your answer against each job. (Use each item ONCE only.)

Counting cars using existing roads	
Making an information booklet	
Analysing a questionnaire	
Designing a bridge	
Estimating the costs	
Writing to contractors	

(SEG, 1993)

▷ **Question 10**   Many supermarkets now use computerized systems to add up sales, produce till receipts and check stock levels.

     Not all shops use computerized systems like the one described above. Explain why such a system is unlikely to be used in a small greengrocery shop.   (NEAB/WJEC)

EXAMINATION ANSWERS

▷ **Answer 1**   A – output
     B – output
     C – main processor
     D – input
     E – communications

▷ **Answer 2**   (a)   A   monitor   output
               B   printer   output
               C   mouse   input
               D   keyboard   input
               E   processor   processing
               F   disk drive   backing storage

(b) (i) keyboard
    (ii) mouse
    (iii) disk drive
    (iv) printer

▷ **Answer 3**   (a)

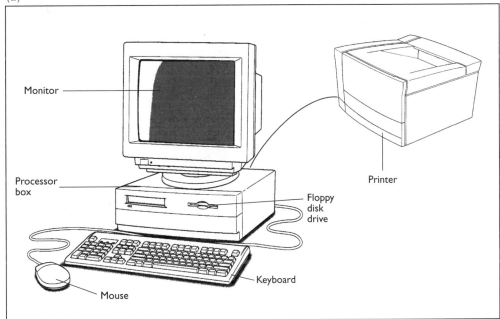

Fig. 3.9

(b) Some examples of things a computer is used for are:

   ▶ store information
   ▶ print information
   ▶ control robots and other devices
   ▶ run a spreadsheet

▷ **Answer 4**   Bleeper – output
              Button – input
              Red light – output

▷ **Answer 5**   (a) Monitor, keyboard, printer, processor box (contains hard disk and floppy disk drive), mouse.
         (b) (i) RAM is Random Access Memory. This is where programs are stored while they are being run and data is stored while it is being processed. RAM is volatile.
             (ii) An Operating System is a program that controls the computer. It is always present when a computer is being used. MSDOS is a popular Operating System for IBM compatible computers.

▷ **Answer 6**   Spreadsheet
              Operating System

▷ **Answer 7**   Mouse, printer

▷ **Answer 8**   Edit and insert corrections (3)
Load the data file (2)
Print a copy (4)
Load and run the software (1)

▷ **Answer 9**   Data logging
DTP
Database
CAD
Spreadsheet
Wordprocessing

▷ **Answer 10**   The cost of setting up the system could be too expensive for a small shop. The small volume of data to be processed does not need a computer to process it as it would not take very long to complete using manual methods.

EXAMINATION QUESTION WITH STUDENT ANSWER

A secretary is using a wordprocessor to write a letter.

(a) Put these tasks in the order they should be done:
   edit the letter
   load wordprocessing software into the computer
   print the letter
   save the letter
   turn off the computer
   open the letter
   turn on the computer
   write the letter

turn on the computer

load wordprocessing software into the computer

open the letter

edit the letter

save the letter

print the letter

write the letter

turn off the computer

(b) Which of the above tasks would be done using a floppy disk or a hard disk?

save the letter

▷ **Examiner's comment**   (a) 'This is essentially correct. However, the student has placed "write the letter" after "print the letter". It should appear before "edit the letter".
(b) This is correct but not complete: "load wordprocessing software into the computer" should also be included.'

SUMMARY

This chapter introduces some important ideas and technical terms that are fundamental to an understanding of IT.

▷ Information Technology is the use of computers and other equipment to store, process and transmit information.

▷ Hardware is the physical equipment.

▷ Software is the programs that control the computer.

▷ Mainframes are large computers.

▷ Microcomputers can be called Personal Computers (PCs), desk top computers, portable, laptops.

▷ Microcomputers typically comprise a monitor, a processor box, a hard disk, a floppy disk drive, a keyboard and a mouse. Multimedia PCs also have a CD-ROM drive and stereo speakers.

    Input is from a mouse, a keyboard.

    Output is to a monitor, a printer and speakers.

    Backing storage is hard disks, floppy disks and CD-ROM.

▷ The computer's memory is installed in the processor box.

▷ Memory size is measured in bytes. A byte is the momery required to store 1 character.

    1 Kbyte = 1024 bytes

    1 Mbyte = 1024 Kybtes

    1 Gbyte = 1024 Mbytes

▷ RAM is volatile memory. This is where programs are stored while they are being run, and data is stored while is being processed.

▷ ROM is non-volatile memory.

▷ Most computers are digital. Data is stored as patterns of 1s and 0s.

▷ Characters are represented using ASCII. Numbers are in binary.

▷ If you want to use software, you would:

    switch on the computer

    load the software into memory

    run the software

    input information

    edit information

    output information

    exit the software

    switch off the computer

Chapter

4

Data capture and input

This chapter should be read if you are preparing for GCSE IT assessment with the following examining boards:

C & G	MEG	NEAB	SEG
London	NDTEF	RSA	WJEC

► GETTING STARTED

Data capture is the collection of data and its input to a computer. The variety of ways in which data can be collected and input is determined by the hardware available. This chapter reviews a range of different methods of data capture and the associated hardware.

The data captured should be accurate and input to the computer without mistakes. Verification and validation ensure that data is accurate and realistic.

C & G	LONDON	MEG	NDTEF	NEAB	RSA	SEG	WJEC	TOPIC	STUDY	REVISION 1	REVISION 2
✓	✓	✓	✓	✓	✓	✓	✓	Questionnaires and other forms			
✓		✓			✓	✓	✓	Verification			
✓	✓	✓	✓	✓	✓	✓	✓	Mark sensing and optical character recognition (OCR)			
✓	✓	✓	✓	✓	✓	✓	✓	Bar codes and light pens or laser scanners			
✓	✓	✓	✓		✓	✓	✓	Kimball tag			
✓	✓	✓	✓	✓	✓	✓	✓	Magnetic ink character recognition			
✓	✓	✓	✓	✓	✓	✓	✓	Magnetic stripe cards			
✓	✓	✓	✓	✓	✓	✓	✓	Voice recognition			
✓	✓	✓	✓	✓	✓	✓	✓	Sound sampling and music			
✓	✓	✓	✓		✓	✓	✓	Joystick			
✓	✓	✓	✓	✓	✓	✓	✓	Mouse			
✓	✓				✓	✓		Tracker ball			
✓	✓	✓	✓	✓	✓	✓	✓	Touch screen			
✓	✓	✓	✓	✓	✓	✓	✓	Graphic pad			
✓	✓	✓	✓	✓	✓	✓	✓	Scanner			
✓	✓	✓	✓	✓	✓	✓	✓	Video digitizers			
✓	✓	✓	✓	✓	✓	✓	✓	Digital camera			
✓	✓	✓	✓	✓	✓	✓	✓	Sensors			
✓	✓	✓	✓	✓	✓	✓	✓	Validation			
✓	✓	✓	✓	✓	✓	✓	✓	Garbage In, Garbage Out			

GLOSSARY

Input Input is the process of supplying data to a computer. For example, you can input characters using a keyboard; you can input a bar code using a laser scanner.

Verification Verification is checking that what is written on a source document (e.g. a questionnaire) is accurately input to a computer.

Validation Validation is checking that the information input is realistic. For example, the number of days in a month is more than 0 and less than 32.

WHAT YOU NEED TO KNOW

Data capture is the collection of data and its input to a computer. There is a wide variety of different methods. Some of these are described in this chapter.

Questionnaires and other forms

Getting people to fill in a questionnaire or form is one way of collecting data. An example of a form that might be filled in when reading an electricity meter is shown in Fig. 4.1.

ELECTRICITY BOARD

'Using character boxes for the name and address'

Account Number   B 025741X

Customer   MR J.B. Priestley

Address   5 Mill Bank Drive

Hexham

HX2 4PD

Previous Meter Reading   5 7 2 1 4

New Meter Reading

Status (please tick one box)

'Using a tick list'

Electricity board meter reader

Other electricity board employee

Customer

Other, please specify ....

Signed ....   Date

Instructions
1. Fill in the New Meter Reading.
2. Check that it is BIGGER than the Previous Meter Reading.
3. If any details have changed, fill in the new details in the boxes on the right hand side.

Fig. 4.1 A data capture form used to read an electricity meter

When designing a questionnaire or form we:

(a) Use simple language so people can easily understand;
(b) Say clearly and unambiguously what is needed;
(c) Provide enough space for the answer;
(d) Provide help in answering if possible;
(e) Give examples if these would be helpful;
(f) Collect all the information that is needed, but no more;
(g) Avoid asking questions that may not be answered truthfully;
(h) Record information in a way which will help computer input, e.g. using character boxes or tick lists;
(i) State why the information is being collected;
(j) Provide space for respondents to sign and date the form.

A questionnaire or form used for data capture is known as a **source document**. The data on a source document must be input *before* it can be processed.

One way to input the information written on a source document is to enter it using a keyboard.

▷ Verification

'The double entry method'

In order to be sure that information on a source document has been accurately input the data is '**verified**' (see Fig. 4.2).

To verify data we use the 'double-entry' method:

Step 1. Input the data.
Step 2. Input the data again.
Step 3. Compare the results of each operation. If these are the same then we have input the data accurately. If they are not the same then we have made a mistake and must correct it.

The advantage of the double-entry method is that the data is accurately input; the disadvantage is that it takes twice as long and, consequently, costs more. For this reason, methods of data capture and input have been developed that *avoid* the need to key-in and verify data. Some of these are described below.

A further disadvantage of double entry vertification is that if the same mistake is made in Steps 1 and 2 then inaccurate data will be input. However, this is very unlikely, especially if Steps 1 and 2 are carried out by different people using different equipment.

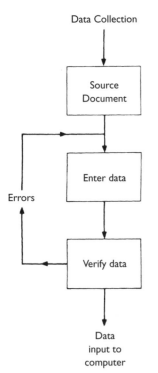

Fig. 4.2 Verification

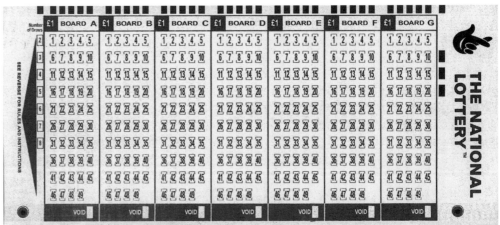

Fig. 4.3 A mark sensing form

▷ Mark sensing and optical character recognition (OCR)

In **mark sensing**, marks are made on a specially designed form or questionnaire using a pencil (see Fig. 4.3). The position of the mark on the form or questionnaire gives it meaning. By shining a light onto the paper and recording the intensity of the reflected light returned to it, a *mark sense reader* attached to the computer reads the data directly into the memory of the computer. This avoids the need to key in the data. There is no verification of the input data. Mark sensing is often used for multiple choice exam papers and National Lottery tickets.

For Optical Character Recognition (OCR), written or printed text is read using a special reader, or scanner, that works in a similar way to a mark sense reader. In OCR it is not the position of the marks on the paper that gives them meaning but the *shape* of the different characters and numbers. OCR can be used to read the pages of a book or a typed A4 sheet directly into the computer. The text input can be wordprocessed. This enables libraries to transfer their books to the computer and offices to store letters on a magnetic disk.

▷ **Bar codes and light pens or laser scanners**

Bar codes and **light pens** or **laser scanners** are most often found in use in supermarket information systems. The light pen or laser scanner is used to *read* the bar code. The bar code is used to *identify* a specific item, e.g. an 850 gram can of baked beans. For an example of a typical bar code see Fig. 4.4. When shopping is taken to the checkout the cashier passes the items over a scanner which will read the bar code. A bar code is printed on most of the items stocked. If there is no bar code on the item then the price is entered on a cash register in the usual way. The cash register and scanner used are connected to a central computer and are known as a Point of Sale terminal (**POS terminal**).

Fig. 4.4 A bar code on a can of baked beans

Country of origin

Check digit

Product

Manufacturer

Fig. 4.5 The information contained in a bar code

```
SPONGE PUDD      0.54
CASSEROLE        4.75
400 STFGRAIN     0.40
BAKED BEANS      0.29
AMERCN GNGR      0.43
DOLMIO SAUCE     0.89
PEAR HALVES      0.37
MUSHROOMS
    0.70lb
  @ 1.32/lb      0.92


TOTAL           31.23
   45 ITEMS
CHEQUE          31.23
CHANGE DUE       0.00
- - - - - - - - - - - - - - - -

   THANK YOU

16/06/94 17:30 011116
      6022   2231
```

Fig. 4.6 Receipt printed at a POS terminal

The bar code contains codes which identify the *country of origin*, the *company* which manufactured the item, the *product* and a *check digit* (see Fig. 4.5). This information is read by the laser scanner and sent to the computer. The description of the item and its price are stored in the computer and instantly sent back to the checkout where they are printed on the receipt (see Fig. 4.6).

Data input using this system is not verified. The likelihood of entering the occasional wrong or damaged bar code is very small, so this is not a problem. If an incorrect bar code is entered it is likely that a *validation check* (see below), using the check digit or matching the input bar codes against a table of valid bar codes, will highlight such errors.

This IT system also provides detailed information on what has been sold, which is useful to the supermarket for stock-keeping, re-ordering and marketing. Staff operating the checkouts need less training and can work faster. They could be paid less as the job is made easier and fewer of them are needed. Alternatively, the supermarket could train staff to improve customer services.

The customer is provided with more detailed information on purchases made. Unfortunately it is likely that the goods will not have individual price labels; this will make shopping more difficult as price comparisons cannot easily be made.

Fig. 4.7 Kimball tag

▷ **Kimball tag**

Kimball tags are small punched cards (see Fig. 4.7). They are commonly found in clothes shops. They usually have printed on them information that identifies the garment they are attached to, e.g. description, size, colour, price and other details. This data is also recorded on the Kimball tag by means of punched holes in a special code. When a garment is sold, the Kimball tag is retained by the shop. The data on the Kimball tag can be input directly to the computer using a *Kimball Tag Reader*. Kimball tags have essentially the same function as bar codes, but they can hold more data. As with bar codes, the data input is not verified. Since Kimball tags can be torn easily this could be a problem. However, they are helpful in keeping accurate stock records.

▷ Magnetic ink character recognition

Magnetic Ink Character Recognition (MICR) is most commonly used with bank cheques (see Fig. 4.8). MICR is only possible with a very restricted font. The font in use in the UK, has only 14 possible characters, including the digits 0 to 9. Numbers are printed in magnetic ink along the bottom of the cheque. These numbers are codes which identify the bank, the customer's account and the cheque. They can be read directly into the computer.

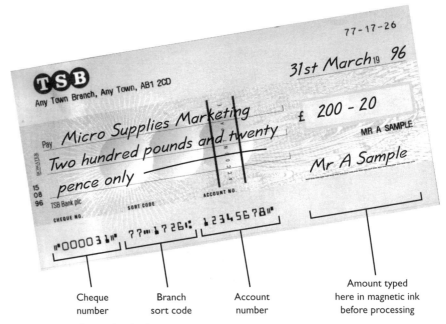

Fig. 4.8 MICR used on a bank cheque

When paying for goods in a shop, the customer fills in a cheque in payment for the goods bought. When the cheque is filled in the amount is written on the cheque by the customer. The customer gives the cheque to the shopkeeper who deposits the cheque at the bank. The MICR reader at the bank cannot read the amount written by the customer in normal ink. This must be typed onto the cheque in *magnetic ink* before it can be processed. The MICR reader will read the information on the cheque directly into the computer.

There is no verification of input data. Cheques can be quite badly damaged before it is necessary to enter the data in some other way. Input can be fast. Up to 2000 cheques per minute is possible. When the cheque is processed, money will be transferred from the customer's account to the shopkeeper's account.

▷ Magnetic stripe cards

A **magnetic stripe** is a short length of magnetic tape sealed into the surface of a plastic card (see Fig. 4.9). Plastic cards containing magnetic stripes are given to customers of banks and credit card companies. These magnetic stripes carry enough information to allow a computer to identify the customer so that their credit limit can be checked.

Magnetic stripe cards are also used as phone cards. Some telephones accept phone cards instead of cash. The number of units unused is recorded on the card. When the user makes a telephone call the units used are deducted from those on the card and the new total recorded on the card.

▷ Voice Recognition

Using a microphone as an input device, computers can be programmed to recognize a limited range of spoken input. This is **voice recognition**. It is a useful method of input for workers whose hands are occupied with other tasks, or for disabled people with little hand movement.

Fig. 4.9 A magnetic stripe on a credit card (from Barclaycard). The stripe is above the signature box.

▷ **Sound sampling and music**

Natural sound can be input and recorded in digital form on a magnetic disk. The sound can be processed. It may be used as part of a musical composition or in sounds for video games.

Music itself can be input, processed and re-played using a computer connected to a synthesizer. The music can be edited as you would edit words using a wordprocessor. Musical scores can be printed and the computer can store the music on floppy disk or other backing storage.

Most computers use **midi** (musical instrument data interface) technology to connect to synthesizers and other midi instruments, such as drum machines. Some computers have built in midi ports, e.g. the Atari ST, but usually you have to buy an external midi interface box.

▷ **Joystick**

Joysticks are widely used for playing games with computers in the home (see Fig. 4.10). They can be made using two small potential dividers (*pots*). These provide voltages of between 0 and 5 volts which are input to the computer. The voltages are converted by an Analog to Digital Converter (ADC) to numbers which the computer can process. One pot provides an X coordinate, the other provides the Y coordinate. The position of a pointer on the screen is found using its X–Y coordinates. When the joystick handle is moved, the voltages input to the computer change, leading to different converted X,Y values. The software responds by moving the screen pointer. In this way the screen pointer can be moved to any part of the screen. Screen pointers can be spaceships, etc., when playing computer games.

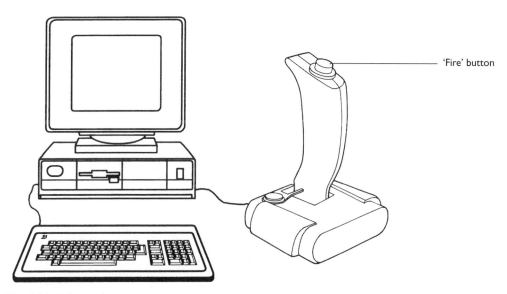

'Fire' button

Fig. 4.10 A joystick

▷ **Mouse**   A **mouse** (see Fig 4.11) is a small hand-held input device with a ball fitted underneath. When the mouse is moved, the signal created by the movement of the ball is transmitted to the computer. This controls a pointer on the screen which moves in a direction corresponding to the direction of the mouse.

There are usually 2 or 3 buttons on the mouse.

Pull-down menus are accessed by pointing at them with the mouse. They consist of lists of features which can be *selected* by *pointing* at them *and clicking* a button on the mouse.

Icons are pictures that suggest the function or feature they represent, e.g. a picture of a floppy disk may give the user the possibility of saving or loading files to/from a disk. The user can select the icon by pointing at it and clicking a button on the mouse.

The mouse has proved to be such a useful, easy-to-use and versatile input device that most computers are sold with one. It is often difficult to use a computer *without* a mouse. A mouse is used with a WIMP screen (see Fig. 4.12). **WIMP** stands for 'Windows, Icons, Menus, Pointers'. WIMP screens are also known as Graphic User Interfaces (**GUIs**).

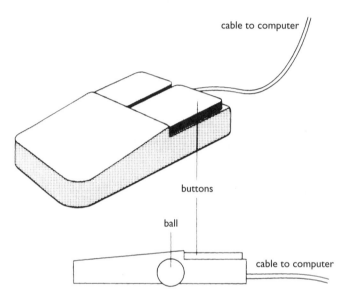

Fig. 4.11 A mouse

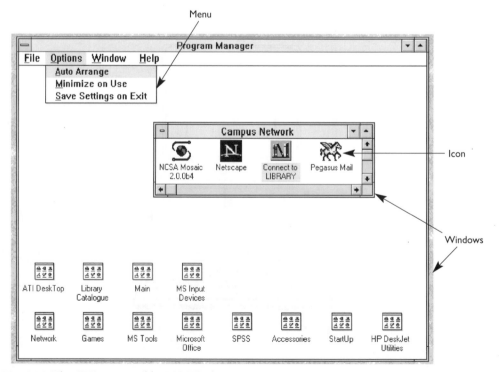

Fig. 4.12 The GUI generated by MS Windows

▷ **Tracker ball** A tracker ball works in a similar way to a mouse. On a tracker ball, the ball is built into the top of the device and it is exposed. You move the ball not the device. There are buttons next to the exposed ball that have the same function as mouse buttons.

You can use the tracker ball to access pull-down menus and select icons as you would with a mouse. You move the pointer on the screen by moving the ball, and select a menu option or icon by clicking the buttons.

Fig. 4.13 A touch pad built into an Apple Powerbook computer

Tracker balls are sometimes used with portable computers. When you are using a portable computer, you may have it balanced on your knees as you sit on the train or in your car. In these circumstances, it is difficult to use a mouse as there may not be a suitable flat surface to move a mouse on. A built-in-tracker ball is ideal. An alternative in a touch pad, as shown in Fig. 4.13.

▷ **Touch screens** A touch screen allows the computer to be operated by touching the monitor screen. There will be a GUI-type display on the screen. The user touches the screen where an icon or menu is displayed. This is then selected.

Touch screens usually have a touch sensitive membrane spread over them. This membrane may be almost invisible and very difficult to detect. The screen may look like a normal screen to the user. Alternatively there may be infrared transmitters and detectors on the monitor around the edge of the screen. Whatever technology is used the principle is the same. When the user touches the screen with a finger or a pen, its position is input to the computer. If it corresponds with an icon or menu option, this is selected.

Touch screens can be very useful where an information service is provided to the public. For example, a Tourist Information Centre may want to make information about accommodation in self-catering cottages available to the public. This could be displayed on a monitor screen that is accessible through a hole cut in a wall, with the rest of the computer kept secure behind the wall. The information service could be made available when the Tourist Information Centre is closed by giving access through an outside wall.

A touch screen is also used with a 'Palmtop' computer or Personal Digital Assistant (PDA), see Fig. 4.14. PDAs are very small computers about the size of a filofax. They are effectively computerized filofaxes. They can hold a wide range of information and access it very quickly. They can recognize handwriting and change it to text. They are also used with a GUI. Instead of moving a mouse to control the pointer on the screen, you touch the screen with a pen in the place you are pointing at. There are no buttons on the pen but there is an icon on the screen that is used to select menu options and other icons. You can use the pen to access pull-down menus and select icons as you would with a mouse.

▷ **Graphics pad**   Using a mouse or tracker ball with a graphics program, it is possible to draw on the screen. However, the technique of using a mouse or tracker ball is quite different from drawing with an ordinary pencil. In order to make drawing easier and more natural, a **graphics pad** can be used. This consists of a flat surface containing a touch-sensitive membrane (see Fig. 4.15). When the user presses on the surface using a rigid stylus, the membrane registers the pressure on the surface and a corresponding mark is displayed on the screen. If paper is placed on the surface of the graphics pad, a normal pen or pencil can be used in place of the stylus and the user can draw on the paper and on the screen at the same time. In this way maps can be traced and diagrams and pictures, etc., can be transferred to the graphics program for further enhancement.

Fig. 4.14 An Amstrad Pen Pad PDA

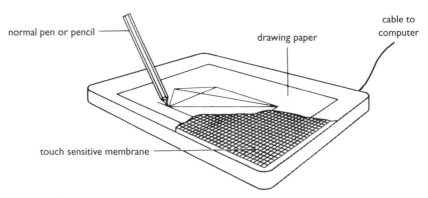

Fig. 4.15 A graphics pad

▷ **Scanner**   **Scanners** are used to input text, diagrams and pictures into the computer. Scanners can be hand-held but more often they are about the size of a desk top photocopier. Printed text can be scanned using OCR software so that it can be wordprocessed. Diagrams and pictures can be scanned and loaded into graphics software where they can be altered or enhanced.

▷ **Video digitizers**

Video **digitizers** convert a video signal into a digitized representation in the memory of the computer. They consist of hardware to intercept the video signal and specialized software. Each frame in the video signal is digitized. At the press of a button, or in response to a pre-programmed sequence, the digitized image is saved onto disk. This can be done for a single frame, or a series of frames. Saving the digitized image of a video frame on disk is known as 'frame grabbing'. Using a video digitizer it is possible to capture a single frame from a video and print it as a picture in a magazine. A series of frames can have graphics or cartoons added using a graphics program. This technique is used to make TV adverts, pop-videos, etc.

▷ **Digital camera**

A **digital camera** takes a picture and stores the image in digital form in a small amount of RAM installed in it. This is in contrast to a 'normal' camera that stores the image on film. The size of RAM in the camera may be very small so that only a small number of pictures can be taken. It is currently usual for the RAM to be fixed in the camera. Once the RAM is full, the pictures must be input to a computer before more are taken. Otherwise, pictures that have been taken earlier are lost. More expensive digital cameras have removable RAM which extends the number of pictures that can be taken. To input pictures to the computer, the digital camera is connected to it and image acquisition software is used to transmit the image from the RAM in the camera to the computer's memory. The images can then be enhanced using graphics software, saved and printed. This is a developing technology. A few digital cameras now use a floppy disk to save pictures.

▷ **Sensors**

There are many types of **sensor** and they have a wide variety of uses. They can be used to record temperature, humidity, light intensity, etc. Sensors usually produce a voltage which must be converted to a digital signal using an Analog to Digital Converter (ADC). The digital signal is interpreted as a binary number which can be used by the software to monitor or display a graph of the 'sensed' condition. A combination of sensors could be used to control a greenhouse, keeping the conditions suitable for optimum plant growth.

▷ **Validation**

'Common validation checks'

All data entered into a computer for processing is validated if at all possible. **Validation** is a check to make sure that **all** the data to be processed is realistic. Some common validation checks are described below:

Table lookup

The input data, for example a bar code, is checked against a table or list of *all* the bar codes that are used. If it is not in the table, then it is not acceptable.

Range check

Numbers input are checked to see if they are either too big or too small. For example, if dates are stored in DDMMYY form, 021293 is a valid date, but 213492 is not, as 34 is not a valid month. Months must lie in the range 01 to 12.

Type check

This is a check that the data to be processed is of the expected type. For example, if the computer expected a date to be input and '£134.96' was input, then obviously there has been a mistake.

There are many different types of data. *Characters* and *numbers* were described in Chapter 3. Technically, these data types may be known as *alphanumeric* and *numeric*, respectively. These and some other data types are listed below with an explanation of what they mean, and correct and incorrect examples.

Data type	Explanation	Correct examples	Incorrect examples
alphanumeric	almost any character string	'23 Main St, Seattle'	control characters
numeric	integer and real numbers (see below)		
integer	a whole number	26, –7, 0	26.7, A13, $6\frac{1}{2}$
real	any number	45.75, –5.125	50%, 24b
date	a valid date in an accepted format, e.g. DDMMYY	131297, 010286	3.125, IX286B, –9

Check digit

A check digit is an extra digit added to a number. The check digit is calculated in a prescribed way that is known to all users. Every time the number is transcribed, possibly read over the telephone, the check digit is re-calculated. If the correct check digit is *not* obtained from the calculation, then an error has been made and the data must be re-checked. The **International Standard Book Number** (ISBN) contains a check digit in the rightmost position.

ISBN	0	631	90057	8
Weight	10	987	65432	1

The check digit has a value that makes the sum of the products of the digits and the weights exactly divisible by 11. In the above example $(0 \times 10) + (6 \times 9) + (3 \times 8) + (1 \times 7) + ... + (8 \times 1)$ is exactly divisible by 11. This is known as a '*weighted modulus 11*' check digit. It can take the values 0 to 9 and 10 (which is represented by an X). You will find an ISBN on every published book, including this one – look at the back cover!

Totals

The use of totals is best explained using an example. Suppose we are doing the payroll for a company. We may have the batch of data shown in Fig. 4.16 to process.

```
Employee number    Name            Hours worked
    34532          Jones               34
    55234          Patel               37
    89686          Singh               29
    45378          Hardcastle          27
    76859          Stratton            40
   ───────                            ────
   301689                              167
```

Fig. 4.16

In the example the employee numbers and the hours worked have been totalled. The total hours worked is a meaningful total. It is the total length of time worked by all these workers. This is known as a **control total**. The total of the employee numbers is meaning-less. This is called a **hash total**. However, provided the details for this group of workers is kept together in a batch, neither of these totals will change. If the totals are re-calculated and they are *not* the same, then the details for some of the workers are either missing or have been changed. This example uses only a few workers to illustrate the use of totals. In large companies with many workers, totals help keep track of all their details.

▷ **Garbage in, garbage out**

'The importance of verification and validation'

It is most important to be certain that the data input for processing is correct. When data is captured on a source document, it must be verified to ensure that what is written on the source document is accurately transferred to a computer-readable medium. When data is input for processing, it should be carefully validated to make sure that it is realistic. If incorrect data is input, then the result of any data processing may be wrong . . . GARBAGE IN, GARBAGE OUT.

▶ EXAMINATION QUESTIONS

▷ **Question 1**   Ring TWO items that can be used to collect data for pupil records.

mouse   keyboard   line printer
optical mark reader   screen   ROM

(MEG)

▷ **Question 2**   Give two ways in which typewritten text can be input to a computer.

(City and Guilds)

▷ **Question 3**   Name the three items that are printed in magnetic ink on a cheque.

(City and Guilds)

▷ **Question 4**   A gas board issues its meter readers with a document for each meter to be read.

REF. NO:	DATE:
NAME:	MAX:
	MIN:
ADDRESS	READING: ☐☐☐☐☐
	CODE: ☐
	Insert N if no reading available
	Insert R if reading outside range

Items in certain fields will be printed by the computer before the document is issued to the meter reader.

(a)   Identify three items that will be printed before issue to the meter reader.
(b)   Identify two items that might be filled in by the meter reader.

(SEG, 1993)

▷ **Question 5**   Many small railway stations now have automatic machines to issue tickets.
(a) Tick ONE change in everyday life caused by this:

Fewer staff are needed in the booking office	
Tickets are more expensive	
Trains run to time more often	

(b) Tick ONE way data is held on the ticket so it can be read by automatic ticket barriers.

Security codes	
Magnetic stripes	
Raised characters	

(SEG, 1993)

▷ **Question 6**   The traffic light system of a large town is to be computerized. The lights at many junctions are to be controlled by a single central computer.

(a) Give two types of input that would be required for the system.
(b) Give two benefits that introducing the system would have.

(SEG, 1993)

▷ **Question 7**   One type of error that could be made when data is typed into a computer system is a transcription error.

(a) A transcription error can be detected by a verification check. Explain how this check is carried out.
(b) A date can be validated as well as verified. A date is to be input in the form 25 APR 1994 (a two digit day, followed by a three letter month, followed by a four digit year). Describe the validation checks that could be carried out on dates in this form.

▷ **Question 8**   A supermarket uses point of sale (POS) terminals. All the products sold carry bar codes.

(a) Name a device used to input bar codes at the checkouts.
(b) Give TWO advantages of this type of system compared with a manual system:
(i) For the shopper.
(ii) For the supermarket manager.

(NEAB)

▷ **Question 9**   (a) What method of data capture would be most suitable for recording the information in each of the following situations? In each case tick the most suitable method.

Situation	Most suitable method of data capture			
A book has been returned to a library after a loan	Bar codes	OMR	Magnetic stripe	OCR
The answers given by pupils in multiple choice exam questions	Bar codes	OMR	Magnetic stripe	OCR
Reading account numbers when a customer pays a gas bill	Bar codes	OMR	Magnetic stripe	OCR

(b) Give one other situation where a different method of data capture is used other than those listed above. Explain how the data is captured and why this method is the most suitable.
(c) A point of sale system in a supermarket includes a scanner attached to each till to read bar codes.
    The bar code on a tin of peas contains the item code and a check digit.
    (i) Why does it not contain the price?
    (ii) What is the purpose of the check digit?
    (iii) The till receipt contains the name of the item and its price. How is this information obtained?
    (iv) What name is given to the mode of operation used to produce the receipt?

(NEAB/WJEC)

▷ **Question 10**   A computer company called Soft Options has just bought a list from Zamco which details names and addresses of companies in the Somerset area. Soft Options wants to identify companies which:

> have more than 500 employees;
> use the Wordprocessing software WORD or WORDPERFECT;
> have a budget of £5000.

Soft Options will target these companies in a sales promotion.
  Design a questionnaire to collect the information for Soft Options.

(City and Guilds)

 EXAMINATION ANSWERS

> **Answer 1**   OMR reader
Keyboard

(MEG)

> **Answer 2**   You can type it in using a keyboard.
You can scan it using OCR software.

> **Answer 3**   The sort code, the account number and the cheque number are printed on a cheque before
it is filled in. The amount is printed on the cheque after it has been filled in.

> **Answer 4**   (a) Ref. No. | Max.
Name | Min.
Address |
(b) Date
Reading
Code

> **Answer 5**   (a) Fewer staff are needed in the booking office.
(b) Magnetic stripes.

> **Answer 6**   (a) Sensors in the road that detect when a car has passed. Push buttons for pedestrians.
(b) Some benefits are:

> The speed of the traffic can be controlled.
> The distribution of traffic can be monitored and controlled so that hold-ups are
avoided or minimized.
> Pedestrians wanting to cross the road can be fitted in with traffic flows.

> **Answer 7**   (a) A verification check consists of:
Step 1: Two different people enter the data.
Step 2: The computer cross-checks the data entered by one person against the data
entered by the other person.
Step 3: Differences are identified and checked against the original data. The
data in the computer is edited until the cross-check identifies no differences.
(b) The two-digit day should be:

> two digits, e.g. 01 not 1.
> larger than 00.
> no more than 28, 29, 30 or 31 depending on the month.

The three letter month should be:

> exactly 3 letters, e.g. APR, not AP or APRIL.
> one of JAN, FEB, . . . , NOV, DEC.

The four digit year should be within a realistic range depending on the application.

▷ **Answer 8**   (a)   Laser scanner, light pen, or bar code reader.
           (b)   (i)   ▶   Receipts are itemized.
                          ▶   Accurate charging with fewer mistakes.
              (ii)   ▶   Checkout staff are more productive, so fewer are needed.
                          ▶   Stock-keeping and re-ordering can be done automatically.

▷ **Answer 9**   (a)   Library – bar codes.
                   Multiple choice exam – OMR.
                   Gas bill – OCR.
           (b)   Situation: Processing bank cheques.
                   Method of data capture: MICR.
                   Suitable because: cheques can be read more quickly and accurately. It is relatively difficult to alter the data on the cheque.
           (c)   (i)   The price is not in the bar code because the price changes. The bar code identifies the product and the price is obtained from the computer. The price held on the computer can easily be changed.
                (ii)   To enable the computer to check that it has read the bar code accurately.
                (iii)   The bar code identifies the item. The name and price of the item are stored on the computer with the bar code. The computer uses the bar code to find the name and price. It then prints them on the receipt.
                (iv)   The computer system is 'on-line' and 'interactive'.

▷ **Answer 10**   The questionnaire should collect this information:

       ▶   the company's name and address
       ▶   the number of employees
       ▶   the wordprocessor used
       ▶   the annual budget

There should be instructions on how to fill in the form and boxes to fill in. The budget could be grouped into 5 or 6 ranges, e.g. £5,000 – £6,000, and tick lists provided.

There should be an explanation of why the data is being collected and the person filling in the form should sign and date it.

EXAMINATION QUESTION WITH STUDENT ANSWER

A newspaper uses a computer to store details of its photographic library. Each photograph has information stored under the following headings: Description, Subject, Date, Negative Number, Photographer, Filmtype.
    The dates are read into the computer in the following format:
DDMMMYY, e.g. 15DEC92

(a)   Each of the following dates has been rejected by a validation program. State which validation check has been used to discover each error.

      AUG2166   *the month is in the wrong place*

      3JAN71   *too short*

      31SEP62   *there are only 30 days in September*

(b)   Produce a comprehensive list of test data to test the date validation checks.

      13Feb91

      19Dec92

      12Jan84

(City and Guilds)

▷ **Examiner's comment**

(a) These answers are correct but do not show that the student knows which errors a computer can detect. Better answers would be:

AUG2166 – the two leftmost characters should be digits.
3JAN71   – each date should be 7 characters in length.
31SEP62 – the two leftmost digits are out of range. In this case they should be between 01 and 30, inclusive.

(b) Part (b) is poorly answered. To construct useful test data you need to have a clear idea of the validation checks you are testing. Generally speaking you should test extreme values and one or two acceptable values for each validation check.

For example, if you were testing a validation check to ensure the date had the correct length, you could use this test data:

30 SEP6 – an extreme value, just too short
30SEP62 – an acceptable value
05JAN 93 – an acceptable value
15FEB955 – an extreme value, just too long

Other validation checks that should be tested would check that:

▶ the two leftmost characters are numbers
▶ the middle three characters are letters
▶ the two rightmost characters are numbers
▶ the day is within range for the month
▶ the month is one of JAN, FEB, ..., DEC
▶ the year is within a sensible range for the application

Clearly, a complete answer is quite extensive. In the exams, your answer may not be complete but should show that you understand validation checks and how to construct the data to test them.

SUMMARY

This chapter reviews a range of different methods of data capture and input.

▷ Questionnaires should be simple, clear, have enough space to answer, give help in answering, and record information in a way that makes input to a computer easier. Character boxes and tick lists should be used. It should be clear why the information is needed, and there should be space for repondents to sign and date the questionnaire.

▷ Information input using a keyboard, from questionnaires or other forms, should be verified.

▷ Verification is checking that what is written on a form is accurately input to a computer.

▷ Double-entry verification ensures accurate input but takes loger and costs more. Consequently, it is avoided if possible.

▷ In mark sensing, the position of a mark on a form gives it meaning. For example, the form used to buy National Lottery tickets.

▷ In Optical Character Recognition (OCR) text is input using a scanner.

▷ Bar codes can be read using a light pen or laser scanner. These are often used in supermarkets and libraries.

▷ Kimball tags are small punched cards. These are sometimes used by clothes shops.

▷ Magnetic Ink Character Recognition (MICR) is used to read bank cheques.

▷ Credit cards and other bank cards are examples of magnetic stripe cards.

▷ Voice recognition is a useful input method for disabled people and workers whose hands are occupied.

▷ Sound and music can be input, processed and re-played using IT.

▷ A joystick, a mouse and a tracker ball can be used for input to a Graphic User Interface (GUI).

▷ Touch screens may be operated using a pen or finger. They are also used with GUIs.

▷ Graphics can be input by drawing on a graphic pad or using a scanner.

▷ Using a video digitizer, single frames or sequences of frames from a video can be captured and input to a computer.

▷ When a digital camera takes a photograph it does not record the image on film. Instead it records the image in a digital form that can be immediately input to a computer.

▷ Sensors can be used to record temperature, humidity, light, wind speed, etc.

▷ Validation is a check that the information input is realistic. Examples are:

    ▷ a table lookup checks that, for example, a customer number is one that is in use:

    ▷ a range check checks that, for example, the day of the month is more than 0 and less than 32;

    ▷ a type check checks that the data input is of the expected type, for example, numeric.

    ▷ a check digit checks that, for example, the ISBN number on a book is correct.

▷ If incorrect data is input, then the results of any processing may be wrong ... Garbage In, Garbage Out.

Memory, files and backing storage

This chapter should be read if you are preparing for GCSE IT assessment with the following examining boards:

| C & G | MEG | NEAB | SEG |
| London | NDTEF | RSA | WJEC |

GETTING STARTED

This chapter reviews the function and purpose of:

▶ RAM and ROM memory;
▶ files and file operations;
▶ backing storage, including floppy disks, hard disks, magnetic tape, and CD-ROM.

Security precautions to protect hardware and software are reviewed, with a particular focus on organizing backups, user identification numbers and passwords, and physical security.

GLOSSARY

Backing storage Backing storage is floppy disks, hard disks, magnetic tape and CD-ROM. It is non-volatile media where files can be saved.

Files Files are saved on backing storage. They can contain any type of information used by a computer. For example, software or data.

Memory Memory is where programs and data are stored while the programs are run and the data is processed. The main memory of a computer is RAM which is volatile.

Volatile Volatile memory loses its contents when a computer is switched off. Non-volatile memory is permanent. RAM is volatile. ROM is non-volatile.

C & G	LONDON	MEG	NDTEF	NEAB	RSA	SEG	WJEC	TOPIC	STUDY	REVISION I	REVISION 2
✓	✓	✓	✓	✓	✓	✓	✓	The memory			
✓	✓	✓	✓	✓	✓	✓	✓	Files			
✓	✓	✓	✓	✓	✓	✓	✓	Backing storage			
✓	✓	✓	✓	✓	✓	✓	✓	Security			

WHAT YOU NEED TO KNOW

▷ **The memory**   Software and data are stored in the memory of the computer, while the programs are run and the data is processed.

Random access memory (RAM)

In a computer the main memory is **Random Access Memory** (RAM). RAM can be *written to* and *read from*. This memory is **volatile**, which means that the programs and data stored in it will be lost when the computer is switched off. When programs and data are loaded from the backing storage, they are temporarily stored in RAM. Software, such as a word-processor, is in RAM while it is being run.

Read only memory (ROM)

Computers may also contain **Read Only Memory** (ROM). ROM, as its name suggests, can *only* be read. It is non-volatile and so retains its contents when the computer is switched off. Unfortunately, the contents of ROM cannot be altered, so it is unsuitable for data that must be changed.

ROM is usually used in microcomputers for programs which it is convenient to have available at any time, in particular when the computer has just been switched on.

In a few microcomputers the Operating System is in ROM. When the computer is switched on, the Operating System in ROM runs immediately. In order to change the Operating System, the actual ROM chip must be removed and another inserted. To do this the computer must be dismantled. In other computers such as IBM compatible PCs, it is usual to load the Operating System from disk into RAM before using other software. This allows the user to run different Operating Systems if required.

Battery backed RAM

Some microcomputers save the date and time on **battery backed RAM**. This is a small amount of RAM memory powered by a battery. The contents of battery backed RAM can be altered, but because it is powered by a battery, these contents are not lost when the computer is switched off. Battery backed RAM is expensive and is suitable for storing only very small volumes of data. The batteries will run out periodically and must be renewed. Backing storage, e.g. magnetic disk, must be used to store larger volumes of data when the computer is switched off.

▷ **Files**   Software and data are kept on backing storage as **files**. Files may contain any type of information used by a computer. For example, data, templates, graphics, programs, etc.

File operations

To store files on backing storage, we save them. When we **save** a file, it is copied from the memory of the computer onto backing storage.

To get the file back once it has been saved, we load the file. When we **load** (or open) a file, it is copied from backing storage into the memory of the computer.

Each file is given a **filename**, which identifies the file and so must be different from any other filename. The filename is used when we need to save or load the file or otherwise refer to it. Files are **created** then they are first set up and given a filename.

When we have two or more files with the *same* structure we may want to **merge** them into one file.

When a file is out of date we **update**, **edit** or **amend** the file, making a completely up-to-date file.

If we no longer need a file and wish to remove it from the disk, we **delete** the file.

If we want another identical copy of a file, we **copy** the file.

If we want to change the filename, we **rename** the file.

To see a list of all the files on a disk we look at the **catalogue** or **directory**. This is a list of all the files on a disk.

▷ Backing storage

Backing storage is long-term storage that is non-volatile. A file stored in RAM memory will be lost when the computer is turned off. However, if this is first saved on backing storage, it is kept intact when the computer is turned off. When it is needed again it can be loaded from backing storage.

Magnetic disks

Magnetic disks vary considerably, depending on the size of computer they are used with. However, they all provide faster access than the corresponding magnetic tape.

Data is stored on a magnetic disk on concentric **tracks** (see Fig. 5.1). Each track is divided into **sectors**, each separated by **inter-sector gaps**. A sector is the unit of data read from or written to the disk by the computer in a single read or write operation.

'Formatting a disk'

When you *format* a disk, it is divided into tracks and sectors on which files can be stored. Formatting a disk which has already been used may also delete any files already saved on the disk. A disk cannot be used until it has been formatted at least once.

Floppy disks

These are flexible, circular, plastic disks coated with a magnetic material. They are contained in a protective sleeve (see Fig. 5.2). The read/write heads access the disk through the read/write hole. The heads are actually in *contact* with the surface of the disk as it spins. This reduces the life span and reliability of the floppy disk. The disk is gripped by the drive at its centre, and spun at approximately 350 revolutions per minute. A high density $3\frac{1}{2}$ inch floppy disk stores 1.44M bytes.

'The write protect mechanism'

The write protect mechanism is used to protect files on the floppy disk. When the write protect mechanism is on, you cannot save files on the disk, delete files saved on the disk nor alter files saved on the disk.

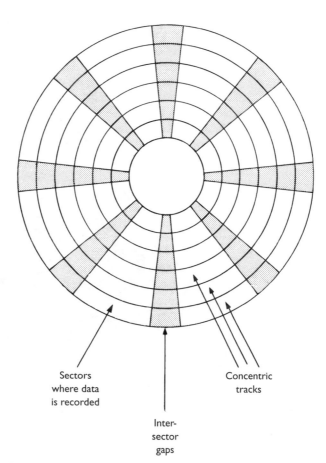

Fig. 5.1 How data is stored on a magnetic disk. There are typically 80 tracks and 10 sectors on a $3\frac{1}{2}$ inch floppy disk

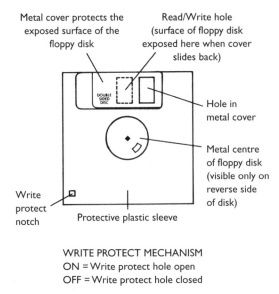

Metal cover protects the exposed surface of the floppy disk

Read/Write hole (surface of floppy disk exposed here when cover slides back)

Hole in metal cover

Metal centre of floppy disk (visible only on reverse side of disk)

Write protect notch

Protective plastic sleeve

WRITE PROTECT MECHANISM
ON = Write protect hole open
OFF = Write protect hole closed

Fig. 5.2 A $3\frac{1}{2}$ inch floppy disk

Hard disks

Hard disks are rigid, inflexible disks. They may be single or stacked as in Fig 5.3. The read/write heads move in unison, floating just above the surface of the hard disk. There is one read/write head for each surface of a disk. When the hard disk is switched on, the disk spins at a uniform, high speed.

The read/write heads are so close to the disk's surface and the disk is spinning so fast that a speck of dust is sufficient to cause a 'head crash' that will destroy the disk. For this reason, hard disks must be used in absolutely clean conditions or sealed into the disk drive unit.

To access a particular sector the read/write heads move to the track it is on. The heads then remain stationary while the disk is spinning. The required sector is accessed as it passes underneath the read/write heads.

Hard disks are not usually visible when you are using a microcomputer. There may be a light that comes on when the hard disk is accessed. Most hard disks are installed inside the

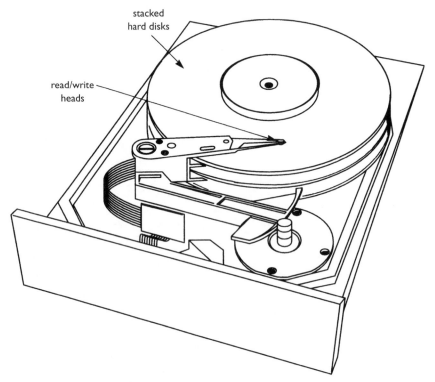

stacked hard disks

read/write heads

Fig. 5.3 A hard disk stack used in a microcomputer

microcomputer when it is assembled and are not normally removed. However, you can obtain removable hard disks.

If you want to buy a hard disk for a computer you can:

► Buy an *external hard disk drive* that connects to one of the computer's external ports using a cable.

► Buy an *internal hard disk drive* that is installed inside the computer. This is like the hard drive that would be installed when the computer is assembled.

Hard disks are used with microcomputers and networks as they are robust and provide sufficiently fast access. For such computer systems, hard disks provide high volume on-line storage at an economic price.

Hard disks are also used with mainframes. These hard disks are more expensive and have larger storage capacities and faster access times than those used with microcomputers. However, they are essentially the same type of backing storage device.

Magnetic tape

'Uses of magnetic tape'

Magnetic tape is a low cost backing storage media. Files stored on it can only be accessed serially or sequentially. Access is relatively slow. Data is stored on magnetic tape as illustrated in Figure 5.4.

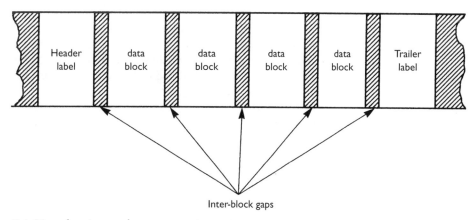

Fig. 5.4 How data is stored on a magnetic tape

The **header label** identifies the tape. **Inter-block gaps** separate the data blocks. A **data block** is the unit of data read from, or written to, the tape by the computer in a single read or write operation. The trailer label is the last on the magnetic tape and gives information such as whether the file continues on another tape.

It is not possible to both *read data from* and *write data to* a file on magnetic tape at the same time.

The computer could not read the entire magnetic tape into its memory as it is likely that the volume of data on the tape would be more than the memory available. The computer accesses the data on the tape a block at a time. When a block has been read, it is processed before another block is read.

Tape cartridges

Magnetic tape is available as a **magnetic tape cartridge**. These are a larger version of the popular audio cassette. They are particularly useful for backing up hard disks when used with microcomputers and network file servers.

Reel-to-reel tape drives

Mainframe computers may use reel-to-reel magnetic tape to store very large amounts of data at a low cost. It is possible to store around 100 million characters on a magnetic tape 3600 feet long, priced at about £20 (a cost of 0.00002 pence per character).

CD-ROM

CD-ROM is the use of compact disc (CD) technology for backing storage for computers. CD-ROM can be used to store very large amounts of data on a relatively robust backing storage medium that can be accessed at speeds comparable with magnetic disks.

'Advantages of CD ROM'

An advantage of CD-ROM disks is their very high on-line storage capacity. A CD-ROM disk can store up to 1000 Mbytes of data. This could be up to 500,000 A4 pages of text, 2000 high resolution colour pictures, 25 hours of recorded speech or a mixture of these.

Another advantage of CD-ROM is the robust nature of the disks. A CD-ROM disk is 12 cms in diameter. This is a relatively compact and easy to handle way of storing such high volumes of data. CD-ROM is an optical medium. It is read by a laser beam which scans tiny pits on the surface of the disk. Consequently the risk of damage when the disk is accessed is reduced as there is no contact between the read mechanism and the disk. The disks are coated with a protective layer that allows them to be handled without erasing the data or damaging the disk. The robust nature of CD-ROM makes them suitable for the long-term storage of data and for data in frequent use.

CD-ROM drives can be used with most microcomputers. They are similar in size to an audio CD drive. They can be installed next to the floppy disk drive or an external drive can be plugged into one of the computer's ports using a cable. Stacks of CD-ROM drives can be attached to networks.

CD-ROM is suitable for storing very large reference works such as dictionaries, encyclopedias, thesauruses, library catalogues, component parts catalogues, etc. These may contain a mix of text, voice, music, photographs, videos, etc. This is known as **multimedia.** Computer technology can be used to make this vast store of information accessible faster and in different ways to those traditionally used. For example, a CD-ROM dictionary can be searched for a word as you would search a database. There is an immediate response compared with a book dictionary where you would slowly search through the dictionary turning pages.

'A disadvantage of CD ROM'

The disadvantage of CD-ROM is that you can only read the information stored on it. In general, you cannot write information to a CD-ROM. However, there are Write Once Read Many (WORM) disks available. You can save data onto a WORM disk once only. The data can then be read as many times as you like. WORM disks are generally used to backup files that need to be stored for a very long time. They are also used by software and multimedia developers.

▷ Security

Files saved on backing storage may be valuable. It may have cost time and money to collect and store them. The files may be of great commercial value to a business. Consequently, it is most important to ensure that they are **secure**.

Backups

The most important security precaution against corruption or loss of files through accident, malicious damage or theft is to keep extra copies of them. These extra copies are known as **backups**.

Magnetic tape is ideal where we need to store large amounts of data and where we have no need to access the data very quickly, or very frequently. It is also a low-cost storage medium. For these reasons magnetic tape is ideal as a backup medium for other magnetic media such as disks.

Both disks and tapes are unrealiable storage media and occasionally files recorded on them will be corrupted or lost in some other way. When data is **corrupted** it is changed so that it is meaningless. When we **backup** a disk onto magnetic tape the files on it are copied, from the disk to the tape. When the data on the disk becomes corrupted, the data files can be **restored** by copying them from the backup tape to the original disk. It is very important to make sure that files are backed-up.

In *large mainframe* computer installations reel-to-reel tapes will be used as the backup medium. For microcomputers magnetic tape cartridges are used. Tape cartridges are used with a **tape streamer**, which is designed to allow easy copying of the files on a disk onto the tape cartridge. They are particularly useful with network hard disks where it is necessary to make frequent, regular backups.

'The ancestral backup system'

Where it is very important to be sure that files are always kept safely, the ancestral backup system is used (see Fig. 5.5).

▷   The **son** is the copy of the files currently in use. This will be backed-up on a regular basis, perhaps daily.

> The **father** is the most recent copy of the son.
> The **grandfather** is the copy of the son that was taken before the father.

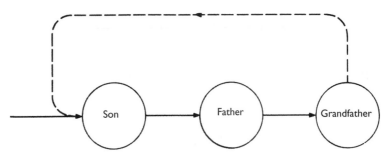

Fig. 5.5 The ancestral system for backups

It is usual to keep the son copies on site where they are easily accessible. The father copies are likely to be stored in a fire-proof safe nearby, probably in the same building as the computer but not in the same room. The grandfather copies should be stored elsewhere, possibly in another town or city. This system is a very effective way of making sure it is always possible to restore files (unless you are extremely careless or unlucky).

It is also possible to use magnetic disks as a backup medium. This is frequently done with microcomputers. The ancestral system for backups is still effective, but floppy disks are used instead of magnetic tapes.

User identification numbers and passwords

Another precaution against loss or damage to files is to restrict the use of the computer system by only allowing registered users to make use of the computer. This is done by giving each user a unique identification number, the **User Id**, and associating a particular **password** with it.

A password is a special sequence of characters, known only to a particular user, that must be presented to the computer system before it will allow access to the system. If every user keeps their User Id and password secret, it is unlikely that anyone else will gain entry to the system.

Passwords should be changed regularly so that, if an unauthorized user does find out a valid User Id and password, these will not be useable for very long.

Physical security

No data file, program or computer system is safe unless it is physically secure. Premises should be made accessible only to registered users. Security guards should be employed and premises should be kept under lock and key. Registered users should have identification cards or similar and these should be checked regularly.

It is not uncommon to find that access to premises where computers are in use is controlled using coded locks, swipe cards, finger or thumb print readers, or voice print readers.

Access to individual computers can also be restricted using similar physical security devices that prevent unauthorized individuals entering the premises.

Floppy disks, etc. should be locked in a secure cabinet, not left lying around.

▶ EXAMINATION QUESTIONS

 Question 1   Which of the following are types of backing storage?

RAM	printer	monitor
floppy disk	MODEM	magnetic tape
CD-ROM	hard disk	software

▷ **Question 2**   Use these words to complete the sentences listed below:

load	sort	rename
merge	sift	uplift
save	select	extend
search	update	reduce

(a) When you _____ a file on disk, you keep it for future use.

(b) Information on a disk cannot be used until you _____ it into the computer's memory.

(c) When you bring the contents of a file up-to-date, you _____ it.

(d) When you _____ a file, you change its filename.

(e) When you _____ two files, there is a new file with all the information in it.

▷ **Question 3**   Explain how a computer is able to display the correct time and date when it has just been switched on.

▷ **Question 4**   The hard disk inside a microcomputer has important files recorded on it.

(i) Explain why these should be backed-up.

(ii) Describe how backups could be done.

▷ **Question 5**   Find the best word in the following list to complete each sentence below. Write the word in the space provided.

| data | field | floppy disk | RAM |
| validation | justification | password | VDU |

(a) _____ is a type of computer memory.

(b) _____ is checking that data is sensible.

(c) A _____ is part of a record.

(d) Unauthorized access to computer files can be prevented by the use of a _____ .

(NEAB)

▷ **Question 6**   You can buy this computer.

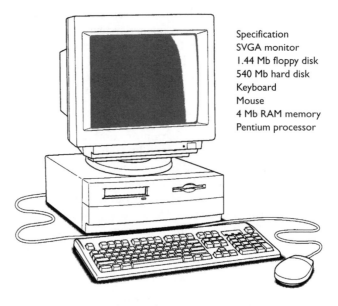

Specification
SVGA monitor
1.44 Mb floppy disk
540 Mb hard disk
Keyboard
Mouse
4 Mb RAM memory
Pentium processor

Fig. 5.6

(a) What backing storage does the computer use?

(b) Which type of disk has the fastest access time?

(c) Explain why you would save your data on backing storage instead of in RAM memory.

(d) The computer's memory can be upgraded from 4 Mb to 8 Mb. Describe an advantage in upgrading the memory.

▷ **Question 7**   An advertising agency uses information technology to prepare text and graphics for brochures and other advertising material.

(a) Which three of the following applications packages would be suitable for this?
    A   communications
    B   desk top publishing
    C   painting and drawing
    D   accounting
    E   payroll
    F   word processing

(b) Four different types of storage are used. Two of these are CD-ROM and RAM. What two other forms of storage would be most suitable in this system?

(c) Explain why each of the following types of storage is necessary.
    (i)   CD-ROM
    (ii) RAM

▷ **Question 8** Why is software stored on a ROM chip and not on a RAM chip?

(City and Guilds)

▷ **Question 9** The Magi-micro has 512 K RAM. How many bytes and bits does the RAM contain?

(City and Guilds)

▷ **Question 10** A program is stored on a floppy disk.

(a) Describe what has to be done so that the program can be run on a computer.

(b) The computer has a hard disk. Describe what has to be done so that the program can be run without using the floppy disk.

EXAMINATION ANSWERS

▷ **Answer 1** floppy disk
CD-ROM
hard disk
magnetic tape

▷ **Answer 2**
(a) save
(b) load
(c) update
(d) rename
(e) merge

▷ **Answer 3** The time and date could be stored in battery-backed RAM. RAM is volatile and is normally cleared when the computer is turned off. However, battery-backed RAM retains its contents.

▷ **Answer 4**
(i)   If they are not backed-up they could be lost due to corruption, hardware breakdown, etc.
(ii) The contents of the hard disk could be copied onto floppy disk or some other backing storage media. This should be done frequently. Backups should be organized using the Ancestral system.

▷ **Answer 5**
(a) RAM
(b) validation
(c) field
(d) password

▷ **Answer 6**
(a) Floppy disk and hard disk.
(b) Hard disk.

(c) Data saved in RAM is lost when the computer is switched off. Data saved on backing storage is permanent.

(d) A bigger memory enables larger programs to be run. Large programs are often large because they have extra programming to make them easier to use. The larger the memory, the more data can be loaded into it. This can reduce the number of disk accesses and speed up program execution.

▷ **Answer 7** (a) B, C, F

(b) Floppy disks and a hard disk.

(c) (i) CD-ROM would be useful for storing high volumes of clip art.

(ii) RAM – this stores the programs and data while they are being used. Without RAM no processing could be done.

▷ **Answer 8** The software stored on a ROM chip cannot be altered and can be used as soon as the computer is switched on. It isn't lost when the computer is switched off. Software stored on a RAM chip is lost when the computer is switched off. It has to be loaded into RAM before it can be used.

▷ **Answer 9**

512 K bytes = 1024×512 bytes
= 524288 bytes
1 byte = 8 bits on most microcomputers
So
512 K = $1024 \times 512 \times 8$ bits
= 4194304 bits
Approximate answers might be acceptable, for example:
512 K = 512,000 bytes
= $512,000 \times 8$ bits

▷ **Answer 10** (a) There are several possible answers, e.g.:
  ▷ switch on the computer
  ▷ put the floppy disk in the disk drive
  ▷ load the program into the computer
  ▷ run the program.

(b) Copy the files on the floppy disk to the hard disk, i.e. install the program on the hard disk.

▷ **EXAMINATION QUESTION WITH STUDENT ANSWER**

MARVELLOUS MEGA-MICRO
Yours for only £1300. The new MEGA-Micro comes with:

▷ *540 MB hard disk*
▷ *3.5 inch floppy disk drive*
▷ *512 K RAM*
▷ *The Operating System in ROM*
▷ *Integrated wordprocessor, spreadsheet, database and graphics software*
▷ *An ink jet printer*

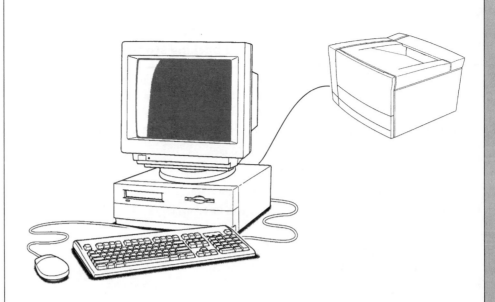

Fig. 5.7

Look at the advertisement for a microcomputer. Explain briefly:

(a) the difference between RAM and ROM;

RAM means Random Access Memory. ROM means Read Only Memory.

(b) the uses of RAM and ROM;

RAM is used for the computer's memory. ROM is used to store programs that are run immediately the computer is switched on.

(c) compare the two disk storage systems, describing their uses and relative advantages;

Floppy discs store less data than hard discs. Access to the data is slower on a floppy disc than a hard disk. They are both used to store programs and data.

(d) how an inkjet printer works.

An inkjet printer squirts jets of ink at the paper.

▷ **Examiner's comment**

(a) True but trivial. A more complete answer would be:
ROM is non-volatile and the information held on it can only be read.
RAM is volatile. Information can be read from it and written to it.

(b) True, but lacking detail. Both RAM and ROM are part of the computer's memory.
RAM is used for the main memory of the computer. It stores the programs and data that are loaded from backing storage.
ROM is used to store programs that are needed as soon as the computer is switched on, e.g. the boot file, which starts up the Operating System.

(c) A good answer. In addition, floppy disks are usually removable whereas hard disks are not usually removable.

(d) True, but the examiner also wants to be told that an inkjet printer forms characters, etc. using a dot matrix print head.

SUMMARY

This chapter looks at memory, files and backing storage.

▷   Programs and data are stored in the computer's memory while the programs are run and the data is processed.

▷   RAM is volatile memory. When programs and data are loaded from backing storage, they are temporarily stored in RAM. When the computer is switched off RAM is cleared.

▷   ROM is non-volatile memory. When the computer is switched off ROM retains its contents.

▷   Software and data are kept on backing storage as files.

▷   Files have a unique filename which is given to them when they are created.

▷   Saving a file is copying it from memory to backing storage.

▷   Loading a file is copying it from backing storage to RAM memory.

▷   Two files can be merged to form one file.

▷   Updating a file is editing or amending it to bring it up-to-date.

▷   Deleting a file is removing it.

▷   Renaming a file is changing its name.

▷   Copying a file is making another, identical copy of it.

▷   A directory or catalogue is a list of all the files on a disk.

▷   Backing storage is floppy disks, hard disks, magnetic tape and CD-ROM. It is non-volatile media where files can be saved.

▷   To keep IT systems secure, you should:

   backup files regularly;

   ensure system security using User Identification Numbers and Passwords;

   ensure physical security using guards, identification cards and locks.

Output

This chapter should be read if you are preparing for GCSE IT assessment with the following examining boards:

C & G	MEG	NEAB	SEG
London	NDTEF	RSA	WJEC

GETTING STARTED

This chapter reviews different methods of output, including monitors, different types of printer (dot matrix, ink jet and laser), printer stationery and printer feed mechanisms. The use of printer buffers and spooling is outlined. A range of other methods of output are reviewed.

GLOSSARY

Interactive Interactive processing takes place when the user and the computer have a 'conversation'. The user inputs information, probably using a mouse and a keyboard. The computer processes this information and displays it on the screen. The user reads the screen and reacts to the information displayed. This cycle of input, processing, output, and user reaction is called interactive processing.

Draft Draft printing is not the best print quality available. It is readable and cheaper to print than the best quality. It is used to print drafts which are to be edited before the final, high quality copy is printed.

NLQ NLQ or 'Near Letter Quality' printing is the best quality print that a dot matrix printer can produce.

C & G	LONDON	MEG	NDTEF	NEAB	RSA	SEG	WJEC	TOPIC	STUDY	REVISION I	REVISION 2
✓	✓	✓	✓	✓	✓	✓	✓	Monitors			
✓	✓	✓	✓	✓	✓	✓	✓	Printers			
✓	✓						✓	Computer output on microfilm			
✓	✓	✓	✓	✓	✓	✓	✓	Graph plotters			
✓	✓	✓	✓	✓	✓	✓	✓	Speech synthesis			
✓	✓	✓	✓	✓	✓	✓	✓	Actuators			

WHAT YOU NEED TO KNOW

Output from computers is familiar to most people even if they have little contact with computers in other ways. A visit to a travel agency, a motor spares stockist or an estate agency may bring us into contact with screen output. Electricity Boards, Gas Boards, Local Councils and a variety of other bodies, all send out bills which have been printed by computer. Libraries often store their indexes on microfiche; historians will use a computer to store plans and maps. This chapter contains a brief, but systematic, review of computer generated output.

▷ Monitors

When using a computer it is likely that you will read the information that is output on a screen. This screen is known as a **monitor**. A monitor looks very much like a television set.

Most microcomputers must have a monitor attached before they can be used. A monitor is probably the most common output peripheral in use with computers. With home computers it is very common to use a television as a monitor. Television sets do not usually give as clear a picture as a monitor.

'Types of monitor'

Monitors can be **high**, **medium** or **low resolution**. The level of resolution is measured in **pixels**. A pixel is the smallest area of the screen that can be changed by the computer. A pixel can be thought of as a dot that makes up a picture, similar to the dots that make up a photograph in a newspaper.

'High resolution'

Using a high resolution monitor it is possible to display a very detailed picture on the screen. In high resolution the screen may display, for example, 800 by 600 pixels, though higher densities are possible. High resolution monitors are used when we want very detailed and accurate screen displays. They are particularly useful for graphic design, computer aided design and related applications. It is also possible to buy high resolution screens that are much bigger than normal screens. For example, in desk top publishing there may be a need to view a whole A4 (the size of this page is A4) or A3 (twice as big as A4) page on the screen for it to be readable. Extra large, high resolution screens make this possible.

'Medium and low resolution'

If high resolution is not required for a particular application, then a medium resolution display could be adequate. A typical medium resolution monitor will display 640 by 200 pixels, much less than the high resolution screen. A low resolution display may be only 320 by 200 pixels. A low resolution display is generally suitable for television sets, and can be used to good effect with computer games at home.

The use of a monitor allows a computer to be used in an **interactive** way. The user *inputs* information. This could be typed in at the keyboard or selected using a mouse. The computer *processes* the information that has just been input, and *outputs* the results to the screen display. The user reads the information output and reacts accordingly.

'Interactive processing'

This cycle of input, processing and output will continue while the computer is being used. **Interactive processing** is very similar to having a conversation with the computer, but instead of *hearing* the conversation we *see* it on the screen. Interactive processing is usual with microcomputers.

▷ Printers

Character printers

Character printers print one character at a time. They are the slowest type of printer. Their speed is measured in **cps**, i.e. characters per second. Speeds of between 80 and 200 cps are usual. Character printers are often used with microcomputers where their slow speed is unimportant, because of the low volume of printed output.

Dot matrix printers

'Draft and NLQ'

These form each character by printing part of a 7 by 5 matrix (see Fig. 6.1). Most dot matrix printers are impact printers. They have a print head consisting of a matrix of steel pins that are projected or withdrawn to form the shape of the character when pressed against an inked ribbon.

The printout produced by these printers is either **draft** print which is of a low quality, or **Near Letter Quality** (NLQ). In NLQ mode each character is printed serveral times, producing a much better quality printout.

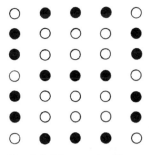

Fig. 6.1 The number 8 formed by a dot matrix print head

Dot matrix printers are reliable, and cheap to buy and run. They are used extensively in schools and offices.

Impact dot matrix printers can also be used with a coloured ribbon to produce printout in several colours. The colour cannot be blended and consequently is not sufficiently adaptable for good quality artwork, but can be used to good effect to emphasize simple graphs and bar charts.

Ink jet printers

These are non-impact dot matrix printers which have been developed to overcome some of the limitations of the impact dot matrix printer. These printers shoot a jet of ink at the paper to form the printed character. Ink jet printers are cheap to buy but expensive to run. They produce much better quality print. The quality and range of the colour printing possible is also improved.

Page printers

'Laser printers are a type of page printer'

Page printers set up a page and then print it. The most common type of page printer is a **laser printer**. These range from small desk top printers used with microcomputers to large, free standing printers used with mainframe computers. Speeds range from 4 pages per minute to 200 ppm; costs vary from £250 to £20,000 or more. Laser printers are able to produce a wide range of type fonts and graphics. They can print in black and white, or colour. It is difficult to distinguish between the best quality colour laser printing and a colour photograph.

Laser printers work by directing a laser beam at an electrostatically-charged surface. The shape of the characters is 'etched' onto the charged surface to make a template of the shapes to be printed. This is then used to transfer the image to the paper. In most cases ordinary paper can be used.

'Benefits of laser printers'

Laser printers are popular as they are flexible, fast and quiet. However, the cost of printing is quite high compared to most other printers. As a result, their use may be restricted in schools and colleges. It is more economical to print draft copies of work on dot matrix printers, only printing the final copy on a laser printer.

Printer paper

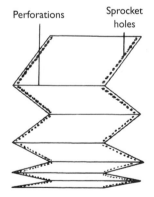

Fig. 6.2 Continous fan-fold printer stationery

'Impact printers and non-impact printers'

Printed output from a computer is called **hard copy**.

Some printers use paper that is **continuous** in the sense that there are many sheets joined together. The paper is **perforated** which makes the sheets easier to separate. The paper is folded into a box in a **fan-fold**. Down the sides of the paper are rows of **sprocket holes** which are used to feed the paper through the printer (see Fig. 6.2).

Other types of printers use A4 plain paper. A4 is the size of this page.

Computer paper may be plain or can be **pre-printed** with other details beforehand. Companies sending out invoices or bills often pre-print their computer stationery with their logo and other details before the computer is used to add the details for each customer (see Fig. 6.3).

Where several copies of the printed output are needed, perhaps for sending to a customer and using in the office, it is possible to print on **multipart** computer paper. Multipart stationery consists of several layers of continuous fan-fold stationery with a layer of carbon paper between. Printing takes place as usual to produce a top-copy, but other copies are produced through the carbon paper.

When using multipart stationery it is necessary to use an **impact** printer. This has a print head that physically hits an inked ribbon onto the printer paper. The impact transfers the ink on the ribbon to the paper. Printers that use ink jets or a thermal print head do not have print heads that hit the paper. These are **non-impact** printers, and cannot print multipart stationery.

Printer paper feed mechanisms

A **tractor feed** consists of two toothed wheels, one positioned at each edge of the paper. These engage the sprocket holes in the edge of the paper and *pull* or *push* it through the printer (see Fig. 6.4).

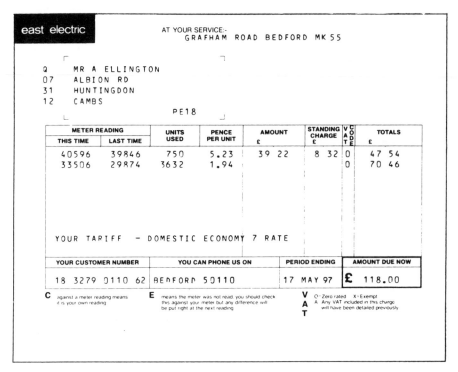

Fig. 6.3 A pre-printed form with details printed on it by the computer

'Types of paper feed
mechanism to printers'

On some printers used with microcomputer systems the tractor feed is either not used, or can be removed. Instead, a **friction feed** is used. This consists of a hard rubber roller, the same width as the paper, that presses against the paper and feeds it through the printer. A friction feed mechanism is not suitable for large volumes of printout on continuous stationery but is very useful if printout on a single sheet of standard A4 is required. The sheet can be fed into the printer by hand. This is a slow and cumbersome method, so **single sheet feeders** have been developed. These supply single A4 sheets to the printer, which are then fed through the printer by the friction feed. This method is increasingly used in small offices where there is no requirement for high volumes of printout, but letters are often printed on single sheets of paper.

Dot matrix printers and printers used with mainframe computers are more likely to use continuous, fan-fold paper pulled through the printer by a tractor feed.

Ink jet printers and laser printers used with microcomputers are more likely to use A4 paper. This is fed through the printer using a single sheet feeder and a friction feed.

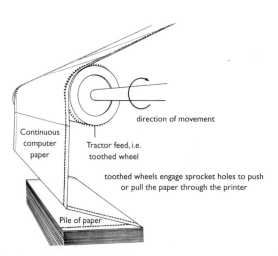

Fig. 6.4 A tractor feed mechanism

Buffers and spooling

All printers are slow compared with the speed of the processor in a computer. Sometimes you have to wait a long time for printing to finish before you can use the computer again, and before other work can continue. Buffers and spooling can reduce the time you have to wait.

Buffers

Most printers make use of **buffers**. They are often built into the printer. A buffer is RAM memory that is used to store output while it is waiting to be printed. A program that needs to use the printer will transfer any printed output to the buffer and then continue processing immediately. The printer then prints the data from the buffer while the program that produced the output, or another program, is being run.

'Buffers and spooling'

Buffers are often able to hold several pages of data waiting to be printed, but even so, their capacity is limited. If there is a large volume of printout to be done then the buffer may be filled. The computer cannot continue until all the data has been printed or transferred to the buffer. This causes the computer to wait for the slower printer.

Buffers are almost always found in use with printers. Even inexpensive printers used with microcomputers have built-in buffers.

Spooling

Waiting for the printer can be avoided by **spooling** the printer output. In spooling, all printed output is first saved as a data file on backing storage. Output to backing storage peripherals such as the hard disk is very fast. Once the data file has been saved, the program can continue processing. The data file now joins the queue for the printer. Printing takes place when the data file reaches the head of the queue. This may take some time on a computer system with high volumes of printed output.

Spooling is used with mainframe computers and networks of microcomputers. It is also used on standalone microcomputers, where printing is done in **background mode.**

▷ Computer output on microfilm

Where it is necessary to keep a record of activities, high volumes of output may need to be kept for perhaps several years. Such records may need to be consulted infrequently, or there may be a legal requirement to keep them. Records printed on paper will take up a large amount of storage space and tend to deteriorate quickly. Instead of storing the output printed on paper it is possible to make a copy of the page on microfilm, as it would have appeared had it been printed. This is **Computer Output on Microfilm (COM)** .

'Advantage of COM'

Microfilm takes up much less storage space and does not deteriorate as quickly as paper. Microfilm is generally available as a roll of film 16 mm or 35 mm wide. The only disadvantage of microfilm is that a special reader must be used, but the expense of this is more than compensated for by lower storage costs.

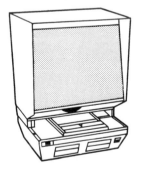

Fig. 6.5 A microfiche reader

COM is also useful where large volumes of information are needed at a variety of locations. A common example of this is the book catalogue in a library. Printed output is again unsuitable because it is bulky, difficult to access and easily torn. Microfilm is not used because it is made up as a roll. Instead, the roll is converted into flat sheets of **microfiche** measuring 105 x 148 mm. The microfiche catalogue can be copied many times and be made available at any location, provided a **microfiche reader** is available (see Fig. 6.5). Microfiche is easily packed and sent through the post. For this reason it is also suitable for applications such as spare parts catalogues for motor vehicles, etc. A visit to a local library, or a motor spares dealer, to see microfiche in use is highly recommended.

▷ Graph plotters

Most printers are unable to print high quality precision graphics on very large sheets of paper. Where these are necessary, a **graph plotter** is used. Graph plotters are very slow, but can draw continuous lines, often in several colours. A **flat bed graph plotter** is illustrated in Figure 6.6. The graph plotter illustrated has three interchangeable pens mounted on the rigid arm. These can be lowered for drawing, one at a time, as required. The pens can be moved from left to right, while the rigid arm can be moved backwards and forwards to allow continuous lines to be drawn on the paper.

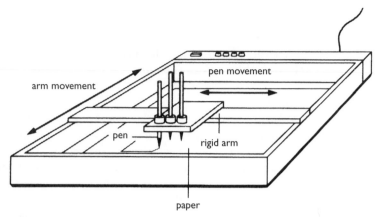

Fig. 6.6 A flat bed graph plotter

Graph plotters are a highly specialised output device. They are especially useful for architectural drawings, building plans and computer aided design applications, where a high quality precision drawing is required, but the volume of output is low.

▷ **Speech synthesis**

'Speech synthesis can help the disabled to use computers'

For some applications printed output, on the screen or on paper is inappropriate. It may be that only a few instructions are required in a situation where reading would be difficult. In any event, some people have difficulty reading, perhaps through disabilities of one form or another. Attempts have been made to get the computer to produce sounds similar to normal speech; this is **speech synthesis**.

Software that attempts to reproduce speech is available for most microcomputers. For example, you can type in a sentence and the computer 'reads' it through a built-in loud speaker. This type of software associates a sound with a particular combination of letters in the words. It usually produces recognizable speech but it does not have the quality of human speech. There are difficulties with words like 'bough' and 'thought' where the same 'ough' spelling has different sounds associated with it. Where only a limited number of words are used, human speech can be recorded in digital form and reproduced by the computer. This is often done in computer games.

▷ **Actuators**

Computers use **control interfaces** to communicate with and control actuators that perform physical actions (see Fig. 6.7). These can be simple electrical devices such as a heater or a fan. However, actuators can also be sources of mechanical power. By communicating with and controlling sources of mechanical power, computers can perform physical tasks. For example, a robot can be made to pick up an object.

The following are some *power sources* used by **actuators**. They make the actuator perform a mechanical task.

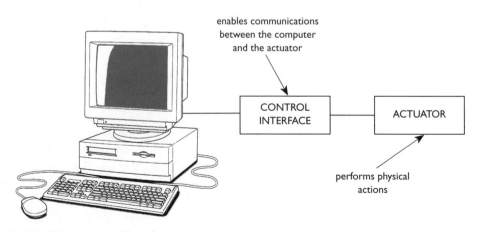

Fig. 6.7 Using a control interface

Hydraulic

Hydraulic systems transmit power using fluids. An hydraulic pump supplies the power. The pressure output from the pump controls the strength of the movement. This is transmitted through pipes to the devices that supply the physical movement.

Pneumatic

Pneumatic systems use compressed air to provide the power needed for movement. A compressor provides air at a constant pressure. Valves are used to supply the compressed air through pipes to the devices that supply the physical movement.

Servo-motor

This is an electric motor that provides continuous, analog power through a system of gears. **Servo-motors** are fast.

Stepper-motor

This is an electric motor that moves in discrete steps in response to digital signals. **Stepper-motors** are slow, low powered devices but they can easily be controlled by a computer.

EXAMINATION QUESTIONS

▷ **Question 1**   A Keyboard
B Screen (VDU)
C Mouse
D Printer
E Joystick

Which TWO of these are output devices?

(NEAB)

▷ **Question 2**   The diagram shows a microcomputer which is used for desktop publishing. The documents produced include text, diagrams and pictures.

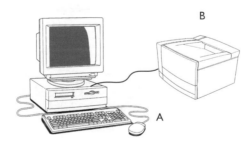

Fig. 6.8

(a) (i)   Name the device labelled **A**
(ii) Describe how you would use this device to open a new document on the screen.
(b) Device **B** is a laser printer. State TWO reasons why a laser printer has been chosen.

(MEG)

▷ **Question 3**   Use these words to complete the sentences below.

alphabetic
character
page

perforations
sprocket
tractor
widget

(a) Putting paper in a printer with a _____ feed can be complicated. You must make sure the teeth go into the _____ holes.

(b) Dot matrix printers can be very slow. Laser printers print a _____ at a time. These can be much faster.

(c) Sheets of continuous computer paper can be separated by tearing them along the _____ . The _____ holes down the side can sometimes be removed in a similar way.

▷ **Question 4**   (a) Name one other input device that a desk top publishing system would need, apart from a keyboard.

(b) Suggest another input or output device that would be useful for a desk top publishing system.

(City and Guilds)

▷ **Question 5**   (a) Name the most important quality of a VDU used for desk top publishing.

(b) Name one other quality of a VDU that would make desk top publishing easier.

(City and Guilds)

▷ **Question 6**   What are the advantages and disadvantages of using a laser printer instead of a dot matrix printer (24 pin, impact)?

▷ **Question 7**

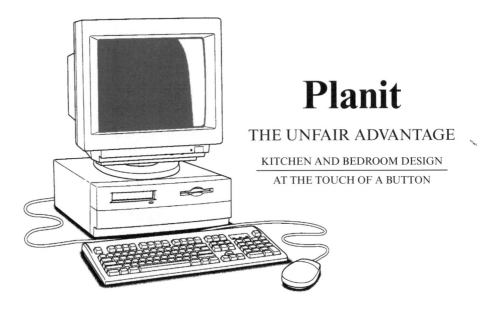

A kitchen design firm uses a computer system to help in planning new kitchens for clients.
  The client will choose the style of units that is required.
  A surveyor will then measure up the kitchen.
  A designer will work out how best to fit the units into the kitchen, and then plan the routes of pipework and wiring.

(a) Name one input device (apart from a keyboard) that the designer could use, and explain why it is suitable.

(b) A high quality plan needs to be drawn by the computer for when the kitchen is being fitted. Name an output device that would produce a high quality plan of the kitchen, and explain why it is suitable.

(c) Describe some other tasks (apart from the actual design of the kitchen) for which the company might use the computer.

(SEG, 1993)

▷ **Question 8** IT systems sometimes accept spoken input and use a voice synthesizer to speak to users.

(a) Name an input device used for voice recognition and an output device used for voice synthesis.
(b) Describe a situation where voice synthesis and voice recognition are an essential part of the IT system being used.

▷ **Question 9** A small company uses a computer.

(a) The company wishes to run two programs.
Program A involves reading names, addresses and dates of birth to print personalized birthday cards.
Program B involves complicated calculations to predict sales figures for next year. The results are to be saved on disk.
How can a multiprogramming operating system help to run the two programs in the shortest possible time?
(b) Why does the company use a laser printer to print letters to its customers and a dot matrix printer to produce employee wage slips?

(MEG)

▷ **Question 10** Read the paragraph below, and then answer the questions:
In a busy local office of a large motoring insurance company there are about ten computerized work stations, linked to each other by a LAN. The system is controlled by a powerful file server with a 30 Gbyte hard disk drive, which is accessible by all work stations. The file server also has a tape streamer attached to it. Each work station has its own dot matrix printer, and there are also two laser printers linked to the network. The word-processing software is capable of mail merge, and also has a spell check facility.

(a) What does LAN stand for?
(b) Why are there both laser printers attached to the network and dot matrix printers for each work station?
(c) (i) What does the spell check facility do?
    (ii) When using the spell check facility, you can add extra words to its dictionary. Why is this important?
(d) (i) What is meant by mail merge?
    (ii) Give a relevant example of when mail merging might be used in this insurance firm.

(SEG, 1993)

EXAMINATION ANSWERS

▷ **Answer 1** Screen
Printer

▷ **Answer 2** (a) (i) Mouse.
               (ii) There are several ways of doing this. For example: open the file menu by pointing at it using the mouse. In the file menu, select 'new'.
           (b) To print faster with multiple copies.
               To print high-resolution copies

(MEG)

▷ **Answer 3**   (a) tractor; sprocket
(b) character
(c) perforations; sprocket

▷ **Answer 4**   (a) A mouse is essential.
(b) A scanner would be useful. This would be used to scan pictures, etc. into the DTP system.

▷ **Answer 5**   (a) High resolution, so that greater detail can be shown.
(b) A larger screen, e.g. an A4 screen, would be useful. Colour is often more useful than black and white.

▷ **Answer 6**   A laser printer can print a wide range of fonts and graphics. It produces a high quality printout. Printing is fast and quiet. However, a laser printer is expensive to buy and to run. A dot matrix printer is cheap to buy and run. However, it produces a lower quality print-out. Printing is slow and noisy.

▷ **Answer 7**   (a) A mouse could be used. It is easier to draw and plan diagrams on the screen using a mouse.
(b) A graph plotter could be used. Often graph plotters draw on A3 (large) sheets of paper. They draw smooth, continuous lines and can draw in colour.
(c) The company could use the computer for payroll; stock control; writing letters, reports, contracts, etc.; sales statistics; etc.

▷ **Answer 8**   (a) input: microphone
output: loudspeaker
(b) Voice synthesis and voice recognition are essential in circumstances where other forms of input and output cannot be used. For example:
▶   for some disabled people
▶   for workers who are using both hands to do their job and cannot break off to use keyboard input, etc.

▷ **Answer 9**   (a) Schedule the computer so that the processor is being used for the calculations in Program B whilst it is printing from Program A
(b) The company wants high-quality impressive documents for its customers. This is not necessary for the employees' wage slips. A dot matrix printer is less expensive to run.
(MEG)

▷ **Answer 10**   (a) LAN = Local Area Network.
(b) The dot matrix printers, which are cheap to run, are used for work within the insurance company. The laser printers, which are expensive to run, are used for letters to customers, etc.
(c) (i)   It checks that words are correctly spelt.
(ii) You may want to add words not in the dictionary, e.g. names, technical terms and abbreviations, etc.
(d) (i)   You set up a standard letter and a data file. When you mail merge them you produce personalized letters.
(ii) You could send personalized letters to customers advertising your insurance services.

> ## EXAMINATION QUESTION WITH STUDENT ANSWER

Output from computers can be presented in many different ways:

(a) Software to log data in a science laboratory can present this data on a screen or as hard copy. State one advantage and one disadvantage of these two methods.

You can see the data on the screen but you have to wait for the hard copy.

(b) In publishing systems it is necessary to combine text and various forms of graphics.
   (i) Why is it often necessary to import graphics files into a DTP package?
   (ii) Why is it becoming increasingly easy to do this?

   (i) You can't create good graphics in DTP software.

   (ii) It is built into the software.

(NEAB/WJEC)

> **Examiner's comment**

The student's answer is too vague and too brief. It lacks some significant details that would clearly show that the student understands the topics being examined.
(a) An advantage of displaying the data on a screen is that you can see what is happening when it is happening. A disadvantage is that data displayed on a screen is not permanent unless it is saved on disk or printed.

An advantage of printing the data is that you have a permanent record of what has been logged. A disadvantage is that you do not necessarily have the data in a form that can later be analysed by computer unless it is input once again.
(b) (i) DTP software often has a restricted range of graphics functions compared with graphics software.
   (ii) Difficulties in importing graphics arise because of different and incompatible file formats. Most software can now import and export files in a much wider variety of formats so it is more likely a compatible format will have been used. Common formats are: WMF, GIF and JPG, etc.

SUMMARY

This chapter reviews different methods of output.

▷ Interactive processing takes place when the user and the computer have a 'conversation'. It is a cycle of input, processing, output, and user reaction. Interactive processing is usual with microcomputers.

▷ A mouse and a keyboard are used to input information.

▷ A monitor screen and a printer are used to output information.

▷ Dot matrix printers are cheap to buy and run. They are slow and the print quality is relatively poor.

▷ Draft printing is not the best print quality available. It is used to print drafts which are to be edited before the final, high quality copy is printed.

▷ Near Letter Quality (NLQ) printing is the best quality print that a dot matrix printer can produce.

▷ Ink jet printers are cheap to buy but expensive to run. They are slow but the print quality is very good.

▷ Laser printers are expensive to buy and run. They are fast and the print quality is excellent.

▷ Continuous, fan-fold paper is separated into sheets by perforations, with sprocket holes down the side. Continuous paper is usually fed through a printer using a tractor feed.

▷ Printer paper can also be sheets of A4 paper. This is fed into the printer using a single sheet feeder and a friction feed.

▷ A buffer is RAM memory built into a printer. It is used to store files while they are waiting to be printed. This releases the computer so that it can continue with other tasks.

▷ Spooling is the queuing of printer files on a hard disk. A file is printed when it reaches the front of the queue. This technique is used to speed up printing on LANs.

▷ Computer output to microfilm (COM) produces compact copies that do not deteriorate as fast as paper when stored for a long time.

▷ Graph plotters can draw high quality designs on large sheets of paper.

▷ Speech synthesis is the output of human speech. This is restricted in range and quality but can be useful in situations where reading a screen is difficult.

▷ Computers use actuators to perform physical tasks. They communicate with them using control interfaces. Actuators can be powered using hydraulics, pneumatics, servo-motors or stepper-motors.

Chapter

7 Operating Systems and networks

This chapter should be read if you are preparing for GCSE IT assessment with the following examining boards:

C & G	MEG	NEAB	SEG
London	NDTEF	RSA	WJEC

 GETTING STARTED

This chapter reviews the purpose and function of Operating Systems and Graphic User Interfaces. Various types of network are illustrated, including LANs, WANs and the Internet. Problems of network security are identified, and ways of preventing breaches of network security are described.

 GLOSSARY

Graphic User Interface These allow computers to be operated using Windows, Icons, Menus and Pointers.

Multitasking Multitasking is running more than one piece of software on the same computer at the same time. For example, you could run a wordprocessor in one window and graphics software in another.

Multiaccess Multiaccess is more than one person accessing the same computer at the same time. For example, travel agents spread throughout the country may access the same mainframe computer to find out travel information.

Local Area Network (LAN) A LAN is a small network, probably in one room or a building.

Wide Area Network (WAN) A WAN is a widespread network, probably national or international. It may use the telephone network for long distance communications.

C & G	LONDON	MEG	NDTEF	NEAB	RSA	SEG	WJEC	TOPIC	STUDY	REVISION I	REVISION 2
✓	✓	✓	✓	✓		✓	✓	Operating Systems			
✓	✓	✓	✓	✓	✓	✓	✓	Graphical user interface (GUI)			
✓	✓	✓	✓	✓	✓	✓	✓	Standalone mode			
✓	✓	✓	✓	✓	✓	✓	✓	Networks			
✓	✓	✓	✓	✓	✓	✓	✓	Network security			

WHAT YOU NEED TO KNOW

▷ **Operating Systems**

What is an Operating System?

The **Operating System** (OS) is a program. It must be available in memory when other software is run. Unless an OS is present a computer cannot normally be used. In the vast majority of computers the operating system is loaded into the memory from disk. In some microcomputers the OS is present in a ROM chip, leaving all the **RAM** memory free for user programs and data.

Many IBM PCs and compatibles, such as RM computers, use the MS-DOS operating system; Apple computers use System 7; Archimedes computers use RISC OS.

Unix is a popular OS for mainframe computers.

What do Operating Systems do?

'The OS interprets commands'

▶ **The OS carries out the commands given to the computer.** Those could be typed in at the keyboard, or come from a program that is being run, or a GUI. An example of an OS command is: DIR A:/w/p.

▶ **The OS supervises programs while they are running.** The Operating System looks after programs while they are being run, making sure no problems arise and helping to overcome them if they do. The OS tries to keep programs running if at all possible.

▶ **The OS makes the hardware easy to use.** User programs run on the OS, which runs between the user program and the hardware (see Fig. 7.1). This makes it possible for the user program to access the hardware using the simplified standard routines provided by the OS. For example, when you press a key on the keyboard a very complex process involving electronics and Operating System software leads to that character appearing on the screen. We would find it tedious to have to program this process directly every time we press a key. Computers would be practically unusable without standard OS routines to ensure key presses result in corresponding character displays on the screen.

'The OS controls input and output'

All access to the hardware from the user programs should be through the standard routines provided by the Operating System.

▶ **The OS helps the user decide what to do.** The Operating System supervises the running of user programs and will display messages telling the user what to do. For example, if the printer has run out of paper the OS will attract the user's attention to this; if the program needs some data, the OS will display a message asking for the data to be provided and may tell the user which file and which disk is needed.

'The OS helps with file management'

▶ **The OS provides utilities to manage the computer system.** When using any computer system it is important to be careful and tidy so that, for example, you do not lose files

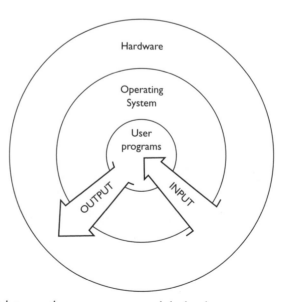

Fig. 7.1 The OS runs between the user programs and the hardware

or get one file confused with another. The OS provides the necessary **utilities** to enable the system to be well managed.

For disks, there will be instructions to *format* the disk and to delete, rename or copy files saved on the disk. When a disk is formatted a skeleton framework is set up of the sectors on the disk in which data and programs will later be saved. On a new (unformatted) disk this framework is not present. The disk must be formatted before it can be used. A file is *deleted* by removing it from the disk. A *renamed* file will have its filename changed, but not the data in the file. A file can be *copied* from one disk to another, so that a copy of the file exists on both disks.

The OS will maintain a **directory** (or *catalogue*) of a disk, which is simply a list of the filenames of all the files on a disk. This directory is itself saved on the disk.

'The OS allocates resources'

▶ **The OS optimizes the use of the computer's resources.** The OS will arrange the use of hardware and software resources, so that optimum use is made of them and all users get a fair share. Users can be given **priorities**, so that if resources are in short supply the Operating System can restrict access to users with a *low* priority and make the resources available to those with a *high* priority.

▶ **The OS keeps a log of users.** A **log** will be kept by the OS which records *who* is using the computer, *how long* they used it and *what* they did. This gives enough information so that users may be charged for the resources they have used.

▶ **The OS makes programs portable from one computer to another.** Operating Systems provide a standardized environment, enabling user programs to use peripherals, such as disk drives, by giving the same instructions on any computer running that Operating System. The disk drives could be of different makes and work differently and the computers could also be different, but still the OS would allow standard instructions to be used. Ideally, this makes programs portable, in other words, they should run on any computer running the OS they were written to be run on.

▶ **The OS helps maintain security.** On larger computers and networks each person who is allowed to use the computer will have a User Identification Number usually known as the **User Id**. Each user also has a **password** which is known only to the user. The OS keeps a register of all the User Ids and passwords and will only allow registered users who give the correct password to use the computer.

Hackers, who are not registered users, will sometimes discover how to break into the system, often by guessing a User Id and password. However, their activities will be logged by the OS, and they can usually be traced and identified. Passwords should be changed regularly so that if hackers do discover a password, they cannot use it for long.

▶ **A Network Operating System (NOS) has extended OS functions** so that it can manage a network. A NOS will allow computers connected to a network to communicate with each other. It will allow users to share software and data stored on a file server. It will organize printer spooling and queues. It will help organize security by maintaining the system of User Ids and passwords.

▷ **Graphical user interface (GUI)**

GUI or WIMP (Windows, Icons, Menus, Pointers) systems have been developed to make it easier for users to make use of a computer. They enable the OS and other programs to be run without the need to type in complex Operating System commands. OS commands are often difficult to remember and it is easy to make mistakes when typing them in at the keyboard. WIMP user interfaces bypass these problems by using a mouse instead of a keyboard (see Figs 4.11 and Fig 4.12).

Windows

'Features of GUI systems'

Windows are rectangular areas of the screen which contain information relating to one task. If a microcomputer supports multitasking, it is possible to run different tasks in different windows, displaying the results on the screen at the same time. For example, a wordprocessor can be run in one window and a database in another, at the same time. It is also possible to open windows on different parts of the same task, for example, different parts of a wordprocessing document and transfer text between them.

Icons

Icons are pictures that represent objects, e.g. floppy disks, or operations that can be performed, e.g., a picture of a dustbin may be used to allow files to be deleted.

Menus

Operations are also made available through **menus**. Menus contain lists of menu options that can be chosen.

Pointers

A **pointer** is used to point at icons and menu options. It is controlled by moving a mouse about a flat surface. The movement of the pointer on the screen corresponds to the movement of the mouse on the flat surface. An icon or menu option can be selected by *pointing* at it and *clicking* one of the buttons on the mouse. When an icon or menu option is selected, the operation it represents is performed. Usually, all the operations available can be accessed using a mouse, without the need to type in text OS commands or other instructions at the keyboard. The pointer will often take different shapes depending on its current function.

▷ Standalone mode

'Multitasking'

Computers used in **standalone mode** are either not connected to a netork or are not using it. Most programs that are run on standalone microcomputers are interactive. In general, microcomputers run one program at a time, but most can run several programs at the same time. On a microcomputer, running several programs at the same time is called **multitasking**.

For example, when using my wordprocessor I may wish to refer to a database to extract information to be put in an article I am writing. If the microcomputer I am using will only run one program at a time I have to save the article on disk, exit from the wordprocessor, load the database, extract the information, save the information, exit from the database, load the wordprocessor, get the document I was using and import the information I extracted from the database. A lengthy process!

If the microcomputer supports multitasking, I simply load the database, extract the information and transfer it into the article. I am able to do this because the wordprocessor and the database will run on the same computer at the same time.

▷ Networks

Computers can be linked together to form networks. There are several ways in which these connections can be made. The shape of the network chosen is determined by the way in which the links are made and the size of the computers attached to the network.

Star network

'Multiaccess'

A star network is common when a mainframe computer is being accessed by many users (see Fig. 7.2). When many users access a computer at the same time, this is known as **multiaccess**.

Users access the network using network stations attached to it. A **network station** is usually a microcomputer with additional hardware and software to enable it to communicate over the network. Network stations are also referred to as 'terminals'.

A network station can be connected directly to the computer network or it can communicate over the telephone network.

'Network stations'

Where a network station is connected directly to the computer network, the additional hardware needed is often called a 'network board' as it is frequently available as a circuit board that plugs into the computer. The additional software is referred to as 'network software'. This software enables the network station to send and receive data over the computer network.

Where two or more computers communicate over the telephone network, communications software and a modem are required.

A **modem** (*mo*dulator/*dem*odulator) converts the digital signal output by the microcomputer to an analog signal that can be transmitted along the telephone lines. A modem also converts the analog signals sent along the telephone lines to digital signals that the computer can process (see Fig. 7.3). The diagram shows two similar microcomputers communicating but, in fact, provided the appropriate communications software is available, any two computers can communicate.

Communications software is a program that can transmit and receive data via the modem and the telephone system. The telephone system is not a reliable means of transmitting data, so when the data is transmitted, it is checked. The modem does a **parity**

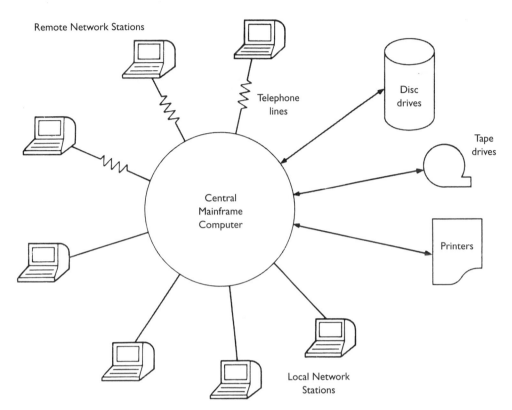

Fig. 7.2 A star network

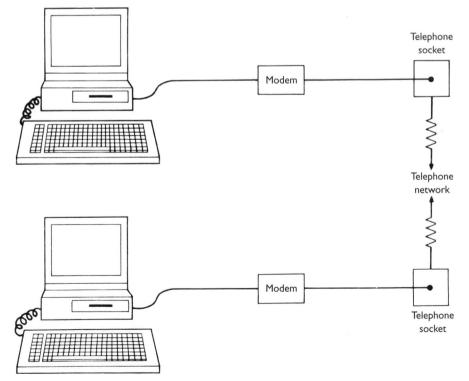

Fig. 7.3 Computers communicating using the telephone network

check automatically as the data is received. To perform a parity check using **even parity**, all the bits representing the received character are added up. If the number of 1s is even the data has been transmitted accurately. To ensure the number of 1s is even, a **parity bit** is added to the bit pattern representing the character. This extra bit is set at 1 or 0 to make the number of 1s even.

For example:

even parity bit	bit pattern	ASCII character
1	101 0010	R
0	101 0011	S

Odd parity is also used. In this case, the parity bit is set to make the number of 1s odd.

Using the telephone system is expensive as a charge is made for the length of time the computers are connected. A microcomputer can be used both as a network station and in standalone mode. Using a microcomputer, it is possible to access a mainframe computer, transfer data from the mainframe to the microcomputer, disconnect, and then use the microcomputer to process the data. This reduces the connection time and the costs involved in communications.

In most Star Networks there will be microcomputers connected to a central mainframe computer via the telephone network; others will be in the same building as the mainframe and connected directly to it. Not all of these terminals and microcomputers will be on-line at the same time.

Line network

A **line network** is used to link several microcomputers, allowing them to communicate with each other and to share data and peripherals (see Fig. 7.4). Each microcomputer uses its own processing power and it is likely that each will be running a different program.

'File servers let computers share programs and data'

On most line networks there will be a **file server** i.e. a computer that organizes access to files saved on the backing storage shared by all the computers connected to the network. Files will be stored on a shared hard disk capable of storing very large volumes of data and accessing it very quickly. Most of the programs run by microcomputers connected to the network will be stored on the hard disk and loaded and run as required.

'Printer servers let computers share printers'

A **printer server** is a microcomputer that organizes access to the printers attached to it for all the stations on the network. The printer server may have one or two printers attached to it. These printers can be used by all the network stations. It is more economical to buy a printer

'Features of a line network'

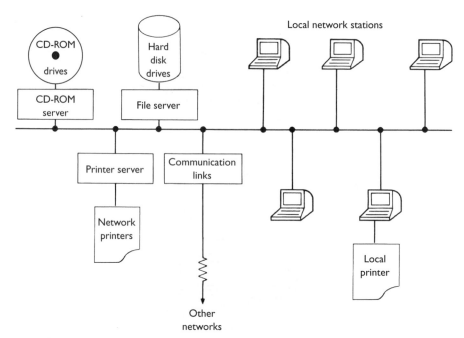

Fig. 7.4 A line network

server and the one or two printers attached to it than to buy a local printer for every station on the network. Local printers would not be in use all the time as printing is done for only a short period of time after the output has been prepared on the network station. The printers attached to the printer server will be in use more often as all the network stations use them.

When a network station uses a printer attached to the printer server, the printed output may not be printed immediately. Printed output is **spooled** to the printer, that is, it is temporarily saved on the hard disk on the printer server where it joins the queue for printing. When it reaches the head of the queue, it is printed. If the printing was sent direct to a printer, the user would have to wait until the printing had been completed before control returned to the network station. However, because the printed output is saved to the hard disk before printing, the network station user does not have to wait long before control returns. Saving to the printer server's hard disk is much faster than waiting for output to be immediately printed.

The advantages of sharing a network printer are that it is more economical, and control returns to the network station faster. The disadvantage is that the printout is not available immediately. It may be necessary to wait some time for printouts.

'CD-ROM servers let computers share CD-ROMS' A **CD-ROM server** is a microcomputer that that enables network stations to share the CD-ROMs loaded on the CD-ROM drives connected to it.

In some networks the file server, printer server and CD-ROM server may be a single microcomputer doing all of these tasks.

Communications links can be made between different networks using bridges, routers and gateways.

A **bridge** connects two similar networks directly, making them appear to be the same network to users. For example, a bridge can connect two similar LANs (see page 90).

A **router** connects two networks that do not have to be similar, and can direct a message received from one network to its destination in another network. For example, a router can connect a LAN to a much larger network.

A **gateway** can perform the tasks of a router. In addition, it can convert information passed between different networks so each network can understand it. A **gateway** can control and monitor access to a network from other networks.

Ring networks

A **ring network** is similar to a line network, except that the ends of the line are joined to form a ring (see Fig. 7.5).

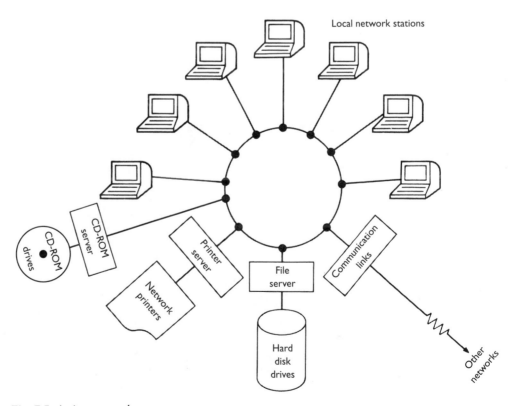

Fig. 7.5 A ring network

On a line network data is sent in both directions along the network whereas on a ring network data is sent in one direction only. Consequently ring networks, generally communicate faster. However, it is often easier to extend line networks as only a single cable is needed to each new network station. This is useful where the complete network cannot be planned in advance because of the need for possible future expansion or where network stations are widely dispersed.

Local area networks (LAN)

A **local area network** or LAN is a network where all the different hardware connected to the network is permanently linked, so that there is no need to use a modem and telephone line to communicate with other network stations. LANs are likely to be Line Networks or Ring Networks. A LAN will be located on one site, possibly in a building such as a school or an office block, perhaps even in a single room.

Wide area networks (WAN)

A **wide area network** or WAN is a network where all the hardware on the network is not permanently connected, due to the wide geographical distribution of network stations. WANs are likely to make use of a modem and telephone lines for regular communications with other parts of the network. A common example of a WAN is a mainframe computer that is accessed from terminals via the telephone system in a star network.

Since the telephone network is worldwide, it is possible and not uncommon for WANs to be international. For example, a newspaper reporter can write articles on a wordprocessor running on a lap top computer powered from a car battery while sitting in a car parked at a remote location (see Fig. 7.6). The article can be saved as a wordprocessing document on a disk. When it is possible to use a telephone, perhaps from a public call box, the reporter can use the telephone system to make a temporary connection between the lap top computer and the WAN used by the newspaper. Once connected, the reporter can send one or more articles, previously prepared for publication, in a few seconds.

This method of working has changed the job of a reporter. There is less need to work from a centralized office. All work can be done in any location from where the telephone network can be accessed. Reporters can now work at home. On the other hand, they may also be required to spend long periods away from home when working on assignments. The cost to the newspaper owner is greater investment in computer technology but this is offset by savings on office accommodation and clerical staff. There may be greater profits due to the increased speed at which news is reported. Customers may well be attracted to a paper that prints news ahead of its rivals.

Fig. 7.6 A reporter using a wide area network (WAN)

The Internet

The **Internet** is an international network made up of smaller networks that are interconnected. It is a public network. Anyone with the appropriate software and hardware is allowed to access it. It is usual to access the Internet using a browser, a modem and the telephone network. Users dial in to an Internet service provider, such as America On Line (AOL). Once connected, they can send e-mail or use **browser** software, such as Internet Explorer or Netscape, to access information servers on the **World Wide Web** (see Fig. 7.7).

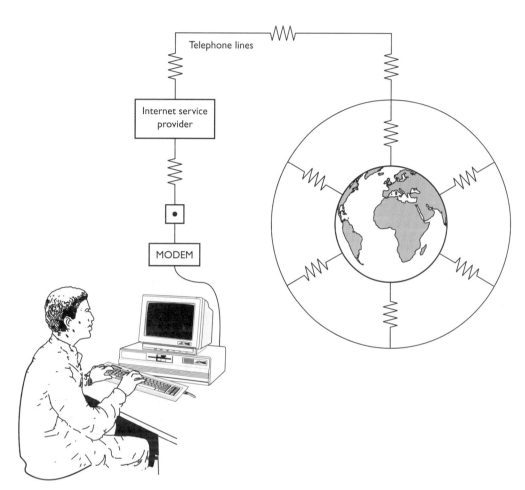

Fig. 7.7 Connecting to the Internet

The advantages and disadvantages of networks

It is cheaper to buy a few complete standalone microcomputer systems, than to set up a LAN with two or three stations. However, once the initial cost of setting up a LAN has been paid, it can be cheaper to add extra stations than to buy standalone microcomputer systems. Expensive peripherals can be shared on a LAN where the cost of purchase for a standalone system might be too great, e.g. a laser printer..

Software stored on hard disks connected to a network can also be shared. This may be cheaper than buying single copies for a number of standalone systems. Networks also enable users to share data.

Some information is only readily available by connecting to large networks, such as the Internet.

▷ **Network security**   Networks create security problems because of their widespread distribution and the increased number of users who have access. Networks share many of the security problems that arise when computers are used in other circumstances but these are exaggerated. Where networks are used, these security precautions should be considered:

- ▶ Users' access to IT rooms should be controlled using **locks** operated by stripe cards or key pads, and usage should be monitored by security guards.
- ▶ The windows of IT rooms should be protected to help prevent forced entry using grills or security laminates.
- ▶ Computers should be attached to desks using clamps, chains or other fittings with a similar purpose.
- ▶ Independent alarm systems should be used on all hardware. These alarms should remain active when the security alarm systems used elsewhere in the building are inactive to allow people to enter.
- ▶ The network cable should be installed where it is inaccessible so that no unauthorized physical connection can be made.
- ▶ Every user should have a unique **User Identification** number and **Password** given to them. Users should be asked to enter these when they log on to the network. Only those users who can correctly enter their User Identification number and Password should be given access to the network. Users should be required to change their passwords frequently. This reduces the length of time an unauthorized user can access the network if a password is discovered.
- ▶ The network OS should keep a **log of users** so that unauthorized activities can be traced.
- ▶ The data on the network should be coded or **encrypted** so that its meaning cannot be easily understood if it is copied by an unauthorized user.
- ▶ Backups of the network file server should be made regularly using the ancestral system.
- ▶ Networks that are connected to the Internet should be protected using **firewalls**. A firewall is a piece of software that monitors access. It can prevent hackers from penetrating an internal network using its connection to the Internet through a Web server.
- ▶ All computers should automatically check RAM memory and hard disks for the presence of viruses when they are used for the first time each day. Floppy disks should be checked automatically when they are put into a disk drive. If viruses are found, they should be removed immediately.

EXAMINATION QUESTIONS

▷ **Question 1**   A secretary is doing the firm's accounts. He logs onto the network and enters his password. He presses the correct letter to select a spreadsheet program from a list on the screen. He then loads in the correct file, enters new data and recalculates the sheet, obtains a printout and saves the new version.

Which of the following is the OPERATING SYSTEM directly responsible for? Tick the appropriate boxes.

(a)   Asking for the password   ☐
(b)   Entering an invoice number   ☐
(c)   Displaying a negative amount in red   ☐
(d)   Calculating a new total   ☐
(e)   Controlling data sent to the printer   ☐
(f)   Selecting a save option   ☐

(NEAB/WJEC)

▷ **Question 2**   Tick TWO ways of protecting personal data:

Laser printing	
Locking disks away	
Sorting data	
Using a data bank	
Using a password	

(SEG, 1993)

▷ **Question 3**   An office worker uses this computer:

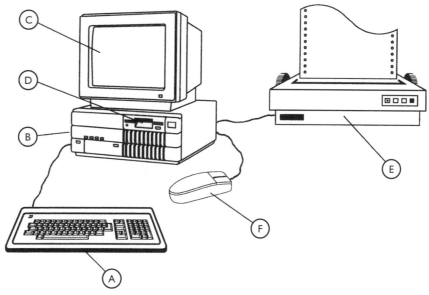

Fig. 7.8

(a) (i)   Write down the labels of the parts used to input information into the computer.
     (ii) Write down the labels of the parts used to output information from the computer.
     (iii) The computer has a hard disk. Write down the label of the part that contains the hard disk.
     (iv) The computer is connected to a Local Area Network using a network card. The network card is installed inside a part of the computer. Write down the label of the part that contains the network card.
(b) When the computer is switched on, the office worker has to enter a password.
     (i)   Explain why passwords are used.
     (ii) The office worker's password has to be changed every week. Explain why passwords should be changed regularly.
     (iii) When the password was changed, the office worker typed in the new password. The password was typed in correctly. The computer asked the office worker to type in the new password again. Explain why the computer asked the office worker to type in the new password again.
(c) The office worker wants to access information on a computer in Australia. Figure 7.9 is part of a flow chart that shows what the office worker has to do to access the information.
     (i)   The box labelled A should contain a question. Write down the question that should be in the box labelled A.
     (ii) The line labelled B should re-join the flowchart. Draw on the flowchart to show where the line labelled B should re-join the flowchart.
(d) Describe how the information can be transmitted from the computer in Australia to the office worker's computer.

(SEG, 1996)

▷ **Question 4**   Describe how, in a modern office system, computers can be connected and managed on a network.

(MEG)

▷ **Question 5**   An order-processing system uses on-line processing, telephone lines and modems.

(a) What is the modem used for?
(b) What is on-line processing?
(c) Some of this information stored on the system is coded. Give TWO reasons why information is coded on a computer file.

(MEG)

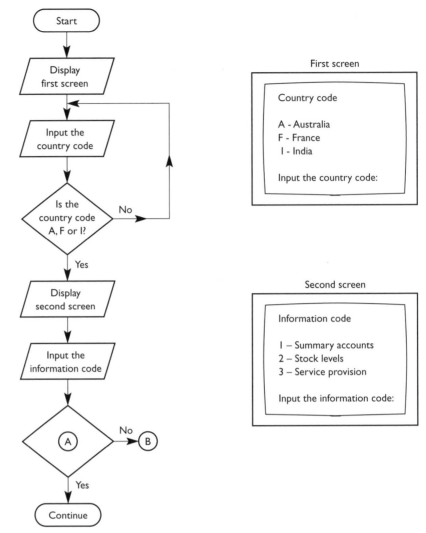

Fig. 7.9

▷ **Question 6** Describe how a computer hacker might do more harm than an office burglar.

(MEG)

▷ **Question 7** A daily newspaper has a local area network which links all the computers in their London headquarters. The headquarters consists of a newsroom, an editorial office and a printing works. The paper also has a wide area network linking it to a regional office in Edinburgh and an overseas office in New York.

(a) The local area network is linked using direct wire connectors. How might the wide area network be linked between:
   (i) Edinburgh and London.
   (ii) London and New York.
(b) Describe how use of LANs has affected work in this daily newspaper.

(City and Guilds)

▷ **Question 8** State two functions which would be carried out by the Operating System.

(City and Guilds)

▷ **Question 9**   A school uses a database system to handle records of pupils.

(a) Give ONE benefit to the school staff of using a computer system.
(b) Describe THREE particular routines that the database software provides.

The office staff use a mouse and windows to interface with the database software.

(c) Write down TWO features that you associate with such a graphical user interface.
(d) Give ONE advantage of using such an interface instead of a traditional command line environment.

(MEG)

▷ **Question 10**   Sainsburys commission a new product from Sprayway Ltd, a facial mineral water spray. Sainsburys launch the product in selected branches throughout the North East of England on a trial basis.

(a) Explain how the Sainsburys head office staff in London are likely to receive the sales information that they require to assess whether the product should be stocked throughout all of their stores.
(b) What information would the Sainsburys head office be looking to extract from their sales database, in order to decide whether to stock the facial spray throughout all of their stores?
(c) How else could Sainsburys have collected sufficient information about the sales of the facial spray to make their stocking decision if they were unable to use information technology?
(d) State TWO advantages information technology would give Sainsburys in making such stocking decisions.

(London)

EXAMINATION ANSWERS

▷ **Answer 1**   The Operating System is directly responsible for (a) and (e).

▷ **Answer 2**   Locking disks away. Using a password.

▷ **Answer 3**   (a) (i)   A, F
(ii)   C, E
(iii) B
(iv) B
(b) (i)   To prevent unauthorized users accessing the software and hardware.
(ii)   If passwords are changed regularly, an unauthorized user who finds out someone's password can only use it for a short time until it is next changed.
(iii) To be sure that the office worker had entered the new password correctly.
(c) (i)   Is the Information Code 1, 2 or 3?
(ii)   The line labelled B should rejoin the flowchart after the first decision box but before the input box containing the message 'Input the information code'.
(d) The information leaving the Australian computer will pass through a MODEM where it will be converted from a digital signal to an analog signal. This analog signal can be transmitted over the international telephone network. The office worker's MODEM converts the analog signal received to a digital signal which can be processed by the office worker's computer.

▷ **Answer 4**   Three from:
Computers would be cabled together and connected to a common file server;
Computers would share a high quality printer or have local printers;
Software would be stored on the file server and shared between users;
Each user would have a secure area to prevent unauthorized access of data.

(MEG)

▷ **Answer 5**   (a) To translate signals from the computer into signals which can be transmitted over the telephone system.
(b) User is in direct contact with the computer. Computer responds to user input.
(c) Two from:
To save space in the computer's memory;
To save data entry time;
To process the data faster.

(MEG)

▷ **Answer 6**   Four from:
Personal data might be viewed and acted upon/sold;
Personal data might be altered;
Personal data might be destroyed;
Software might be deleted;
Viruses could be introduced into a system and spread.

(MEG)

▷ **Answer 7**   (a) (i)   telephone line or microwave link
(ii) satellite link
(b) LANs, especially those linked via WANs, enable:
▶ reporters to send articles to the newspaper from around the world;
▶ the newspaper to communicate with its employees faster, using e-mail;
▶ all employees can share resources on the network, including on-line databases, etc.

▷ **Answer 8**   An Operating System:
▶ controls the input and output;
▶ deals with errors while the computer is running;
▶ provides system utilities, e.g. format.

▷ **Answer 9**   (a) Faster access to pupil information.
(b) Three from:
Searching for specified information;
Different layouts for printed output;
Sorting data into a variety of orders;
Specifying what data to display;
Any other functions.
(c) Two from:
Windows to position on the screen;
Icons to select applications;
Mouse control of the pointer;
Pointer on the screen.
(d) One from:
Very little typing;
Fewer commands to memorize;
Ability to drag data from one application to another;
Easy transfer of data;
Any suitable advantage.

(MEG)

▷ **Answer 10**   (a) Sales information about all product sales is likely to be recorded in electronic form. This information will be sent to Head Office in electronic form across a WAN.
(b) The sales information about the new product will be extracted from the sales information about all products. The Head Office will want to know how much of the product has been sold, where it was sold, at what times it sold most and if different pricing affected sales.
(c) They could manually record the sales of the new product. One method is to have a

sales assistant handing out the product and recording sales. This method is often used to promote new products.

(d) The advantages of using IT are:

▶ the information is collected and sent to Head Office much faster;

▶ the information is in a form that assists statistical analysis using IT tools;

▶ the analysis is carried out faster using IT.

▷ EXAMINATION QUESTION WITH STUDENT ANSWER

A school is setting up a new IT resource base, with 16 standalone computers, for pupils.

The school could have installed a network, but decided against this option. Discuss the possible reasons for this decision.

The network in our school is always breaking down. None of the computers work and we cannot do our work on the computers. This could be why the school didn't have a network.

(NEAB/WJEC)

▷ **Examiner's comment**

That is one good reason to avoid installing a network. There are others:

▶ information stored on a network is less secure;

▶ it can be difficult and expensive to link computers in different rooms in the school;

▶ computers using a network can be slowed down if the network is heavily used;

▶ if pupils' work is stored on the network file server, the amount they can store will be limited.

There are also many good reasons to install networks that are not mentioned here!

SUMMARY

This chapter reviews what Operating Systems and networks do and why they are needed.

An **Operating System** (OS):

▷ Carries out the commands you give it. You can give commands throgh a GUI or type them in on a command line, e.g. COPY C:\ACCESS\DATA\AGENTS A:

▷ Supervises programs while they are running. The OS will try to keep programs running whatever difficulties occur. For example, if the OS tries to load a file from a disk and cannot, it does not continue trying or crash, but returns control to you, and explains the problem.

▷ Makes hardware easy to use. You do not have to worry about the internal complexities of the computer system.

▷ Helps you decide what to do. For example, if the printer is unavailable when you want to print, it will tell you and ask you what you want to do, perhaps suggesting alternatives.

▷ Provides utilities to manage the computer system. For example, to format floppy disks.

▷ Optimizes the use of the computer's resources. For example, so that printing can be done while you are doing other tasks on the computer.

▷ Makes programs portable, so that they can be run on different computers with the same OS.

In addition, a **Network Operating System** (NOS):

▷ Allows networked computers to communicate e.g. using-e-mail.

▷ Allows you to use software and data stored on a fileserver. For example, you can use a wordprocessor stored on a fileserver from a network station.

▷ Manages printer queues and spooling. When you send a file to the printer, the NOS puts it in the printer queue on the fileserver. Your file is printed out when it gets to the front of the queue.

▷ Organizes user Ids and passwords.

▷ Keeps a log of who uses the network.

Networks can be star network, line networks, ring networks or combinations of these.

▷ Computers used in standalone mode are either not connected to a network or are not using the network.

▷ Computers can be directly connected to a Local Area Network (LAN), or connected to a Wide Area Network (WAN) using a Moderm and the telephone network.

▷ Using a network you can share software stored on a fileserver's hard disk, use networked printers, access CD-ROMs through a CD-ROM server, and communicate with other networks.

▷ Communication links can be made between different networks using bridges, routes and gateways.

▷ The Internet is an international network made up of smaller networks that are interconnected.

Networks create security problems because of their widespread distribution and large numbers of users. To make networks and other computer facilities more secure, you should:

▷ Use locks and guards to control access to IT rooms.

▷ Put grills or security laminates on the windows of IT rooms.

▷ Attach computers to desks or walls using clamps and chains.

▷ Use alarm systems that are always active on all computers, in addition to other alarm systems.

▷ Install the network cable where it is inaccessible.

▷ Give users unique User Ids and passwords, and change passwords frequently.

▷ Keep a log of users.

▷ Use data encryption.

▷ Back up files regularly.

▷ Use firewalls.

▷ Use automatic virus checks.

Communicating information

This chapter should be read if you are preparing for GCSE IT assessment with the following examining boards:

C & G	MEG	NEAB	SEG
London	NDTEF	RSA	WJEC

GETTING STARTED

When communicating information you should try to be clear, simple and interesting, and present information in a straight forward and logical way. You should take into account your audience and the extent to which it is likely to understand what you are communicating. All IT software can extend and enhance the effectiveness of your communication skills. This chapter reviews the function and purpose of software that is particularly useful for **communicating information**. That is, software for wordprocessing, graphics, desk top publishing (DTP), e-mail, multimedia and conferencing.

GLOSSARY

Audience When you communicate information it is most important to get the attention of your audience, and to communicate with it in a way that helps it understand you.

Clip art Clip art comprises pictures, cartoons, photographs, diagrams and other images that can be imported into the software you are using to illustrate your work. There are thousands of high quality, copyright-free clip art images available on floppy disk and CD-ROM.

Font A font is a set of consistently shaped characters. Common examples are the Times New Roman font and the Arial font.

Scrolling When you make a document disappear at the top of the screen and appear at the bottom, you are scrolling down it. You can also scroll up it and scroll horizontally.

C & G	LONDON	MEG	NDTEF	NEAB	RSA	SEG	WJEC	TOPIC	STUDY	REVISION I	REVISION 2
✓	✓	✓	✓	✓	✓	✓	✓	Audience			
✓	✓	✓	✓	✓	✓	✓	✓	Wordprocessing			
✓	✓	✓	✓	✓	✓	✓	✓	Graphics			
✓	✓	✓	✓	✓	✓	✓	✓	Desk top publishing (DTP)			
✓		✓	✓	✓	✓	✓	✓	E-mail			
		✓	✓	✓	✓	✓	✓	Multimedia			
✓		✓	✓		✓	✓	✓	Conferencing			

WHAT YOU NEED TO KNOW

IT extends and enhances our ability to *communicate*. In this chapter, we look at software that is mainly used to communicate information, e.g. software for wordprocessing, graphics and desk top publishing (DTP). This software does not replace traditional methods of communication, it extends and enhances them. It is most important to remember that using IT is no substitute for a clear, simple, interesting presentation of the information being communicated in a straight forward and logical manner. Your use of IT should improve the effectiveness of your communication skills. It may not teach you those skills.

'Communication is the key'

For example, **wordprocessors** do not replace handwriting, although they may very well replace manual and electronic typewriters. Wordprocessors extend what we can do and allow us to do what we already do in new and better ways. Wordprocessors are not being used to their full potential if they are just used for making a neat copy of work that has already been written out. They should be used for drafting and re-drafting text. For example, writing a long essay (or a book!) involves planning the way in which large volumes of written material are presented. Sometimes you will want to move a sentence or a paragraph to a new position in the essay. If you have handwritten or typed your essay, this can be difficult. You may have to re-write or re-type sections or cut out a section and stick it in somewhere else. With a wordprocessor, you can simply move the text to its new position. You can include pictures, diagrams and other graphics in most wordprocessors. These could be photographs or printed diagrams from books that you have scanned into the computer. Desk top publishing (DTP) software will enable you to re-arrange the text and graphics you have produced into a layout similar to that of a newspaper or magazine.

'Wordprocessors extend what we can do'

These IT tools and techniques can be very useful for developing and producing coursework for GCSE exams. They are also widely used throughout commerce and industry.

▷ Audience

When you are communicating information, by whatever means, it is important to consider the effects of what you do on your **audience**. You should do this for all forms of communication by whatever media you are using.

'Think about the audience'

You will need to take into account the extent to which your audience understands the material you are communicating. For example, if you are explaining how a nuclear power station works, your explanation to children in primary school would need to be more straight forward than if you were giving an explanation to a group of A-level physics students. If the complexity of the material presented does not match the understanding of your audience, they will be bored, confused and annoyed. It is unlikely they will enjoy your explanation.

As the purpose of communication is to *inform* your audience, they should not fall asleep because your means of communication is dull. If you can use humour and metaphor effectively, your audience might be more interested in the material you are communicating. The use of colour images instead of black and white; video instead of still pictures; sound and music as well as pictures can motivate audiences.

Teachers in schools have to consider their audience when planning their lessons. How often have you been bored because the lesson was too easy or frustrated because the material was too hard? Which teachers do you find interesting? Why? If you remember these experiences when you are trying to communicate information to your audience you may produce more effective work yourself.

▷ Wordprocessing

Wordprocessors, i.e. computers running wordprocessing software, have now largely replaced the traditional, mechanical or electronic typewriter. Wordprocessors can do any task carried out on a typewriter. They also make such tasks easier, and have additional, more powerful facilities.

A wordprocessor will typically consist of a microcomputer, monitor, mouse, disk drive, printer and wordprocessing software. Many, but not all, wordprocessors can be operated either from the keyboard alone or using the keyboard and a mouse. A mouse improves the ease and speed of operation of a wordprocessor. The quality of the printed output is determined by the type of printer used. For high quality output, high speed graphics and a wide variety of character styles or fonts, a laser printer is needed. For inexpensive, low quality printout, a dot matrix printer is appropriate.

'Wordprocessing software'

Wordprocessing software is extensive and varied. There is very often a choice of word-processors for a particular computer and many wordprocessors will run on several different makes of computer.

For example, Word and Wordperfect are wordprocessors suitable for IBM compatible computers (see Fig 8.1). In addition, Word is available for Apple computers.

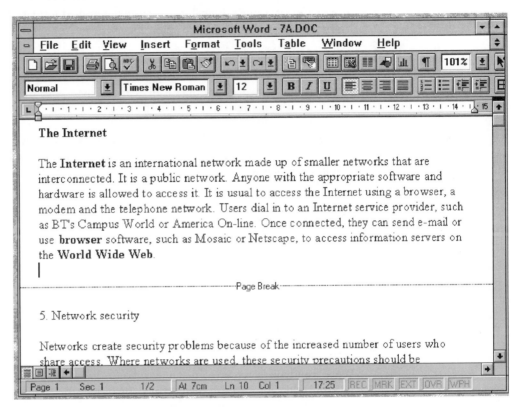

Fig. 8.1 The screen displayed by Word software running on an IBM compatible PC

What a wordprocessor can be used for

Wordprocessors can be used to prepare a wide variety of printed material. The range of tasks that can be done is so extensive that only a few can be mentioned here. These are some of the tasks that a wordprocessor could be used for:

'Some uses of the wordprocessor'

▶ Writing a letter, memo, leaflet, brochure. essay, article, book, etc.
▶ Preparing a curriculum vitae (c.v.), questionnaire, work sheet, exam paper, etc.
▶ Keeping a list of names and addresses so that they can be printed out on sticky labels which can then be stuck on envelopes.
▶ Printing personalized letters to be sent to customers, patients, subscribers, donors, etc.
▶ Helping disabled people communicate, particularly the deaf.

What wordprocessors do

Different wordprocessors do the same tasks but may be operated in different ways. Some wordprocessors will have more facilities and be easier to use than others. The facilities described below are available on most wordprocessors. You should look for these facilities on the wordprocessor you use and make sure you can use them.

Create a document

'Creating a document'

A document is a file of words or text to be processed, for example, an article or a letter. When a new document is needed it is **created**. When you are creating a document, the screen displayed will be blank to begin with. The text is typed into the document from the keyboard and appears on the screen as it is typed. The point at which you are entering text on the screen will be marked by a cursor. This may be a solid rectangle, the size of one character, that may be flashing. The end of the document may be marked in some way, possibly by a horizontal line across the screen. If you want to keep the document you have created then you will have to save it (see below).

What You See Is What You Get (WYSIWYG)

'WYSIWYG'

WYSIWYG or What You See Is What You Get means that the document you see on the screen of the wordprocessor is exactly as it will look when it is printed. This is a most desirable feature. It is often difficult to visualize the printed format of a document if you are using a wordprocessor that does not display documents in WYSIWYG form on the screen.

Wordwrap

'Wordwrap'

When entering text, at the end of each line, as you type beyond the right margin, the word that you type in will be automatically carried over onto the next line. This is **wordwrap**. You need take no action to ensure that wordwrap takes place. In most wordprocessors, wordwrap is entirely automatic.

'Marking the end of a paragraph'

   If you are used to using a typewriter, you may be inclined to press <RETURN> at the end of each line. Do NOT do this. You should only press <RETURN> at the end of a paragraph. Pressing <RETURN> marks the end of a paragraph.

Scrolling

'Scrolling'

Since it is likely that a document will be too big for all of it to be displayed on the screen at the same time, the document will **scroll**, that is, if you are viewing an existing document, text will disappear at the top of the screen while more text appears at the bottom, when you move down the document. You will notice the opposite effect when moving up the document. You have not lost the text when it is not displayed on the screen. The entire document is stored in the memory of the computer but we can only see part of it on the screen. Scrolling takes place automatically when you are entering text. You need not take any action to ensure it happens.

Moving around a document

When you have entered the document, you may want to **move around** it to view and edit it. To do this you can use the cursor control keys or 'arrow keys'. However, this will be quite slow, particularly if you want to move from the start of a long document to the end. Your wordprocessor may provide quicker ways of moving around a document. For example, it is not uncommon to press the <PGUP> key to move up the document one screen and to press the <PGDN> key to move down a document by one screen.

'Cursor control keys'

Delete, insert and edit text

When a document has been entered, it may have mistakes in it, e.g. spelling mistakes, or you may decide you want to re-write parts of it. You can delete or insert text when editing it on the screen. Delete means 'remove existing characters'; insert means 'put in new characters'. Editing text is done by a combination of deleting and inserting text. All wordprocessors allow text to be edited.

Control characters

Your document may contain 'invisible' characters that you have entered at the keyboard but do not see on the screen. These are known as **control characters** as they are used to control the operation of the word processor. The most obvious of these is the character that represents a single press of the <RETURN> key, though there will be others to represent different style and format commands. You might find it useful to know where you have pressed the <RETURN> key in your document as this key is pressed at the end of a paragraph and to insert blank lines. Many wordprocessors will allow you to choose whether to display the control characters on the screen.

'Control characters'

Block delete, move, cut, copy and paste

You can define a block of text then delete (or cut) it, move (or cut and paste) it to a different position in the document, or make another copy of it in a different position, perhaps in another document. A block can be a character, a paragraph , a graphic image, or the whole document. A block is defined by highlighting it using the mouse or a combination of function keys. The ability to delete, move, cut, copy and paste large blocks of text is a very useful facility when re-drafting or re-writing large documents.

Text style

'*Different fonts*'

Various **style** facilities are available in most wordprocessors to improve the appearance of the text. For example, text can be underlined, bold or italic or a combination of these. You can have different sizes of text or different fonts. The size of a character is measured in points. A **font** is a particular style of the characters printed. Some text styles are illustrated in Fig. 8.2.

You can change text style before entering text. All text subsequently entered will be in the style chosen. You can change text style after you have entered the text by highlighting the block to be re-styled and then selecting the new style.

You can generate word art in some wordprocessors (see Fig. 8.3)

Times New Roman font, 10 point, normal

Times New Roman font, 14 point, normal

Times New Roman font, 18 point, normal

Times New Roman font, 22 point, normal

Times New Roman font, 14 point, italic

Times New Roman font, 14 point, italic, underlined

~~Times New Roman font, 14 point, strike through~~

Arial font, 10 point, normal

Arial font, 14 point, normal

Arial font, 22 point, normal

Arial font, 14 point, italic

Arial font, 14 point, underlined

~~Arial font, 14 point, strike through~~

Fig. 8.2 Different styles of text

Fig. 8.3 Word art

Format

Formatting facilities control the layout of text in the document. There will be a variety of formatting facilities. For example, text can be centred on a line; margins can be justified so that the right and left margins are aligned; text can be indented; text can be printed in several columns instead of the usual across the page format; the width and length of the page can be altered; page numbers can be automatically inserted.

Frames

In some wordprocessors it is possible to draw a simple, rectangular **frame** or border around text to emphasise it. However, it is more usual to put in features that enhance the presentation of a document using DTP software.

Search and replace

The **search** facility is used to find particular words or character strings in a document. The **search and replace** facility is used to find a particular word and replace it with another. For example, if a word has been spelt incorrectly, every occurrence of the word can be located and the incorrect spelling automatically replaced by the correct spelling.

Spelling check

The spelling of words can be checked against an extensive dictionary which can be added to or changed as you wish. Spellings can be checked as you type in the words or you can check the whole document when you want to. It is also possible to check grammar, though grammar checkers are less common and less reliable than spelling checkers.

Save and load documents

When a document has been created it can be **saved** on backing storage, e.g. magnetic disk. The computer can then be switched off but the document will not be lost as there is a copy of it on the disk. When the document is needed at a later date, it can be **loaded** from the disk into the computer.

Printing

Documents can be **printed** on a printer connected to the wordprocessor. The quality of the printed output from a wordprocessor is determined by the type of printer used. For high speed, good quality and a wide variety of character styles, fonts and graphics a laser printer is needed; for inexpensive, lower quality printout a dot matrix printer is appropriate.

Many inexpensive dot matrix printers will now print a variety of fonts, in draft and Near Letter Quality (NLQ). Draft printing is fast, but low quality as you can easily see the dots that form each character. NLQ is much better quality than draft. You cannot easily see the dots that form each character and there may be more than one font available. As ink jet and laser printers fall in price, they are rapidly replacing dot matrix printers for most purposes.

Mail merge

'Mail merge can be useful'

Companies regularly send letters to customers in which the content of each letter is the same but the name, address and other limited details change.

A **standard letter** contains the part of the document that does not change from letter to letter. In the standard letter the position of the data that does change can be indicated using markers. A **marker** will be replaced by data read from a separate **data file**. For example, a standard letter can be merged with a data file of customers' names and addresses to print a personalized letter for each customer.

To use mail merge to send a personalized, standard letter to customers, you proceed as follows. You should note that although the principles of doing a mail merge are the same in all wordprocessors, the actual method of doing it will differ, perhaps considerably.

1. Create a standard letter with markers

You should note that different wordprocessors use different ways of inserting the markers. The standard letter should be saved on disk. An example of a standard letter is shown below:

DIY Magazine
25 Wakefield Rd
Halifax HX2 5GR
25/6/96

Dear <marker 1>,

I am writing to remind you that your annual subscription is due later this month. I am sure you have enjoyed DIY Magazine this year. You can look forward to a host of interesting articles and other features in the coming year that will help you keep your home at <marker 2> in good shape.

Please renew your subscription as soon as possible.

Yours sincerely,

Daniel Merlin
Circulation Department

2. *Create a data file*

Next, build up a file of data to replace the markers when the letters are printed. Different wordprocessors do this in different ways. The data file corresponding to the above standard letter is shown below:

marker 1, marker 2
John Smith, Stanbury
Rizwan Malik, Bradford
Bodan Jovanovich, Halifax
Jennie Jones, Oxenhope

3. *Do the mailmerge*

You now have a standard letter and a data file and are ready to do a mailmerge. To print the personalized letters, you will have to identify the standard letter and the data file, then activate the mail merge. The letters will be printed for the customers whose details are stored in the data file. In this example, four letters would be printed as there are four records in the data file. One example of a personalized letter printed using mail merge is shown below. Notice that the markers have been replaced by the data.

DIY Magazine
25 Wakefield Rd
Halifax HX2 5GR
25/6/97

Dear Bodan Jovanovich,

I am writing to remind you that your annual subscription is due later this month. I am sure you have enjoyed DIY magazine this year. You can look forward to a host of interesting articles and other features in the coming year that will help you keep your home at Halifax in good shape.

Please renew your subscription as soon as possible.

Yours sincerely,

Daniel Merlin
Circulation Department

'Exporting and importing'

Exporting and importing

Saving a document with the intention of loading it into, for example, DTP software, is known as **exporting** the document. Loading a document that has been prepared on, for example, a different wordprocessor, is known as **importing**.

You may be able to import a wordprocessed document into DTP software without modifying the form in which it is saved on disk. However, it is likely that you will have to ensure that the form in which the document is exported matches one of the forms in which the DTP software can import it. If you can match the form of an exported document with a form in which it can be imported, then all the control characters will be understood by the receiving software. This means that all text styling will be kept. If you cannot match the form of the exported and imported documents then the control characters will not be understood and text styling may be lost. Documents can always be exported and imported in ASCII form but, in this case, all text styling, etc. will be lost.

'Compatibility problems'

You can import graphics into some wordprocessors. You will need to be sure that the form in which the graphic has been exported matches a form in which it can be imported.

'Clip art'

Some wordprocessors are supplied with a library of clip art, e.g. Microsoft Word for Windows. Clip art is art work that has been prepared by a professional artist and saved on disk. A clip art library will contain useful graphics such as borders for restaurant menus, cartoon characters to put in newsletters, etc. Clip art can easily be imported into the wordprocessor it has been prepared for.

You may also be able to import a spreadsheet or a database into a wordprocessed document. This is useful for preparing business accounts, etc.

Quit

When you have finished using the wordprocessor, you will want to exit from it and switch off the computer. It is important to exit from the software using the commands provided as there will be a check built into the wordprocessor to remind you to save your document if you have not done so. If you do not save your document *before* quitting, it will not be available if you want to use it in the future.

How wordprocessing has changed the job of a typist

The job of an office typist has changed greatly due to the introduction of wordprocessors. Compared to using a manual or electronic typewriter, with a word processor there is much less need to re-type letters and less routine copy typing. More attention can be given to the presentation of work and more style and format facilities are available to encourage this. Correspondence does not have to be stored printed on paper in filing cabinets but can be saved on disk until needed. Consequently, much less manual filing of correspondence in filing cabinets is necessary and it is easier to locate the documents saved on disk.

Wordprocessors increase the productivity of typists, allowing them to complete *more* work of a *higher* standard. This may lead to fewer typists being employed. The operation of a wordprocessor demands different skills from those necessary to use a typewriter so that typists have had to re-train, learning new skills. Not all have easily adapted to the new technology. However, those who have learned wordprocessing skills benefit from higher pay and status. The client has also benefited from the use of wordprocessors. Replies to letters can be quicker and more personalized. Correspondence will be more likely to be clearly printed and error free. The cost of the service is also likely to be held or reduced, allowing savings to be passed on to the customer.

▷ Graphics

Graphics software provides a means of drawing pictures on the computer screen. It varies in complexity and capability and must be carefully selected depending on the use to be made of it.

Most graphics software in schools is 2-dimensional, i.e. there is no attempt to represent solid objects. For convenient use of graphics software a mouse is essential as a GUI will almost certainly be used. The facilities available are likely to be represented by icons or listed in menus. They can be activated by pointing at an icon or menu option with the mouse-controlled pointer and clicking the button on the mouse to select it.

What graphics software can be used for

Graphics software can be used to prepare a wide variety of illustrated material. The range of tasks that can be done is extensive. These are some of the tasks that can be done using graphics software:

▶ Drawing a picture, diagram, cartoon, etc.
▶ Drawing a map, a plan of a house, etc.
▶ Designing patterns for wallpaper, textiles, etc.
▶ Producing posters and other advertising materials

What graphics software will do

The facilities described below are available in most graphics software. You should look for these facilities in the graphics software you use and make sure you can use them.

'Common facilities of graphic design software'

▶ **Draw** on the screen. A line can be drawn freehand on the screen by moving the mouse. The line corresponds to the movement of the mouse. Various types of standard line may be selected, e.g. straight or dotted, in a variety of patterns. You can choose different widths of line.
▶ **Colours**. A variety of colours will be available on a colour monitor. There will be a range of standard colours to choose from and perhaps the facility to mix colours to produce a unique blend. These colours can be used in combination with other features of the software. For example, to draw coloured lines.
▶ **Fill**. Closed shapes can be filled with patterns. These patterns may be standard, or designed by the user, perhaps in several colours.
▶ **Airbrush**. Fill patterns or colours can be applied in a texture that mimics the effect of an airbrush or spray gun. Different brush patterns can be selected or designed by the user.
▶ **Text**. Words and characters can be typed in a variety of styles or fonts. It may be possible for the user to customize an existing font or design a new one.
▶ **Circles and boxes**. Circles and boxes can be drawn. These may be in outline or they could be filled in with a colour or pattern.
▶ **Blocks**. An area of the screen can be defined as a *block*. This block can then be moved or copied to another part of the screen. Blocks can be transformed by stretching, enlarging, reflecting or rotating them.
▶ **Zoom**. Areas of the screen can be magnified, or zoomed in on, to allow very fine detail to be added or changed.

Pictures and clip art

Pictures can be saved on disk and imported. These could be drawings; diagrams; plans; maps; images that have been scanned from a photograph; video frames that have been digitized. It is sometimes useful to have available a library of images (**clip art**) that have been prepared by a professional artist with a specific purpose in mind. For example, a circuit designer would find it useful to have a clip art library containing the symbols used in drawing electronic circuits; the secretary of a sports centre might find a clip art library of sports equipment useful. Clip art can be prepared on graphics software for importing to a wordprocessor.

Exporting and importing

Pictures may be **imported** for inclusion in a current composition; scanned images may be imported so that they can be enhanced or otherwise edited. The final image may be **exported** for importing to a newsletter or an advert being prepared on DTP software.

Save and load documents

Pictures can be **saved** on backing storage and **loaded** when required.

Printing

Pictures can be **printed**. A laser printer will produce high quality graphics. A dot matrix printer will produce lower quality graphics.

Colour printing is still expensive, although colour ink-jet printers are available at a reasonable price. It is difficult to get an accurate printout on paper of the colour seen on the screen. The printout provided by a laser printer is adequate if a black and white print is acceptable.

Quit

When you have finished, you will want to exit and switch off the computer. It is important to exit from the software using the commands provided as there will be a check built into the graphics software to remind you to save your work if you have not done so. If you do not save your work before quitting, it will not be available if you want to use it in the future.

The above facilities should be available in most graphic design software. Using such facilities it is possible to do textile design (see Fig. 8.4), wallpaper design and produce high quality business cards and tickets for dances, etc. Typical systems are IBM PC compatibles running Paintbrush or Corel Draw, and Apple computers using MacPaint or MacDraw.

'More specialized facilities of graphic design software'

More specialized facilities are sometimes available for specific tasks. For example, some graphics software will accept images captured by a video camera when input via a video digitizer. These images can be changed or enhanced using the facilities of the graphics software. This technique can be used to add text to video film or to create a mixed sequence of video and graphic designs such as cartoons.

'Computer aided design (CAD)'

Three-dimensional objects can be designed with some specialized graphics software. These objects can be displayed on the screen as wire frame images, or as solid objects which can be rotated or viewed in plan and elevation.

In manufacturing, graphics software can be used to design products. A library of standard components can be provided so that the new design can be made up from existing manufactured parts as far as possible. It becomes relatively easy to redesign products as their designs are easily changed using graphics software without the need to redraw the entire design.

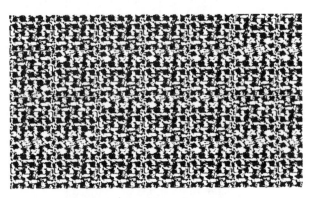

Fig. 8.4 A textile design produced using graphics software

▷ Desk top publishing (DTP)

Desk top publishing software allows the user to produce printout in the style of a newspaper (see Fig. 8.5). That is, in columns with pictures and other graphics.

DTP software can be thought of as integrated wordprocessing and graphics, with additional features to enable pages to be laid out in columns and illustrations to be inserted where necessary. Different character sizes and fonts will be needed on the same page. Some facility to import photographs and images will be required.

Often, DTP software will have only primitive wordprocessing and graphics facilities. The DTP software provides only the structure to manipulate documents into columns, etc. and to cut and position graphics as required. In this case the DTP software is relying on the user to use the specialized facilities of wordprocessor and graphics software to prepare documents and illustrations before importing these into the DTP software for placing in the desired page format. DTP software is run on a microcomputer system with a laser printer for high quality, fast printout. A mouse is essential, as DTP is inevitably run in a WIMP environment. A scanner will be needed to import photographs and possibly a video digitizer to capture video images.

Typical systems are Pagemaker and Timeworks on IBM compatible microcomputers; Pagemaker and QuarkXPress on Apple computers.

What DTP software can be used for

DTP software can be used to prepare a wide variety of good quality printed material with a range of text sizes, styles and fonts, and graphics. DTP software is mainly used

Fig. 8.5 Desk top publishing

for constructing page layouts for newsletters, magazines, etc. where an attractive and interesting blend of text and graphics is important.

What DTP software can do

Different DTP software does the same tasks but may be operated in different ways. The facilities described below are available in most DTP software. You should look for these facilities in the DTP software you use and make sure you can use them.

Create and layout a page

DTP software is page based. It focuses on identifying which areas of a page will contain text and which will contain graphics. This is called **page layout**.

When a new page is **created**, one of the most important tasks to be done is to layout the page. To begin with the screen displayed will contain an outline of the page. The page itself will not have text or graphics on it. Text and graphics are placed on the page as it is constructed. They can be moved and the shape of the frame they are in adjusted, as required. The page layout may be changed at any time.

Text

Text is typed onto the page from the keyboard or imported from a wordprocessing document. Text can be processed in DTP software as it can be in a wordprocessor, however, the screen view in DTP often makes this difficult. Text is usually best imported from a wordprocessor. The DTP software can be used to enhance the style of the imported text.

Graphics

Graphics are usually imported. The ability to generate graphics in DTP software is often limited in comparison with graphics software. DTP software will allow you to draw lines and put frames round text and imported graphics and to re-size a graphic and crop its overall size. This allows you to select a part of an imported graphic and change its size to suit your page layout. You can move graphics around on the page.

Page views

'Page view can help'

It is important that you should be able to *see* the page you are constructing before printing it out. However, laying out an A4 page using a standard monitor creates difficulties. If you display the whole page on the screen, you will not be able to see it in sufficient detail to read the text or make fine adjustments to the graphics. If you display only part of the page, you will not see the layout of the whole page. One solution to these problems is to provide menu options that allow you to move very quickly from a view of the whole page to a view of part of the page. A more expensive solution is to buy a larger, A4 monitor.

Page measurements and column guides
Most DTP software displays horizontal and vertical rulers to help you layout the page exactly. To help you place your text and graphics, column guides are provided. These save you working out where the columns should be placed. The aligning of text and graphics to the column guides can be done automatically.

Column flow
When placing text on the page, you may need to continue at the bottom of a column into the top of the next column. DTP software will handle the flow of text from the bottom of one column into the top of the next column.

Moving around a document
You may want to move around the page to view and edit it. To do this you can use the cursor control keys or 'arrow keys'. However, as most DTP software is operated using a mouse and a GUI, you may find that using the vertical and horizontal sliders in the GUI is faster.

Save and load documents
Pages can be saved on backing storage and loaded when required.

Printing
Pages can be printed. A laser printer will produce the high quality needed for DTP use.

Quit
When you have finished, you will want to exit and switch off the computer. It is important to exit from the software using the commands provided as there will be a check built into the DTP software to remind you to save your work if you have not done so. If you do not save your work before quitting, it will not be available if you want to use it in the future.

▷ E-mail

You can send a message to someone using your computer to send information to another computer over a network (see Fig. 8.6) The sender logs on to the sender's e-mail server and sends a message. This message is automatically transmitted from the sender's e-mail server to the receiver's e-mail server. Sometimes later the receiver logs on to the receiver's e-mail server and reads the message.

Using **e-mail servers** avoids the need for the sending and receiving computers to be in direct contact. Mail can be sent to an e-mail server which is always available. At a later date this mail can be accessed whenever it is convenient to do so. This is the basis of most electronic mail systems, for example, those based on Pegasus e-mail software.

E-mail can be distributed from one sending computer to several receiving computers. This can involve an e-mail server but may not do so. For example, companies can prepare their mail on a wordprocessor during the day. Each letter to be mailed is stored along with the telephone number of the receiving computer to which the document must be sent. At night, the computer automatically dials up the receiving computers and transfers their mail to them. This method of communication is used by some household appliance service departments to send details of the next day's work to service engineers who work in widely dispersed areas. Each service engineer has a microcomputer which must be ready to receive e-mail at a predetermined time during the night. At this time, the documents prepared at the central computer location during the day are transferred.

'Advantages of electronic mail'

One advantage of e-mail is that large volumes of data can be transmitted quickly over the national and international telephone networks at local call rates. This is much faster and cheaper than voice transmission, and complex reports, diagrams and pictures can be included.

▷ Multimedia

Multimedia is a developing means of communicating information. Multimedia combines wordprocessed text and graphics in a format similar to DTP with the addition of moving video and sound. Multimedia can be used to produce computer based learning materials,

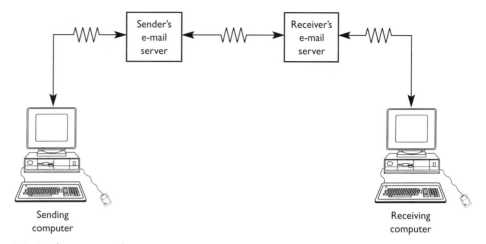

Fig. 8.6 Sending an e-mail message

encyclopedias, etc. that have a richer, more comprehensive content than has previously been possible. Multimedia applications often use CD-ROM backing storage as they require fast access to very large volumes of data.

For example, consider an encyclopedia of birds. If the encyclopedia was in book form, it would contain written descriptions of the birds, habitat, etc. and still pictures of the birds. Multimedia provides this information and, in addition, will offer recordings of bird song and video of the birds flying, etc. This is closer to what we experience when we observe birds and can be expected to be of more help in identifying them. As the information is available on a computer, it can be copied into other computer software, such as a wordprocessor. Access to the information can be more like accessing a database than reading a book.

▷ Conferencing

'The rise of conferencing'

Conferencing is conducting a meeting or conference using IT. If you want to join the conference, you log on to the central computer where the conference is being held. You do not have to meet with the other people involved in the same room at the same time. You can join the conference at any time and leave it when you want to. The central computer keeps a record of what everyone has said.

For example, suppose I wanted to join a conference about the GCSE exams, I would use my desk top computer to log on to the remote computer where the conference was being held. The conference could have been going on for several years. There would probably be a menu of seminars I could join. For example, there could be seminars on each of the different GCSE subjects and the various tasks GCSE boards have to do, such as awarding the grades. I might choose to join the seminar on IT. Within this conference seminar I would expect to find articles, questions, ideas, etc. about IT. I would read through all this material, perhaps making my own comments. If I knew the answers to questions other people were asking, I would type them in. I might leave questions of my own for other people to answer. I then log off. I might return to the conference again in a few weeks to see if there is any additional material of interest to me. A conference could continue indefinitely. The computer stores all the contributions people make. You do not know who will join the conference and when they will join it.

An electronic conference proceeds more slowly than a live conference. It can bring together people from anywhere in the world who might not otherwise have the chance to meet. You have a chance to say what you want to, when you want to, at your own pace. No one can interrupt you. You can think carefully about what you want to say before typing it into the computer.

EXAMINATION QUESTIONS

▷ **Question 1**   Tick TWO advantages to the school secretary of using a wordprocessor rather than a typewriter.

	ADVANTAGES Tick 2
The ribbon is changed automatically.	
It uses less paper.	
Work can be checked on the screen before printing.	
The keyboard is smaller.	
You can edit documents without making a mess.	

(MEG)

▷ **Question 2**   You are asked to include a picture in a letter. Which software would you use to combine text and graphics?

(City and Guilds)

▷ **Question 3**   In your letter you realize that paragraph 2 should follow paragraph 3. Which one of the following techniques would be the most efficient to carry out this correction? Put a tick inside the round brackets of one technique only.

text over writing   (   )

deleting and retyping   (   )

block move – cut and paste   (   )

(City and Guilds)

▷ **Question 4**   In order to advertise the Xmas fayre, the secretary created the following poster using a wordprocessor:

> # XMAS FAYRE
> ## Come and visit *Santa*
> ## At
> ## Middlebridge School
>
> ## Sat. December 4th 1996
> ## 2.00pm start

Fig. 8.7

To improve the appearance of this poster, it was decided to use a desk top publishing package and the resulting poster is shown below.

Fig. 8.8

Describe the changes to the poster which have been made by using the desk top publishing package.

(NEAB/WJEC)

▷ **Question 5** Desums, a firm of accountants, decides to introduce electronic mail to link all their offices across the country.

(a) What is meant by the term *electronic mail*?
(b) Give ONE advantage that Desums will gain by using electronic mail rather than the normal postal service.
(c) Give ONE disadvantage in using electronic mail.
(d) Give ONE example of when Desums would use electronic mail even though a fax machine is available.

(WJEC)

▷ **Question 6** Chris has decided to purchase a desk top publishing system to produce recipe books and leaflets.

(a) Chris does not write good English. Describe, with examples, two ways in which software with good wordprocessing facilities would help him to produce better work.
(b) Give examples of what a DTP set-up might be used for. What would it do that software with ordinary wordprocessing facilities would not do?
(c) What hardware/software would be necessary for him to produce high quality hard copy?

(RSA)

▷ **Question 7**   Describe how teletext services benefit house-bound people.

(MEG)

▷ **Question 8**   There are many ways in which computers help newspaper reporters to prepare text for presentation to the printer.

(a)   Describe TWO such ways that have been used.
(b)   Describe how the job of a newspaper reporter has changed through developments in information technology.

(MEG)

▷ **Question 9**   A company employs door-to-door sales representatives. They enter their orders into portable computers during the day. The orders are transmitted to head office each evening.

(a)   Describe how the representatives would transmit their orders to head office.
(b)   Describe the operation of an electronic mail system which is used by the representatives.

(MEG)

▷ **Question 10**   In order to produce the monthly company newsletter inhouse, the Personnel Department acquire desk top publishing facilities. Explain THREE facilities/functions of such a package that would help produce an effective newsletter.

(London)

 EXAMINATION ANSWERS

▷ **Answer 1**   Work can be checked on the screen before printing.
You can edit documents without making a mess.

(MEG)

▷ **Answer 2**   Desk top publishing (DTP) software is used to combine text and graphics. However, most wordprocessors now permit the inclusion of graphics.

▷ **Answer 3**   Block move – cut and paste.

▷ **Answer 4**   Some changes made using DTP are, as follows:

▶   The text size and font has been changed.
▶   A picture has been imported.
▶   The text has been repositioned.

▷ **Answer 5**   (a)   Electronic mail (e-mail) is used for sending messages from one computer to another over computer networks. Usually, the sender logs on to his/her e-mail server and sends a message. This message is automatically transmitted to the receiver's e-mail server. The receiver logs on to his/her e-mail server and receives the message.
(b)   E-mail is transmitted faster than the postal service (often referred to as 'snail mail'). The cost of sending e-mail messages can be much less. These advantages are more exaggerated over longer distances.
(c)   The software, hardware and networks used to send e-mail are expensive to set-up.
(d)   When a fax is received, it is usually printed, whereas an e-mail message is in a form that can be processed by a computer. Desums may wish to transfer spreadsheets from one office to another in a form in which they can be worked on using a computer.

▷ **Answer 6** (a) Chris would find a grammar checker and a spelling checker useful. He could use a large, clear font and print his work. He might be encouraged by the clear, neat presentation of his work with neither spelling nor grammatical errors.

(b) DTP could be used for producing posters, newsletters, etc.

DTP has these facilities that are not found in most wordprocessors:
  ▶ You can import graphics, and modify them.
  ▶ You can layout a page in columns, and easily place or re-position text and graphics on the page.

(c) A laser printer.

▷ **Answer 7** No need to leave house to find out information.
Data updated regularly.   (MEG)

▷ **Answer 8** (a) Send complete story using a portable computer and a modem. Reporter types in story in office and it's stored on the central computer. Typesetting is done by picking up all stories and putting them together using DTP.

(b) Portable computer with modem means more work can be done where the action is. Teletext systems means that some information is available by television rather than searching elsewhere.

Answers describing benefits of telex, fax, electronic data exchange, the Internet.
                                                                          (MEG)

▷ **Answer 9** (a) Two from:
Connect the computer to a telephone line.
Log in to the head office computer.
Transmit data file to head office.
Log off system.

(b) Two from:
Reps log on to the system through the telephone and computer.
Messages are left for other reps.
Other reps have to log on and look at their messages.
                                                                          (MEG)

▷ **Answer 10** Some facilities/functions of DTP that help produce a newsletter.

  ▶ You can place text and graphics in whatever position you wish and reposition them wherever you wish.
  ▶ You can apply a variety of text style features, e.g. bold, underline, different sizes of text, etc.
  ▶ You can create borders, tint backgrounds, etc. using the built-in graphic facilities.
  ▶ You can import clip art, scanned images, etc.
  ▶ You can import text from one or more wordprocessors, or type it directly into the DTP software.

EXAMINATION QUESTION WITH STUDENT ANSWER

Middlebridge School is holding its annual Xmas fayre and the following text has been drafted using a wordprocessing package.

Dear parent/guardian
We are holding the school Xmas fayre on Saturday December 4th and we need volunteers to help with the stalls and donations of items to sell on the stalls. We plan to have the following stalls: Cakes, Sweets, Toys, Tombola, Books, Plants, White Elephant, Crafts. As you know this is our main fund-raising event of the year and we plan to spend the money raised on increasing the number of computers within the school. Items can be left in the school office at any time and if you are interested in helping on the day please leave your name with the school secretary .
Yours faithfully
J. Smith
Headteacher

The Headteacher has decided that the sentence starting 'As you know . . .' should be moved so that it becomes the last sentence of the letter.

Explain how you would do this without re-typing the sentence.

You would use the mouse. Then you would go to the end of the letter. Then you would move the sentence.

▷ **Examiner's comment**

This answer is probably correct but it is not expressed very clearly. Because the student avoids technical language, the answer appears vague. There are several acceptable answers to this question. This is one possible answer, giving a sequence of actions:

▶ Highlight the sentence
▶ Move the cursor to the new position, in this case, just after the sentence ending 'school secretary'
▶ Select the block move function.

SUMMARY

▷ All information is communicated for a purpose, to an audience. You should take into account your audience and the extent to which it is likely to understand what you are communicating. When communicating information you should try to be clear, simple and interesting, and present information in a straightforward and logical way.

▷ This chapter reviews the function and purpose of software that is particularly useful for *communicating information*. That is, software for wordprocessing, graphics, desk top publishing (DTP), e-mail, multimedia and conferencing. This software has overlapping capabilities but each has distinctive features. Some of these are described below:

▷ Using a wordprocessor, you can:

  ▷ Write a letter, a leaflet, an essay, a c.v., a questionnaire, etc.

  ▷ Create, save or load, open or close, and print wordprocessing documents.

  ▷ Move around a document by scrolling up and down it, and scrolling sideways.

  ▷ Insert, delete and edit text.

  ▷ Use different text fonts and sizes, and generate word art.

  ▷ Move, cut, copy and paste blocks of text and graphics.

  ▷ Import and export text, clip art and other graphics, database reports, and spreadsheets.

  ▷ Generate personalized mail using the mail merge facility.

▷ Using graphics software, you can:

  ▷ Create, save or load, open or close, and print graphics files.

  ▷ Draw on the screen using a variety of colours.

  ▷ Use different brushes, and different sizes and densities of brush stroke.

  ▷ Draw freehand shapes, and generate regular shapes, e.g. circles and boxes.

  ▷ Fill shapes with patterns and colours.

  ▷ Use different text fonts and sizes.

  ▷ Zoom in and out to edit text and graphics.

  ▷ Move, cut, copy and paste blocks of text and graphics.

  ▷ Import and export scanned images, video frames, clip art and other graphics.

▷ Using desk top publishing (DTP) software, you can:

  ▷ Lay out the pages of a newsletter, magazine, etc. with some precision.

  ▷ Create, save or load, open or close, and print DTP pages.

  ▷ Import text, scanned images, video frames, clip art and other graphics, database reports, and spreadsheets.

  ▷ View the page in different magnifications, zoom in and out.

  ▷ Move around a page by scrolling up and down it, and scrolling sideways.

  ▷ Move, cut, copy and paste blocks of text and graphics to arrange information on a page.

  ▷ Use different text fonts and sizes, and generate word art.

▷ Using e-mail software, you can:

  ▷ Send and receive messages, nationally and internationally using the Internet.

▷ Using multimedia software, you can:

  ▷ Produce and view multimedia encyclopedias, etc.

  ▷ Combine graphics, text, video and sound in a format similar to DTP.

▷ Using software for conferencing, you can:

  ▷ Take part in a continuing debate on subjects that interest you.

  ▷ Read what others have to say.

  ▷ Make your own contribution.

Chapter 9

Databases and handling information

This chapter should be read if you are preparing for GCSE IT assessment with the following examining boards:

C & G	MEG	NEAB	SEG
London	NDTEF	RSA	WJEC

GETTING STARTED

IT is useful for handling information. This is especially so when there is a large volume of information or access to the information you want is difficult or time consuming. Using a **database** you can **search** through information very quickly, **select** only the information you want, sort it and **report** on what you have found. Databases usually handle text but they can also include graphics, and multimedia.

Other ways of accessing information are:

▶ **Teletext**. For example, Ceefax and Oracle.
▶ The **World Wide Web** (The Web).
▶ **Expert systems** that allow users to recognize particular situations and advise on appropriate action. For example, for medical diagnosis.

GLOSSARY

File A database file is a collection of related records. For example, a file of information about customers.

Record A record is a collection of related fields. In records of the same type, the fields are in the same order. For example, each customer's record might include their name, address, telephone number, etc. in the same order.

Field A field is an item of information. For example, a customer's name.

Key field A key field uniquely identifies a record. For example, each customer will have a unique customer number that uniquely identifies the customer and their record in the database.

3C & G	LONDON	MEG	NDTEF	NEAB	RSA	SEG	WJEC	TOPIC	STUDY	REVISION I	REVISION 2
✓	✓	✓	✓	✓	✓	✓	✓	Databases			
✓	✓	✓	✓	✓	✓	✓	✓	Membership records for a squash club			
✓	✓	✓	✓	✓	✓	✓	✓	A telephone enquiry service			
✓	✓	✓	✓	✓	✓	✓	✓	Videotext			
✓	✓	✓	✓	✓	✓	✓	✓	The World Wide Web			
✓	✓	✓	✓	✓	✓	✓	✓	Expert systems			

▷ **WHAT YOU NEED TO KNOW**

When there is a very high volume of information to handle or the information is complex, IT will increase the speed at which you can access the information in order to find answers to your questions.

Databases enable the user to search through large volumes of data, select information using search conditions and display it on the screen or print it in whatever format or order is required.

▷ **Databases**

'Files, records and fields'

A **database** is an organized collection of structured data. The data will usually be structured in the form of files, records and fields.

A database **file** contains one or more related *records*. A **record** is a collection of related data and contains several *fields*. A **field** is a single item of data. Fields within records of the same type will be in the same order. Each record will usually contain a **key field**. The key field is different in each record in a file; often it is an identification number that identifies the record and, in the case of personal data, also identifies the person.

For example, a squash club will have a **file** containing a separate record for each member of the club. Within each member's **record** will be **fields** for their membership number, name, address, date of birth, etc. The membership number may also be the key field.

Database software is often supplied to the user without files of data. The user is expected to create and maintain any data files required.

What databases can be used for

Databases can be used for a wide variety of tasks such as:

'Some uses of databases'

▷ Car and vehicle records; nationally and, for example, of all the cars likely to be parked in the school car park.
▷ Criminal records; national and local police.
▷ Stock keeping; shops and warehouses of all types.
▷ Customer records; all types of business.
▷ Membership lists for sports clubs, etc.
▷ Estate agents' files of houses for sale.
▷ Recording information about hotels, etc. for tourists.
▷ School records of pupils, staff, exam results, etc.
▷ Libraries: for book issues and catalogues.
▷ Census data; for statistical analysis by historians, etc.
▷ Information about plants, animals, etc. for biologists, etc.

What databases do

'Flat file databases'

Different databases do the same tasks but may be operated in different ways.

Flat file databases are relatively straight forward and easy to use. They handle one data file at a time containing records with the same record specification and provide facilities to sort, search and print reports. They are not usually programmable. It is this type of database that is most often used up to GCSE. Examples are the databases in Microsoft Works for IBM compatibles and Claris Works for Apple computers.

'Relational databases'

Relational databases are more complex to use. They offer the same features as a flat file database but, in addition, can handle more than one data file at a time. The data files may have different record specifications. They are usually programmable. Different levels of access can be set for different groups of users. Menus can be written specifically for a group of users, and passwords can control access. If you use a relational database at GCSE, it is unlikely that you will be expected to use the features of it that go beyond those available in a flat file database. Examples are Access and Superbase for IBM compatibles.

Databases consist of information handling software and data files. In order to set up, maintain and search the data files and produce meaningful reports, the information handling software must have the facilities described below. They are available on most flat file databases. You should look for them on the database you use and make sure you can use them.

Create

The user must be able to **create** (i.e. set up) a data file in which data can be stored. This involves, at least, giving the file a filename and specifying the structure of each record in the record specification.

The **record specification** will include:

'The record specification'

▶ A list of the fields in each record in the order they appear in every record.
▶ A key field.
▶ For each field in the record:
  a unique field name
  a description of what the field contains
  the data type and format of the data
  the field length

A variety of **data types** and **formats** will be available. Some of the more common ones are:

'Some data types and formats'

▶ Character strings, e.g. 'Bradford City AFC'.
▶ Numbers in integer form, e.g. 24, –6.
▶ Numbers in real form, e.g. 238.67, –4.235, 0.56.
▶ Number formats specifying the number of decimal places, if a £ sign is needed, etc., e.g. £999.99.
▶ Date formats specifying how the date will be displayed, e.g. 5 JUN 94, 940605.

Edit: insert, delete and amend

'Aspects of editing'

Having created a record specification, it should be possible to **insert** (i.e. add) a record. A data entry screen will be displayed showing the record specification. You enter data into the empty fields, setting up the record. You can add records to the database at any time. When you have set up several records, you may want to **delete** (i.e. remove) some of them. It should also be possible to **amend**, (i.e. change) the data that you previously entered into a field.

Data entry using a keyboard is slow and can be inaccurate. This may cause problems where there are large volumes of data to be input. Consequently, other methods of entering data are used where possible. For example, when setting up a library management information system, it is necessary to create a database containing details about all the books in the library. There will be a large number of books and a relatively large amount of text based information about each book to be input. An alternative method to entering this data using a keyboard is to read the ISBN numbers using a bar code reader. The ISBN numbers are then matched with those on a CD-ROM. The CD-ROM contains ISBN numbers for all the books published in Great Britain. All the other details about the books are also on the CD-ROM. A new database is created, using the information on the CD-ROM, that contains details about only the books in the library.

Search or interrogate

A database will often contain a very large number of records. You will want to **search** the database to get only the information you need. You can search or **interrogate** the data file for the information you want by defining a **search condition** or query. This search condition is used to select the required records.

Examples of search conditions are:

'Examples of search conditions'

▶ Name begins with 'CR'.
▶ Number plate contains '4CH'.
▶ Code is '23R-5X'.
▶ Balance < 0.
▶ Hair is NOT 'brown'.
▶ Schoolcode = 37141 AND Exams passed contains 'Information Technology'.
▶ Licence is 'provisional' OR vehicle type contains 'cycle'.
▶ Code NOT = 'Z-23' AND Credit is 500 OR Balance > 1000.

'Uses of wildcards'

You can often use *wildcards* in search conditions. Suppose we are trying to identify a car that has been in an accident. We noticed that the car was N registration and the number plate contained the characters '2' and 'L' in that order but not together. A suitable search condition might be: Numberplate is 'N*2*L*'. The *s are being used as wildcards. They indicate that there may be some or no characters in that position. All the number plates starting with 'N' and with a '2' followed by an 'L' will be selected. Asterisks (*) are often used as wildcards, though different databases use other characters.

You will have to understand **precedence rules** if you want to use complex search conditions. These define the order in which the logical operators AND and OR are evaluated. For example, consider this sentence: John AND Shahid OR Jestin are going to the cinema. This could mean:

1. John is going with one of Shahid or Jestin, or all three are going.
2. John and Shahid are going together or Jestin is going alone, or all three are going.

Most databases interpret the sentence as in item 2 above, unless told otherwise. The easiest way to be sure you have expressed exactly what you intend is to use brackets. You would define the meanings expressed in 1 and 2 above as:

John AND (Shahid OR Jestin) are going to the cinema.
(John AND Shahid) OR Jestin are going to the cinema.

Search conditions tend to be written in slightly different syntax in different databases. You will need to find out how to set up search conditions in the database you are using. Using the search condition you set up, the file would be looked at and all the records that satisfy the search condition will be selected.

Sort

It may be helpful to **sort** the records selected into some order, e.g. alphabetic order on the name, before reporting on the results of a search. Sorts can be ascending or descending. **Ascending** means upwards. An ascending alphabetic sort on names would put the names in the order A to Z. Descending means downwards. A **descending** alphabetic sort on names would put the names in the order Z to A.

Report

Having searched the file, perhaps sorting the records selected, a **report** to the user on the results of the search is required. This report could be displayed on the monitor screen, saved as a file on disk, or printed. In either case a report can be constructed that contains either all or some of the fields in each record selected. The report could be in **record** format (see Fig. 9.5), i.e. with the fields printed out in a format similar to the data entry screen, or in columns (see Fig. 9.7). In a report in **column** format, each row will contain the details extracted from one record. The format of a report should be under the control of the user.

Some databases will add up numeric fields and print group, page and report totals. Other calculations, such as averages, may be possible.

Bar charts, pie charts and line graphs can be printed from some databases. These can be used to display visual summaries of the information stored on the database.

Serial and sequential files

The order in which records are stored on backing storage, and the way the records can be accessed, varies.

In a **serial file** the records are not stored in any particular order.

In a **sequential file** the records are sorted into some order, usually on a key field.

In both serial and sequential files, it is only possible to access a record by first reading through *all* the previous records on the file.

Direct access files

In a **direct access file** it is possible to read the required record, without first accessing other stored data. In other words, we can access the required record *directly*. Direct access files are also called **random access files**.

Direct access files, serial files and sequential files are all found on magnetic disk. On magnetic tape, only serial files and sequential files are used. Direct access files cannot be used on magnetic tape, since it is always necessary to start at the beginning of a magnetic tape and read through it until the required record is found.

Example: A part of a school's pupil information file

The following data is taken from an entirely fictitious file of pupils attending a Bradford school.

'Each pupil has a different key field'

> 85123: SHARP: LOUISE: 820601: 109 HAVELOCH ST.: THORNTON: BD13 4PY
> 85145: PATEL: SANDIP: 841223: 12 HOLLY DRIVE: QUEENSTOWN: BD13 2AB
> 86234: MOORSIDE: JAMES: 830913: 3 STONES LANE: ALLERTON: BD6 9QX

▶ Within each record there are seven fields.
▶ There are three records shown; one for each pupil.
▶ The fields are in the same order in each record.
▶ The pupil number is the key field.

Using the first record as an example, we have:

85123	pupil number (key field)
SHARP	family name
LOUISE	first name
820601	date of birth, i.e. the 1st of June 1982
109 HAVELOCH ST	street
THORNTON	town
BD13 4PY	Post code

A colon (:) has been used to separate the fields. In practice, the end of a field would be indicated by an end of field marker inserted by the software. How this is done need not concern us here, but an **end of field marker** is needed because there can be **variable length fields**. For example 'family name' may vary considerably in length from record to record. Without such a marker, confusion may arise as to *exactly* where the field ends. Fields such as 'date of birth' are described as **fixed length** because they have the same length in every record.

The pupil number is the key field. It is different for each pupil and identifies both the *record* and the *pupil*.

'Note how the date is coded'

Notice how the date is coded in YYMMDD format. This means that the first two digits starting at the left-hand side represent the year, the next two digits represent the month and the last two digits, the day. The day, DD, always occupies two digits. For example, the 13th day would be coded as 13; the 6th day as 06. The month, MM, is coded so that January is 01, February is 02, November is 11, etc. If the year, YY, is 1989, this is coded as 89. The date is coded like this for several reasons. Firstly, it saves storage space when the file is saved on backing storage. Secondly, as the date is coded as a number in YYMMDD format, the records can be easily sorted into date of birth order. Thirdly, validation is easier. Simple range checks can be used to make sure the date is valid, i.e. DD lies between 01 and 31 inclusive, MM is between 01 and 12. A type check could be used to make sure the date only has numbers in it.

▷ **Membership records for a squash club**

This example of an IT **system using a database** tackles the problem of keeping *membership records* for a squash club. It is also used to report summaries of useful information derived from the database.

This example of a database used by a fictitious squash club contains information about a small number of members. Sufficient records have been set up to illustrate how such an information system would work. In practice a much larger volume of information would be handled.

The squash club has different classes of membership, i.e. young people, ordinary members (adults), unwaged (adults who are not in full time employment), honorary members and life members. Each membership class pays an appropriate subscription. Young people pay £5 per year; ordinary members, £20; unwaged, £10; honorary and life members do not pay a subscription.

The squash club has separate competition ladders for male and female members. The position of a member in the competition ladders is used to select teams for league matches and other competitions.

The database was set up so that the club treasurer could use it to keep track of members who have not paid their subscriptions. There are a variety of other useful tasks that the database can also be used for.

'A flowchart can help'

A flowchart showing how the information system is organised is shown in Fig. 9.1. The system is based on a flat file database.

Input

New members fill in an **application form** (Fig. 9.2) when they join the squash club. This application form is used to collect the information needed about the new member. Notice that the form is as simple as possible. The order in which the information is asked for is repeated on the data entry screen for the database and in the record structure of the database. This assists accurate data entry and cross-checking.

The application form is used as a data entry form when the new member's record is set up on the database for the first time.

The record specification looks like this:

field name	description of field	data type	length
member	membership number	integer	4
surname	surname and initials	string	20
address	address and post code	string	40
phone	telephone number	string	20
date	date of birth in YYMMDD form	integer	6
sex	sex M = male F = female	string	1
ladder	position in ladder	integer	2

class	membership class:
	    Y = young person
	    O = ordinary member
	    U = unwaged
	    H = honorary member
	    L = life member
		string	1

subs	subscription outstanding	real, 2 decimal places	7

Notice that the member's sex and their membership class are to be coded as single characters. This will reduce the size of the file. There is no loss of meaning provided you know what each code stands for.

There is also a field to store the position of the member in the competition ladder. This field is updated each week by the secretary. The secretary receives a list of the current positions in the competition ladder on the positions form (see Fig. 9.3) and goes through the database updating the corresponding field.

Each member of the squash club has a membership card (see Fig. 9.4). The membership card has on it the name of the member and their membership number. This identifies the member and reminds the member of his or her membership number. The IT system generates the membership card from the membership record. The membership card may never be used in conjunction with the IT system described here. However, it may be important to the squash club that members have some form of identification that they can carry with them. It is a feature of IT systems that they can generate information, such as membership cards, that could be useful in the social context which the IT system supports but are not useful in relation to the system itself.

'Uses of the membership card'

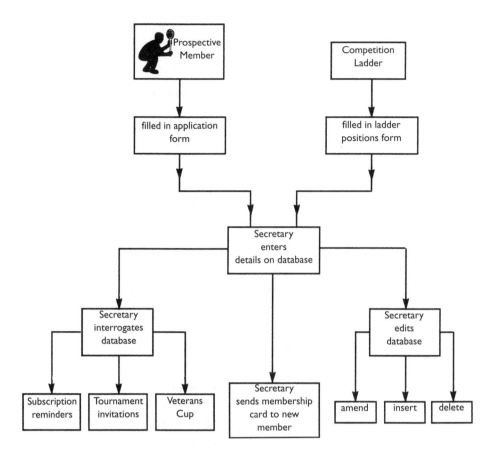

Fig. 9.1 The IT system used by the squash club

'Setting up the database'

The secretary can enter membership data over several sessions. In the first session the record specification is created and data entered. At the end of the session the database is saved. The secretary begins all the following sessions by loading the database. Membership records can then be inserted, deleted or amended as members join the squash club, leave it or change their membership details respectively. At the end of each session the secretary saves the database again. Fig. 9.5 shows some of the records that have been entered into the example IT system.

It is important that the secretary keeps the database up-to-date. The information on the application forms filled in by new members and the positions of current members in the competition ladders should be input on a regular basis, at least weekly. Deletions and amendments should be made promptly. If the database is not up-to-date or the data on it is corrupted, the information extracted from it will be incorrect. This is an example of Garbage In, Garbage Out (GIGO).

Processing

All the **processing** that is required is done by the database software. Processing consists of selecting some records using a search condition and sorting the selected records into a convenient order.

'Setting up the search conditions'

The secretary will have to set up the search conditions. Search conditions are logical statements that determine which records will be selected from the database. For example, suppose we wanted to know who was top of the competition ladder. The field called 'ladder' contains the position of the member in the competition ladder. The member who is top of the competition ladder will have the number 1 in the field called 'ladder'. The question 'who is top of the ladder' can be rewritten as the search condition 'ladder equals 1'.

'Carefully define the search conditions'

The importance of carefully defining search conditions is illustrated by this example. You might expect that the search condition 'ladder equals 1' would pick out the record of the person who is top of the ladder. In fact, there will be two records selected. This is because there are two competition ladders; one for males and one for females. If you want to select only the top of the men's ladder (or only the top of the women's ladder) you will need to modify the search condition. The search condition for the top of the men's ladder is 'ladder equals 1 AND sex is 'M' '; the search condition for the top of the women's ladder is 'ladder equals 1 AND sex is 'F' '.

HIGH PRESSURE SQUASH CLUB

MEMBERSHIP APPLICATION FORM

SURNAME | J O N E S |

INITIALS | F |

ADDRESS | 3 4 | R O D I N | A V E N U E |

| B R I E R L E Y |

POSTCODE | B R 1 5 | 3 R T |

TEL. No | 0 1 2 3 9 - 5 2 7 1 0 4 |

SUBSCRIPTION

	YOUNG PERSON	£5
	ORDINARY MEMBER (Adult)	£20
✓	UNWAGED (Adult)	£10
	HONORARY MEMBER	NONE
	LIFE MEMBER	NONE

SEX ~~MALE~~/FEMALE   DATE OF BIRTH | 1 2 / 0 8 / 6 5 |
(Please delete)

SIGN *F Jones*   DATE 27/11/96

FOR OFFICE USE ONLY

MEMBERSHIP NUMBER | |

Fig. 9.2 The membership application form

POSITIONS FORM

WEEK COMMENCING

MEN'S COMPETITION LADDER

NAME	POSITION

WOMAN'S COMPETITION LADDER

NAME	POSITION

FILLED IN BY: _____

Fig. 9.3 The positions form

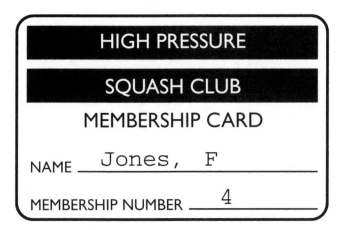

Fig. 9.4 The membership card

Search conditions are very important when using any database as they control what information is selected from it. The usefulness of a database depends on writing search conditions that will provide the information required.

```
                      A PRINTOUT OF ALL THE RECORDS ON THE DATABASE
            May  21, 1996                                              Page 1


            MEMBER          1
            SURNAME         MASON, T
            ADDRESS         56 HILL VIEW, APPLEBY, AP12 3DU
            TELEPHONE       01234 453322
            DATE OF BIRTH   760621
            SEX             F
            LADDER          4
            CLASS           O
            SUBS            £  20.00


            MEMBER          2
            SURNAME         JONES, M
            ADDRESS         34 RODIN AV., BRIERLEY, BR5 3RT
            TELEPHONE       01923 456321
            DATE OF BIRTH   861123
            SEX             M
            LADDER          2
            CLASS           Y
            SUBS            £   5.00


            MEMBER          3
            SURNAME         JONES, P
            ADDRESS         34 RODIN AV., BRIERLEY BR5 3RT
            TELEPHONE       01923 456321
            DATE OF BIRTH   630304
            SEX             M
            LADDER          6
            CLASS           O
            SUBS            £


            MEMBER          4
            SURNAME         JONES, F
            ADDRESS         34 RODIN AV., BRIERLEY BR5 3RT
            TELEPHONE       01923 456321
            DATE OF BIRTH   650812
            SEX             F
            LADDER          2
            CLASS           U
            SUBS            £  10.00


            MEMBER          5
            SURNAME         GOWER, N
            ADDRESS         6 STATION RD., STEETON ST4 6TY
            TELEPHONE       01234 563987
            DATE OF BIRTH   710502
            SEX             M
            LADDER          1
            CLASS           O
            SUBS            £  20.00
```

Fig. 9.5 A sample page from a printout of all the records on the database. Similar information would be shown for every member of the club.

Output

Control of the **output** from a database is restricted to choosing which records and fields will be displayed, the format of the output and the output medium to be used, i.e. printout, screen display or disk file.

At most, you can only display all the fields in a member's record, but you could decide to display just a few fields. For example, if the secretary was printing a list of members to telephone to invite to a surprise tournament to be held that evening, only the member's name and telephone number would be needed. The membership number might be included to be sure the identity of the member was absolutely correct.

The different output formats that can be selected depend on those that are available in the database. Some databases allow you to vary the format as you wish; however, others. restrict you to only a few different layouts.

Some of the tasks the secretary of the Squash Club can do using the database are described below. There are many others.

Secretary's task: subscription reminders

One of the most important jobs that the secretary has to do is to make sure all the members **pay their subscriptions**. Some members are nearly always late in paying their subscriptions and the secretary has constantly to remind them. The secretary finds it more effective to telephone members than to send written reminders, however some members are not on the telephone and these will have to be sent a reminder through the post.

'Using the database to remind members to pay their subscriptions'

To do this job the secretary would find it helpful to have a printed list showing the membership number, name, address and telephone number of those members who still owe the club subscriptions. This list should be in alphabetical order.

A printed list is particularly useful for this job as it allows the secretary to work away from the computer, so that the job can be done in a variety of locations at a time to suit the secretary. It is unlikely that a squash club would have a full time secretary so that the job of reminding members that their subscriptions have not been paid may have to be done when the secretary has a few minutes free time, for example, in the lunch hour at work, in a telephone kiosk while waiting for a train, at home during the evening, etc. If a printed list is not available, the job may be much more difficult to fit conveniently into the time the secretary has access to the computer and may not be done regularly. This could seriously affect the income of the squash club.

```
                          SUBSCRIPTIONS OUTSTANDING
        May  21, 1996                                              Page 1


        NAME           FARR, M                 AMOUNT UNPAID  £   10.00
        TELEPHONE      01435 777656            MEMBERSHIP NO. 19
        ADDRESS        FLAT 4, HIGHVIEW, QUEENSBURY QU4 8TH
        _____

        NAME           FORD, T                 AMOUNT UNPAID  £   20.00
        TELEPHONE      01473 964213            MEMBERSHIP NO. 12
        ADDRESS        34 LOW FOLD, ALLERTON AL3 5CX
        _____

        NAME           GOWER, N                AMOUNT UNPAID  £   20.00
        TELEPHONE      01234 563987            MEMBERSHIP NO.  5
        ADDRESS        6 STATION RD., STEETON ST4 6TY
        _____

        NAME           HILL, J                 AMOUNT UNPAID  £   10.00
        TELEPHONE      01788 777454            MEMBERSHIP NO. 13
        ADDRESS        22 GREEN LANE, THORNTON TH5 7UY
        _____

        NAME           JONES, F                AMOUNT UNPAID  £   10.00
        TELEPHONE      01923 456321            MEMBERSHIP NO.  4
        ADDRESS        34 RODIN AV., BRIERLEY BR5 3RT
        _____

        NAME           JONES, M                AMOUNT UNPAID  £    5.00
        TELEPHONE      01923 456321            MEMBERSHIP NO.  2
        ADDRESS        34 RODIN AV., BRIERLEY, BR5 3RT
        _____

        NAME           MASON, T                AMOUNT UNPAID  £   20.00
        TELEPHONE      01234 453322            MEMBERSHIP NO.  1
        ADDRESS        56 HILL VIEW, APPLEBY, AP12 3DU
        _____

        NAME           MOONEY, G               AMOUNT UNPAID  £    5.00
        TELEPHONE      01222 598777            MEMBERSHIP NO. 23
        ADDRESS        4 BACK LANE, QUEENSBURY QU9 4KL
        _____

        NAME           SCHACK, R               AMOUNT UNPAID  £   20.00
        TELEPHONE                              MEMBERSHIP NO.  8
        ADDRESS        3 WALTON RD., ALLERTON AL12 6BN
        _____

        NAME           SMITH, J                AMOUNT UNPAID  £    5.00
        TELEPHONE      01121 987980            MEMBERSHIP NO.  7
        ADDRESS        13 CROSSLEY RD., APPLEBY AP2 4FG
        _____

        NAME           TODD, B                 AMOUNT UNPAID  £    5.00
        TELEPHONE      01344 343434            MEMBERSHIP NO. 14
        ADDRESS        16 MALT LANE, QUEENSBURY QU11 6MN
```

Fig. 9.6 A list of members with overdue subscriptions

To provide the information needed, the secretary has to decide on the search conditions, field selection and output format to be used. Members who have not paid their subscriptions will have a number greater than zero in the 'subs' field. One way of selecting those members who still have subscriptions to pay is to use the search condition 'subs is greater than zero'.

Only those fields that will be used need to be printed, that is, the membership number, name, address, telephone number and the amount of subscriptions still unpaid.

The secretary finds it convenient to have the extracted records sorted into alphabetic order on the name field before printing. This helps in finding a member's details given the name of the member.

The list of members with overdue subscriptions is shown in Fig. 9.6.

Secretary's task: tournament invitations

'Using the database to issue invitations to a tournament'

Occasionally the secretary receives an invitation to enter teams from the club in interclub knockout competitions. Often these invitations arrive too late to allow invitations to individual members to be sent by mail. Usually there are separate competitions for male and female players.

The secretary has been asked to send a team of three female players and a team of three male players to a local knockout competition. The secretary receives the invitation at very short notice. To do the job the secretary sits down at the computer with the telephone at hand.

The secretary wants to send the best players the club has, in this case the top three male and female players. These will be those players with positions 1 to 3 in the club's competition ladder. One possible search condition is 'ladder is greater than zero' AND 'ladder is less than 4'. However, as the secretary is in a hurry and members must be contacted by telephone, those members who are not on the telephone will not be invited. The search condition will need some alteration. One solution would be to change the search condition to exclude members with no telephone. Alternatively, the top five or six members could be displayed, which would allow the secretary some flexibility in deciding who to contact.

Since the secretary will need the name of the member and their telephone number, these fields should be displayed. The sex and position in the club's competition ladder should also be displayed as this is relevant to the job the secretary is doing. The membership number might also be useful for identification purposes.

The secretary might find the extracted information easier to understand if it is displayed in some order that emphasizes the job being done. The data relating to male and female players will need to be separate and should be printed in the order of the player's position in the club's competition ladder. That is, the output should be displayed in order of sex, females followed by males, and within this in order of position in the club's competition ladder, with the higher positions first.

The information extracted can be neatly displayed in table form on the monitor screen (see Fig. 9.7).

```
                          THE TOP PLAYERS IN BOTH COMPETITION LADDERS
         May   21, 1996                                                    Page 1

                              MEMBER                         LADDER
         NAME                 NO.     TELEPHONE NO.          POSITION SEX

         WORTH, A             9       01223 454344           5        F

         MASON, T             1       01234 453322           4        F

         DOWNS, S             6       01222 457342           3        F

         JONES, F             4       01923 456321           2        F

         PEARSON, L           18      01434 899775           1        F

         WORTH, N             10      01223 454344           5        M

         SMITH, J             7       01121 987980           4        M

         SCHACK, R            8                              3        M

         JONES, M             2       01923 456321           2        M

         GOWER, N             5       01234 563987           1        M
```

Fig. 9.7 The top players in both competition ladders

Secretary's task: veterans' presentation cup

At the annual general meeting held each year, the veterans' presentation cup is given to the oldest life member or honorary member of the squash club.

Members should be over thirty-five and life members or honorary members. This is expressed as the search condition 'age is greater than 35 AND (membership class is life OR membership class is honorary)'.

The fields selected identify the members, confirm the search condition and allow the members to be contacted. The membership number, membership class, age, name, address and telephone number of each member are displayed.

The output is displayed as shown in Fig. 9.8.

```
                THE VETERANS' CUP AND THE AWARD OF COMMEMORATIVE BADGES
        May  21, 1996                                                      Page 1


        NAME       PATEL, R                           DATE OF BIRTH 580302
        ADDRESS    34 SUNBRIDGE RD., STEETON ST8 4AS  MEMBER NO.    15
        TELEPHONE 01145 567788                        MEMBERCLASS   L
```

Fig. 9.8 The veterans' cup award

Other tasks

'Backups'

The secretary will need to do some tasks that are useful in maintaining the computer system but that are not useful in providing information the squash club needs. One of the most important of these tasks is backing up the database. Copies of the database must be made on a regular basis, at least weekly. The ancestral method of organizing file backups should be used.

'Printing address labels'

Another task that the squash club database might be used for is to print address labels for sticking on letters to be sent to club members. As the database is set up at present this would not be possible as there is only one address line. Addresses are currently printed as, for example:

FLAT 4, HIGHVIEW HOUSE, QUEENSBURY QU4 8TH

This is not the usual format for addressing letters. We would expect the address on a letter to look like:

FLAT 4
HIGHVIEW HOUSE
QUEENSBURY
QU4 8TH

To print the address in this format, the database should have been set up with at least four fields for the address, i.e. one field for each line of the address. Had this been done originally, address labels could have been printed. To make this change once the database has been created you may have to re-enter the address of every member. If this use had been planned for originally, there would be no extra time spent on it, but if an existing database has to be changed this could be extremely time consuming.

'Sending letters to members'

In addition, the secretary will probably want to use the computer to print out personalized letters to members. This requires the use of a wordprocessor with a mail merge facility. A standard letter is set up with personal details omitted. These are obtained from the database when the letters are printed. Not all wordprocessors will allow you to do mail merge and many of those that do are not integrated with a database. If it is important to use the information on the database in a mail merge, a database that is integrated with a wordprocessor should be used. Claris Works is a good example of integrated software, including a wordprocessor and database. It is available for both Apple and IBM compatible computers.

Some databases will allow you to display graphs, pie diagrams or bar charts to illustrate or summarize data stored on the file. For example, you might want to look at the age distribution of members. This information could be effectively displayed in a bar chart where the height of each bar was proportional to the number of members in a given age range (see Fig. 9.9).

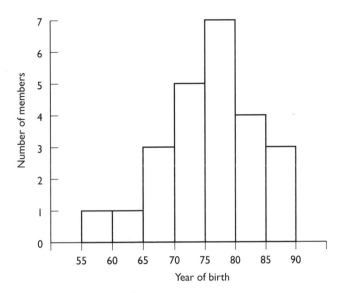

Fig. 9.9 The age distribution of members

A telephone enquiry service Databases are useful when it is necessary to extract information very quickly from large volumes of data. For example, an Electricity Board has a very large number of customers. A record containing the details for each customer will be stored in a file. The details stored for each customer will include the name, address, customer number, details of previous electricity meter readings, method of payment and credit status.

Fig. 9.10 A telephone enquiry service

'A fast response is
needed'

The customer file will be used when calculating bills and mailing them to customers. Some of the bills will be calculated from new meter readings and some will be estimates based on previous meter readings. For various reasons, customers may wish to query their bills. They may also contact the Electricity Board to arrange for the supply to be connected or disconnected. Many customers will use the telephone to make their enquiries (see Fig. 9.10). Telephone enquiries demand the fast response times provided by a database.

A customer who telephones the Electricity Board will speak to a telephone operator wearing a headset. This allows the operator's hands to be free to use the keyboard of one of the terminals connected to the mainframe computer that is running the database. Ideally, the customer will tell the operator their customer number, so that this can be used as a search condition to locate their record. Unfortunately, many customers will not know their number. In these cases the operator will ask the customer their name and make a search of the database, extracting all those customers with that name. Next, the customer will be asked their address to confirm that the correct record has been found. Customer enquiries over the telephone are only practical because of the search facilities and fast response available using the database.

▷ Videotext

Videotext is a page-based information retrieval system. When displayed on the screen, one page occupies the whole screen. Each page has a number and can be accessed using it. There is usually some form of index that directs the user to the page containing the information required. For example, a page may contain a weather report; other pages may contain stock market reports, etc.

Teletext

Teletext is a form of videotext (see Fig. 9.11) broadcast by television and received on a modified domestic TV or using a teletext receiver connected to a microcomputer. Ceefax (broadcast by the BBC) and Oracle (from ITV) are teletext systems. Teletext pages are broadcast interleaved with the television signal in a repeated cycle of page numbers. Pages are broadcast constantly whether they have been selected or not. When a page number has been selected, the user must wait until that page is broadcast in the cycle before it will be displayed. Once displayed, the page is updated every time it is rebroadcast.

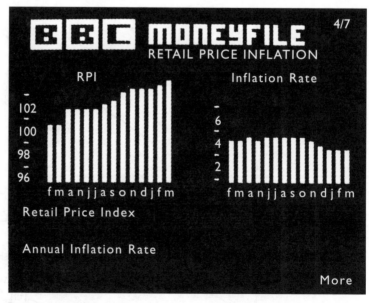

Fig. 9.11 A page of teletext

Fastext

Fastext is teletext received using a TV with built-in memory. When a page is selected it is displayed on the TV screen and stored in memory. At the same time several pages adjacent to it are also stored in memory. When the user moves from one page to the next page in sequence, the page is already in memory and is displayed immediately. You can move one or two pages backwards as well as forwards with Fastext. If you select a page outside of the range of pages stored in memory, you will have to wait as long as you would wait on a teletext TV without Fastext.

'Advantages of receiving via a computer'

The advantages in receiving teletext using a computer rather than a TV are that the computer can store pages on disk for later use and can print pages if requested. Computer software can be downloaded from teletext, saved on disk and run when needed.

Viewdata

Viewdata is another form of videotext. It is like teletext in that it is also a page-based system and its appearance on the screen is similar. However, viewdata is a two-way system; data can be both received and transmitted. Teletext is usually one-way, pages can only be received. Viewdata software is run on a mainframe computer. An example is Minitel in France.

To access a viewdata system, a microcomputer and modem are preferable, although very basic hardware involving a simple numeric keypad can be used. Pages are only transmitted when requested. Access to some pages may be charged for by the information provider and access may be restricted in some cases by requiring a password. The information stored on viewdata systems and the services provided are more extensive than those transmitted by a teletext system. For example, goods can be bought by mail order by providing a credit card number and money can be transferred between bank accounts.

Viewdata or teletext emulators

These are available for some microcomputers and allow users to set up their own videotext system. Typically, they provide indexes and can be made to display a repeated cycle of pages. It is sometimes possible to download pages from Ceefax or Oracle into the emulator. Emulators are useful for providing local information in libraries and other information centres.

▷ The World Wide Web (WWW, the Web)

Users connected to the Internet can use a **browser**, such as Internet Explorer or Netscape, to access information servers on the **World Wide Web**. These provide an astonishingly wide range of information and other services, such as on-line shopping. For example, most universities have Web servers that provide information about the courses they offer (see Fig. 9.12).

Information on the Web is not well indexed. There is a wealth of information but it is difficult to find it. One way to find information is by **surfing the Web**. Surfing is looking at one Web server after another until you find the information you want. This can be very time consuming. To help users find the information they want, some Web servers are **search engines** (e.g. Alta Vista). These provide a means of searching for information across the entire Web. The user enters a search conditon similar to those used to search a database. The search engine returns the location of any relevant information it find on Web information servers throughout the world.

▷ Expert systems

An **expert system** or Intelligent Knowledge-Based System (IKBS) allows users to benefit from the accumulated knowledge of human experts. It consists of software that enables users to recognize particular situations and advise on the appropriate action to take.

For example, an expert system used in medicine for diagnosis of diseases will ask the doctors who use it a variety of questions concerning the symptoms of the patient. Using the answers given, the expert system will identify the specific disease or provide a list of possible illnesses. It will then suggest appropriate action to be taken to cure the disease.

The knowledge built into an IKBS is only as good as the knowledge of the experts who set up the system. As experience grows, or new knowledge is discovered, the IKBS will need to be changed to include this. Some IKBSs do not incorporate any knowledge when

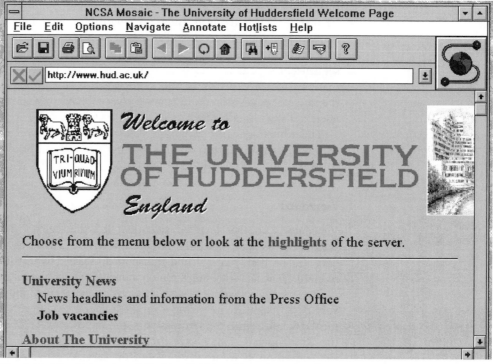

Fig. 9.12 The University of Huddersfield World Wide Web information server accessed using the Mosaic Browser

first used, but have been acquired by experts to help them build their own methods and ways of working into a coherent system.

The full potential of expert systems has not yet been exploited. They have the potential to give everyone access to the most advanced human thinking, but due to the difficulties in setting up such systems this is still only a possibility.

EXAMINATION QUESTIONS

 Question 1   An estate agent keeps a file of property for sale on computer. Some of the information stored on each property is shown in the table below:

Code	Type	Class	Price	Number of Bedrooms
AXY123	House	D	91420	4
AXY917	Bungalow	S	80000	3
AXX134	House	S	47500	3
AXY912	Bungalow	D	120000	4

(a) (i)   State how many records there are in the file.
     (ii) State how many fields there are in each record.
(b) The CLASS field uses a single letter:
     D is a detached property;
     S is a semi-detached property.
     Suggest a helpful code for a terraced property.
(c) Name the key field
(d) Every week the estate agent needs to update the file.
     (i)   What does update mean?
     (ii) Which field is most likely to be affected when the estate agent updates the file?
(e) The estate agent decides to sort the records in his file on PRICE in **ascending** order.
     Complete the following table to show the order after sorting:

Order before sorting	Order after sorting
AXY123	
AXY917	
AXX134	
AXZ912	

(WJEC)

▷ **Question 2**   A video-film club hires films to members. The club uses separate database files to store details about:

   films,
   members,
   films hired.

The screen below shows part of the FILMS database file.

Film number	Film name	Film category	Rating	Hire charge
0123	Mermaids	Comedy	15	£2.00
0124	JFK	Drama	15	£2.50
0254	Star Wars	Adventure	U	£1.50
0361	Mad Max 2	Adventure	18	£2.00
0422	City Slickers	Comedy	15	£125
0744	Die Hard 2	Adventure	18	£1.50
0813	Blackadder	Drama	15	£1.50

(a) If you look at the information in the table about the film Blackadder you will spot a mistake. Drama should be Comedy.
Put three of the following steps in the best order to correct the mistake.
A Print the whole database.
B Save the changes.
C Correct the mistake.
D Delete the whole database.
E Select the Blackadder record.
Step 1 ....
Step 2 ....
Step 3 ....
(b) Look again at the information in the table. Which other piece of information is probably a mistake?

(NEAB/WJEC)

▷ **Question 3**   When you start school you are asked, with your parents, to complete a data sheet. (See sample below.)

Name	Address
Tel No.	Contact in Emergency
Tutor Group	Contact's Tel No.
Any Special Medications	
Doctor's Name	Doctor's Address
Doctor's Tel No.	

(a) Why does the school need this information?

(b) Explain two circumstances in which this information may be important to you or your family.

(c) As well as the school needing to keep information on you, name one other person or place that may want to keep these sort of details about you and explain why.

(NDTEF)

▷ **Question 4**   QUESTION DATA:

SURNAME	FIRST NAME	SEX	DATE OF BIRTH
Acland	Simon	M	11–09–78
Addis	Joy	Y	26–05–80
Anders	Jane	F	03–01–80
Archer	Sandra	F	22–07–77
Basey	Michael	M	17–04–79
Bates	Faith	F	28–11–75
Boyer	Peter	M	21–07–79
Brodie	Carole	F	09–02–77
Davis	Jean	F	10–01–79
Dawkins	John	M	19–01–78
Dawkins	Peter	M	29–12–80
Dawkins	Peter	M	15–04–77
Dawkins	Simon	M	29–12–80

(a) St Saviour's School has recently decided to computerize their information systems. The first step has been to create a database file of pupil data. Using the extract from this database file given above:

(i) Write down two of the field names.

(ii) Write down one complete record.

(b) The school secretary asks you how you get a list of all female pupils. Write down the query command to display the surnames and first names of all female pupils.

(City and Guilds)

▷ **Question 5**   A hospital radio station has been given a collection of old records, unfortunately they are all mixed up. The producer needs to be able to find a record with a particular title, singer, composer, band or released in a particular year. They decide to use a computer database to help them.

(a) Give an example of one advantage and one disadvantage of inputting this information on a computer.

(b) Draw up the format for this database.

(c) State which are files, fields and records in your format.

(d) The hospital wanted to add some other information about the tapes and CDs that they have to the database. Describe how they can alter the database (using a method that you have used).

(NDTEF)

▷ **Question 6**   A company uses a computer to put buyers of second-hand cars in touch with people who are selling cars. It collects information from sellers by getting the sellers to complete a form. Buyers can then ring up and ask for a list of people who have the sort of car they want.

(a) Design a form for the input of information for a SELLER.

(b) Describe clearly the processes required to get a list (in price order) of all Ford Escort cars less than 5 years old in the price range £3000 to £4000.

(c) Explain why a manual card index might be better than a computer for a second-hand car dealer who usually has between 8 and 10 cars for sale.

(SEG, 1993)

▷ **Question 7** A large shop sells bicycles. The information about each bicycle in stock is held in a database on a computer. Part of the information is shown below:

Maker	Model	Type	Colour	Price
Peugeot	Elite	Racing	Blue	200.00
Butler	Junior	Racing	Green	175.00
Holdsworth	Espada	Mountain	Red	220.00
Molton	Mini	Folding	Green	109.50
Muddy Fox	Shappell	Mountain	Blue	0.225
Butler	Norfolk	Touring	Red	180.00

(a) Explain why it is important to check carefully all information put into a computer.
(b) (i)   There is an obvious error in the data above. Put a ring round the error.
     (ii) The correct data should be:...
     (iii) Describe a check that could be carried out automatically to find errors like this.
     (iv) Give an example of a likely error in this column that could NOT be found out by the checking method you have described.
(c) A customer is only interested in mountain bikes. List the steps you would go through to get a printed list of all mountain bikes from the computer.
(d) An advertisement is being designed for one of the bicycles. The first draft is shown below.

> Peugeot Racing Bike
> Elite Model
> Blue
> Only £200
> Credit terms available

Give three improvements that could be made to make the advertisement more effective.
(e) The shop also sells second-hand bikes. Give two other items of information that might be useful to have in the database for the second-hand bikes.

(SEG, 1993)

▷ **Question 8** A school uses a computer system to help with administration.

(a) The computer has a database which stores data about the teachers, pupils and rooms. Describe THREE different ways of presenting the output from the database.
(b) A new pupil joins the school. How could the computer system be used to help to fit the pupil into suitable classes?
(c) The computer system stores personal information about the new pupil. State ONE way that the school office staff can use the personal information stored about pupils on the computer.

(MEG)

▷ **Question 9** A company of estate agents, with a main branch in one town and several branches in nearby towns, is planning to change from a manual system to a computerized one.

(a) The company plans to set-up a computer file with details of houses that are for sale. This file will store the name of the owner, the address, the 'phone number and type for each house. Suggest four other fields that might be included on file.
(b) Explain why some of the data in the fields in this file is stored in a coded form.

(c) The file will store details of several thousand houses. People interested in buying any house should be able to obtain a print-out of the details by simply calling in at a branch of the company. What type of backing storage would be needed for the file? Give two reasons for your choice.

(d) Some of the fields in this file are of fixed length, others are of variable length.
   (i) Give one advantage of using fixed length fields.
   (ii) Give one disadvantage of using fixed length fields.

(e) Describe the hardware the company will need to install in each of its branches and in the main office for the new computerized system.

(NEAB/WJEC)

▷ **Question 10**   Study the extract from the FRUGRO database given below. The full database hold records on over 20,000 different fruits and vegetables and also contains more information on each item such as growing conditions, fertilization etc.

Fruit	Name	Cropping	Size	Virus Resistant	Yield	Quality	Producer
S	Ghenghis Khan	Late	2–4	y	high	excellent flavour	Pearson Brothers
S	Glentham Delight	Main	2–4	y	high	excellent flavour	Porter Produce
R	Frenchay Runner	Main	1–2.5	y	medium/ high	superb	Frenchay Brothers
R	Frenchay Early	Early	1–2.5	n	high	excellent	Frenchay Brothers
S	Pilgrim's Progress	Late	2–5	y	medium	superb	Kent Billham
S	Pershings Pleasure	Late	2–6	y	medium	excellent	Pearson Brothers
R	Ladbrook Largesse	V Late	2–4	n	medium	superb	Kent Billham

(a) Explain why some items on the database have been coded. What is the purpose of the coding?

(b) In what way might using the database be of more use than another way of storing the data?

(c) There may be other specialist 'on-line' databases available. Explain with the use of diagrams what the term 'on-line' means in this context. How would these be of use compared to another way of accessing the data needed?

(d) Give a way in which an 'on-line' database could be accessed by Chris. What is the main difference between an 'on-line' database and one held on CDROM at the area Agricultural College?

(RSA)

▷ **Question 11**   A dentist wishes to set up a simple computer system to provide information about her patients' teeth; their appointments; the treatment they have; and the money they owe her. She can afford a desk top computer with a hard disk, a monochrome monitor, a keyboard, a mouse and a dot matrix printer.

(a) State the type or types of application software that you would recommend. Explain your choice.

(b) Describe how the system might handle the information, including the results it could produce for the dentist, the regular entry of data, the structure of the stored data and the processing carried out.

(c) Explain the benefits of using a generic application package rather than a specially pro-grammed system, and state any likely limitations in its ease of use and efficiency of operation.

(d) Suggest possible improvements to the system if the dentist could afford different peripherals and specially programmed software.

(e) State a potential advantage of the computer system to each of the following:
the dentist;
the nurse;
the receptionist.

(f) State a disadvantage that might be there for any two of these people.

(RSA)

EXAMINATION ANSWERS

▷ **Answer 1**   (a) (i) Four records are shown. Theoretically, up to 17,576,000 records are possible but this is unlikely in practice.
(ii) Five fields are shown.
(b) 'T' could be a terraced property.
(c) 'Code' would be the key field.
(d) (i) 'Update' means bring up-to-date.
(ii) Of the five fields shown only the price is likely to change.
(e) AXX134
AXY123
AXY917
AXZ912

▷ **Answer 2**   (a) E, C, B.
(b) The hire charge of £125 for City Slickers.

▷ **Answer 3**   (a) Some of the reasons the school needs this information are:
▶ To know who to contact in emergencies.
▶ To know what medicines a pupil uses.
(b) Some of the reasons why this information may be important to you are:
▶ You could have an accident and the school would need to contact your family.
▶ The school will need your address to send letters to your parents.
(c) Some of the others needing this information are:
▶ Your doctor – to keep a record of patients.
▶ The library – to keep a record of members.

▷ **Answer 4**   (a) (i) Field names are: surname, first name, sex and date of birth.
(ii) Any single line of the table is a complete record, e.g. 'Dawkins; Simon; M; 29–12–80.
(b) Query command: An example would be:

IF SEX IS F
THEN DISPLAY SURNAME, FIRST NAME.

This command would not display the details for Joy Addis and Sandra Archer as their sex has been entered incorrectly.

▷ **Answer 5**   (a) Some advantages are:
▶ Fast, easy access to the information.
▶ Easy to edit.
Some disadvantages are:
▶ To access the information, you have to know how to use a computer.
▶ A computer must be available to use.

(b) These are some of the fields that would be in each record:

field name	type	length	example
title	character	25	12 Gold Bars
band	character	25	Status Quo
year	number	4	1984

There would also be fields for the singer, composer and location. There would be a key field, possibly the record number.

(c) The fields are shown in (b) above. There is one record for each old record. All the records make up a file.

(d) These are some of the ways in which you can alter a database:
▶   Add more fields to a record.
▶   Add records to the file.

▷ **Answer 6**   (a) The form asks for the seller's name and 'phone number and details about the car for sale, such as; maker, model, year, mileage, colour, etc. The form should use the following techniques where appropriate:
▶   character boxes to fill in, e.g. [A] [ ] [J] [O] [N] [E] [S] [ ] [ ]
▶   tick lists, e.g.

Mileage: up to 10,000   ☐
            10,000–20,000   ☐
            20,000–30,000   ☐
            30,000–40,000   ☐
            40,000–50,000   ☐
            over 50,000   ☐

The form should explain simply and clearly why the information is being collected and should be signed and dated by the person filling it in. There should be simple examples of how to fill in the form where these are needed. The design should look like a form.

(b) Assuming the database is running on the computer, you would:
▶   Query the file using a search condition, such as:
CAR IS FORD AND MODEL IS ESCORT
AND AGE IS LESS THAN 5
AND PRICE IS MORE THAN £3000
AND PRICE IS LESS THAN £4000
▶   Sort those records selected by the query into some sensible order, such as, descending order on price.
▶   Print or display on the screen the details required from the selected records, e.g. model, year, mileage, price, seller's name and 'phone numbers.

(c) If only 8 to 10 cars are for sale it would be better to record their details on cards because:
▶   You don't need a computer to access them.
▶   You could carry them with you all the time.
▶   It might be faster to find the information you want.

▷ **Answer 7**   (a) The accuracy of the information output depends on the accuracy of the information input (see GIGO).

(b) (i)   Ring the cell containing 0.225.
    (ii)   Probably 225.00.
    (iii) A validation check, specifying the range of acceptable prices, would detect this error.
    (iv)   A price error within acceptable limits would not be detected, e.g. £185.00 instead of £180.00.

(c) You would use the search condition:
'Type is Mountain'
to select the mountain bikes, then print a report showing the details of those records selected.

(d) You could enhance the appearance of the advert by using different text styles and fonts, including graphics, and using colour.

(e) Name; address and 'phone number of the previous owner.

▷ **Answer 8** (a) Three from:
Form lists for teachers.
Teacher lists.
Classroom timetables.
Subject options lists.
Pupil timetables.
Any other suitable list.

(b) Using a timetabling program to produce a timetable for the pupil. Try out various patterns to see which fit. See where there are spaces in classes.

(c) One from:
Storing contact names in case of illness.
Storing doctor's name in case of illness.
Correct spelling of name and address to check whether the pupil has brothers/sisters in the school.
Any other suitable record.

(MEG)

▷ **Answer 9** (a) Any four of:
Number of bedrooms.
Fields showing if the house has:
▶ central heating
▶ double glazing
▶ a garage
▶ a garden

(b) Information about the garage facilities could be coded, e.g.:
N – no garage
S – single garage
D – double garage
Coded fields take up less space on backing storage and are typed in faster when the data is being entered into the computer.

(c) The file would be stored on a hard disk. It is faster to read/write data from/to a hard disk than other types of backing storage. Files on hard disk can be direct access files. A record in a direct access file can be found faster than records in other types of file.

(d) (i) A fixed length field has the same length in every record. For example, a date is a fixed length in every record when it is written in YYMMDD form. As the computer knows it's length, it can be processed faster.

(ii) If fixed length fields are used for fields such as names and addresses, storage space is wasted if the data is shorter than the field length. If the data is longer than the field length, all the data cannot be stored.

(e) The company will need this hardware in each of its branches:
▶ Computer(s) (monitor, processor, floppy disk drive, hard disk drive, keyboard, mouse).
▶ Local printers.
▶ MODEM.
▶ Scanner.
▶ Hardware to do backups.
The company will need this hardware at the main office:
▶ Mainframe computers (processor, hard disk drives, magnetic tape drives, operators console, line printers, local terminals).
▶ Communications front end and MODEMS.

▷ **Answer 10** (a) Coded fields take up less storage space on backing storage and are typed in faster when the data is being entered into the computer.

(b) The data could be stored on a card file. However, using a database enables a user to:
- ▶ Search for and find one record faster.
- ▶ Search for and find a group of records faster, e.g. late cropping vegetables with a high yield.
- ▶ Sort the information into a different order very quickly.
- ▶ Print out selected information from the database, e.g., the producers and names of late cropping vegetables with a high yield.

(c) 'On-line' means connected to and in communication with (usually) a mainframe computer.
 An on-line database (Fig. 9.13) should be relatively up-to-date compared to a database on CD-ROM. The speed of access should be faster using an on-line database compared with teletext. A variety of on-line databases are available all over the world. You only pay for the time you are connected to them and the information used.

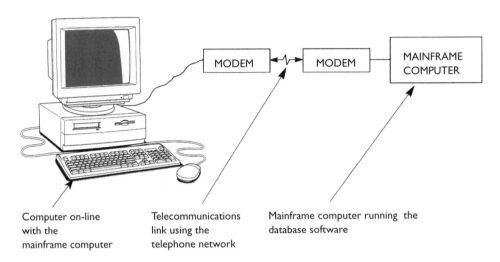

Fig. 9.13 Database

(d) Chris would have to use a MODEM and the telephone network to access an on-line database. An on-line database should be relatively up-to-date compared with CD-ROM.

▷ **Answer 11** (a) Database.
 The dentist can find information about a patient quickly, select various categories of patient and print appropriate reports.
 (b) Description covering:
- ▶ Record specification.
- ▶ Editing records and fields.
- ▶ Searching.
- ▶ Sorting.
- ▶ Reporting.
 (c) Benefits:
- ▶ Immediately available.
- ▶ Very little re-programming needed.
- ▶ Guarantee it will work.
- ▶ Skills transferable to other information handling applications.
 Limitations:
- ▶ If it does not meet your needs you may not be able to adapt it.
- ▶ The facilities available could be too simple or too complex and consequently obstruct you in using the database.
 (d) The dentist could purchase:
- ▶ A colour monitor – colour is often used to make software easier to use.
- ▶ A laser printer – this would save time as it prints faster than a dot matrix printer. It also produces better quality output.
 Specially programmed software could help the dentist with stock keeping and payroll. These extra functions could be integrated with the patient database.

(e) Potential advantages are:
   Dentist: More accurate record keeping.
   Nurse: Immediate access to the patient's records.
   Receptionist: Easy access to daily record of appointments.
(f) Disadvantages are:
   Dentist: Cost of installation and maintenance of computer system.
   Nurse: No records available if the computer breaks down.
   Receptionist: May lack IT skills.

EXAMINATION QUESTION WITH STUDENT ANSWER

ALLCARS is a vehicle rental company
ALLCARS uses a database to store information about its customers and the cars they rent

(a) Tick TWO boxes to show which items of information should be included in each customer's record.

	Tick TWO boxes
The customer's weight.	✓
The customer's name.	✓
The number of the car rented.	✓
The customer's income.	
The length of the car.	

(b) ALLCARS classify customers as occasional, regular or frequent.
   This information is coded before it is stored on the database.
   (i) Design a suitable coding system for this information.

   OCC = occasional

   REG = regular

   FRE = frequent

   (ii) Explain why this information is coded.

   To stop people who don't know the code finding out what it means

(c) Tick TWO boxes to show which of these statements are most likely to be true.

	Tick TWO boxes
The database is used to find out which customer has rented a car.	✓
The database displays the bus timetable.	
The database stores the customer's name as a code.	
The database prints a list of cars showing how many times each car has been rented.	✓
The database is also used by the newsagent shop next door.	

(d) The manager wants to display all the blue cars.
   The manager uses this search condition   Colour is blue.

Tick TWO boxes to show why the search condition might display most, but not all, of the blue cars.

	Tick TWO boxes
The data entry clerk is colour blind.	
The colour of some of the blue cars was entered incorrectly.	✓
All the blue cars were serviced last week.	
Some of the white cars were recently re-painted red.	
Some of the white cars were recently re-painted blue.	✓

(e) ALLCARS wants to know if customers are satisfied with the cars they rent. You are asked to design a questionnaire to collect this information for input to the computer. Design a suitable questionnaire.

ALLCARS

Customer Satisfaction Survey

What is your name? _____

Which car did you rent? _____

Did you like it? YES/NO _____

Signed _____ Date _____

(SEG, 1996)

▷ **Examiner's comment**

(a) Two of these answers are correct but one is wrong (the customer's weight is irrelevant). The question asks for two boxes to be ticked, not three. It is unlikely that full marks would be awarded.

(b) (i) Coding systems should be meaningful and as short as possible. This is a better answer:
   O = occasional
   R = regular
   F = frequent

   (ii) It is unlikely that ALLCARS codes this information to keep it confidential. Coding this type of information saves space on backing storage. As a result, less backing storage is needed, and access to the file could be faster.

(c) Correct. The database could display the bus timetable, and the newsagents might also make use of it, but this is not very likely. Coding customer's names is not done as the shortest, meaningful code is likely to be the name itself.

(d) Correct. If the database is to display all the blue cars, then their colours must be recorded accurately and be up-to-date on the database.

(e) There are some good points and some weaknesses in this answer.
   It is clear what the form is for. If the name is to be given, perhaps character boxes should be provided as we are collecting information for input to a computer. However, customer surveys are often anonymous so that customers will feel more able to comment freely.
   It is not clear how to answer the question 'Which car did you rent?'. Should the car number be given? The next question clearly indicates how to answer it. However, the question itself is too vague. Signing and dating a questionnaire is excellent unless, as is probable here, the customers should be allowed to remain anonymous.

SUMMARY

This chapter looks at information handling using databases, videotext, the World Wide Web, and expert systems.

▷ A databse **file** is a collection of related records. For example, a file of information about customers.

▷ A **record** in a database file is a collection of related fields. In records of the same type, the fields are in the same order. For example, each customer's record might include their name, address, telephone number, etc. in the same order.

▷ A **field** is an item of information. For example, a customer's name.

▷ A **key field** uniquely identified a record. For example, each customer will have a unique customer number that uniquely identifies the customer and their record in the database.

▷ Field may be coded. **Codes** should be short yet meaningful. For examaple, they way in which a customer pays could be coded:

way a customer pays	code
cash	ca
credit card, e.g. visa	cr
cheque	ch
debit card	de
store card	st

▷ Using a databse, you can:

    ▷ Keep records of customers criminals, books stock, pupils, teachers, houses for sale, etc.

    ▷ Use a **search condition** to look for information, for example, PostCode is 'BC12 3SY'.

    ▷ **Sort** the information into some order. For example, descending alphabetic order, i.e. Z to A.

    ▷ **Select** the information to include in your report from the information you have found.

    ▷ **Report** on what you have found.

▷ **Videotext** is a simple way of handling information using a page based system. **Teletext** is a type of videotext. For example, Ceefax and Oracle. Using teletext you can select pages of information. Pages are broadcast in cycle. They can be received and displayed on a TV or using a computer. Using a computer, pages can be saved and printed. Teletext is not usually interactive.

▷ The **World Wide Web** gives you access to an extensive range of information and services throughout the world. You can access the Web using a **browser**, such as Netscape, and find information by surfing the Web or using a search engine such as Alta Vista.

▷ **Expert systems** allow users to build a structured database of their knowledge and experience that can be used to recognize particular situations and advise on appropriate action. For example, an expert system for medical diagnosis.

Spreadsheets and modelling

This chapter should be read if you are preparing for GCSE IT assessment with the following examining boards:

C & G	MEG	NEAB	SEG
London	NDTEF	RSA	WJEC

GETTING STARTED

Spreadsheets can be used for the wide variety of tasks that involve calculations laid out in rows and columns. They can generate a wide variety of useful graphs. Spreadsheets are often used for financial applications and in mathematics. They can be used to record information but they are also used for modelling.

GLOSSARY

Cell	A cell is the intersection of a horizontal row and a vertical column.
An absolute cell reference	An absolute call reference does not change when cells are moved or copied.
A relative cell reference	A relative cell reference changes when cells are moved or copied so that the references it makes to other cells are adjusted relative to its new position.
Modelling	When a spreadsheet is used for modelling, it is being used to explore the situation it describes or to predict what will happen.

C & G	LONDON	MEG	NDTEF	NEAB	RSA	SEG	WJEC	TOPIC	STUDY	REVISION I	REVISION 2
✓	✓	✓	✓	✓	✓	✓	✓	Models			
✓	✓	✓	✓	✓	✓	✓	✓	Spreadsheets			
✓	✓	✓	✓	✓	✓	✓	✓	Stock keeping in a small shop			
✓	✓	✓	✓	✓	✓	✓	✓	Modelling			
✓	✓	✓	✓	✓	✓	✓	✓	Price forecast model			
✓	✓	✓	✓	✓	✓	✓	✓	Supermarket queue model			
✓	✓	✓	✓	✓	✓	✓	✓	Break even model			
✓	✓	✓	✓	✓	✓	✓	✓	Predator/prey model			

▶ **WHAT YOU NEED TO KNOW**

▷ **Models**

Models are representations of the real world. Our earliest introduction to modelling is likely to be moulding plasticine or clay to make representations of people or animals. You can buy toy soldiers and model cars; dolls and dolls houses. They are all models, that is, representations of the real world.

Models in some form are used throughout commerce and industry. You can build a physical model of a shopping centre or other building project to demonstrate the architectural style and layout of the planned development. Models of such developments can also be built using computer software. Computer models of large scale developments are relatively complex and expensive to build, though it is not uncommon for an architect to use computer aided design (CAD) software to plan in detail the design and construction of a new building.

'Models you can set up are our main interest here'

The computer models you may encounter are likely to fall into two distinctive groups. There will be models that you set up and manipulate yourself. These models will be constructed using a spreadsheet. It is this type of model that is the focus of this chapter. Spreadsheets are widely used in many different types of activity, especially in recording and organizing financial models. They provide a well structured layout and facilities for storing text and numerical data and doing calculations. Spreadsheets can vary considerably in complexity and size.

You may also encounter models that are *set up for you*, providing you with a simulation of a real situation. For example, you may use a computer-based simulation of an oil spill in the North Sea. The computer will give you control over factors that limit the spread of the oil slick such as the number of workers tackling it, the quantity of detergent available, the placement of floating booms, etc. You could have a limited budget to spend to get the oil slick cleared up. The computer will simulate the effects of the weather and the tide. Using such a model will help your understanding of the constraints and difficulties that arise in such a situation. This model could be used for training people to tackle real oil slicks.

'Computer games can be realistic'

Computer games are like models. Some games present you with realistic situations but many do not. Computer games often present fantasy in a context that is apparently real. It is important to distinguish between a model which tries to represent the real world as exactly as it is possible, and a computer game which may make no attempt to do so.

It is essential to remember that a model is a *representation* of the real world. It is *not* the real world. You cannot expect reality to be exactly like a model of it. The better the model, the more exactly it copies reality. The advantage of using models is that they allow us to experiment. We can try out strategies and forecast what will happen. However, a forecast is based on experience of the past. The future may not mimic the past. Consequently, we must treat forecasts based on models with care.

▷ **Spreadsheets**

When you are doing calculations using a sheet of paper and a pen or pencil, you will find that it is often easier to understand what you are doing if you work in *rows* and *columns*. Columns are up and down the page; rows are across the page.

'Spreadsheets are used where rows and columns are involved'

For example, you may layout the calculations you do in Maths at school in columns. Maths teachers often insist on this! If you have studied Accounting, you will have come across situations where you have amounts of money in columns with a description of what each sum is beside it. A supermarket receipt is a good example of this type of layout (see Fig. 10.1). There is a description of the items bought, the unit price, the quantity and the amount paid for the items. At the bottom of the receipt, the total to be paid for all the items bought is printed. This style of layout is widely used throughout industry and commerce for a variety of calculations.

A **spreadsheet** is the computerized equivalent of a piece of paper divided into rows and columns. A typical screen display from a spreadsheet is shown in Fig. 10.2. Notice that the rows are numbered from 1 to 19 down the left-hand side of the screen and the columns are numbered from A to I along the top of the screen. There are actually many more rows and columns in the spreadsheet. What is seen on the screen is just part of the spreadsheet. We are looking through a 'window' in which we can see only some of the rows and columns available. All spreadsheets have similar rows and columns.

As this particular layout is so useful there are very many different spreadsheets available. For example, there are Excel and Lotus 1–2–3 for IBM compatibles, and Claris Works for Apple computers.

What a spreadsheet can be used for

Spreadsheets can be used for the wide variety of tasks where the division of the screen into rows and columns is useful. They can be used to do any calculations that may be needed. They are especially useful for doing accounts and forecasting expenditure. These are some of the many tasks where spreadsheets are used:

'Uses of spreadsheets'

- ▶ stock keeping in a shop
- ▶ organizing milk deliveries
- ▶ company accounts
- ▶ school tuck shop income, expenses and profits
- ▶ payroll, sales information and forecasting
- ▶ models of supermarket queues, etc.

Morrisons Supermarkets

	unit price	quantity	price
baked beans	0.30	2	0.60
rice	0.56	4	2.24
ice cream	1.47	1	1.47
meat	4.52	1	4.52
magazine	0.65	1	0.65
biscuits	0.25	5	1.25
			10.73

21.02.96

THANK YOU FOR YOUR CUSTOM

Fig. 10.1 A supermarket receipt

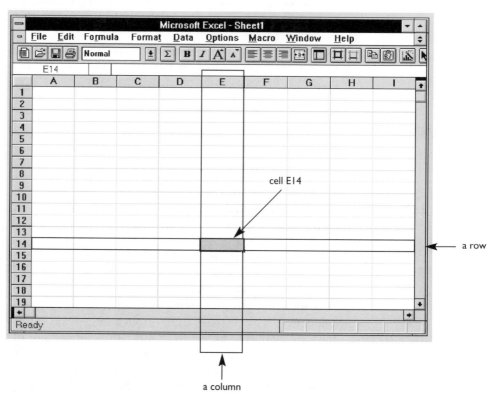

Fig. 10.2 The screen display from a spreadsheet

What spreadsheets do

Spreadsheets are the computerized equivalent of a piece of paper divided into rows and columns. The layouts available and the calculations you can do on a piece of paper can also be represented on a spreadsheet. However, as you might anticipate, a spreadsheet is more flexible and extends what you can do.

Different spreadsheets do the same tasks but may be operated in different ways. The facilities described below are available on most spreadsheets. You should look for the following facilities on the spreadsheet you use and make sure you can use them.

Cell references

Spreadsheets are divided into rows and columns (see Fig. 10.2). Where a column and a row intersect is a rectangular box known as a *cell*. A cell is referred to by giving the column it is in and the row it is in. In Fig. 10.2 the cell which is at the intersection of row 14 and column E has the **cell reference**, E14 (column E, row 14). Every cell has a different cell reference so that if a cell reference is given it names only one cell.

Cell range references

It is often useful to refer to a *range* of cells, for example, all the cells in column D between rows 5 and 17. To refer to cells in column D between rows 5 and 17, you could use the **cell range reference** D5:D17.

To refer to a rectangular block of cells it is usual to specify the cell reference of the top left hand corner and the cell reference of the bottom right hand corner. For example, to refer to the block of cells in columns A to D, starting at row 5 and going down as far as row 17, you could use the cell range reference A5:D17.

Cell contents

Cells can contain character strings, numbers, formulae, dates or times.

'Contents of cells'

Character strings may be used for column and row headings that say what is in that particular column or row, e.g. 'item price'.

Numbers may be amounts of money or other quantities. Numbers can be integers, e.g. 4, –1, 0, 45, or real numbers, e.g. 2.354, –34.6.

Formulae can be programmed into a cell allowing the contents of the cell to be calculated from the contents of other cells. For example, if in column D, rows 5 to 17 there are money values, these could be added together and their total displayed in the cell at column D, row 20 by entering an appropriate formula in that cell. The formula SUM(D5:D17) can be used to add the contents of cells D5 to D17. The formula itself will not be displayed on the screen in the cell at D20 but the total value calculated will be displayed.

'Types of formulae'

Formulae may be arithmetic calculations, sums or more complex functions to work out averages and square roots, generate random numbers, etc. You may also be able to use programming statements, such as IF/THEN, and logical functions, such as, AND, OR and NOT. The variety of functions you can use will vary depending on the spreadsheet you are using.

Automatic re-calculation

The value of a formula will be **automatically re-calculated** when the contents of one or more cells that the formulae refers to are altered. Automatic re-calculation is one of the most important features of a spreadsheet that extends it beyond being merely an electronic sheet of paper.

Protecting cells

'You can protect cells'

Setting up a spreadsheet can be a time consuming task. You may want to **protect** some of the cell contents you have entered from accidental corruption. In particular, if you are setting up the spreadsheet for someone else to use, you will not want them to change column headings and formulae. Cells can be protected to prevent their contents being changed. The contents of a protected cell cannot be altered until the protection is removed.

Cell display formats

You may want to **display** the data in a cell in various **formats**. The following are some common display formats:

> ▶ Right and left justify: all cell contents are lined up with the right- or left-hand edge of the column, respectively.
> ▶ Centre: all cell contents are positioned midway between the right-hand edge of the column and the left-hand edge.
> ▶ Dates can be displayed in various forms, for example, 930612, 12 Jun 1993, etc.
> ▶ Numbers can be displayed rounded to a fixed number of decimal places with a £ sign or a minus sign, as required.

'Different data formats'

Column width

When the spreadsheet is first displayed on the screen, all the **columns** will probably be the same number of characters **wide**. You may want to alter this arrangement so that some columns are wider and some are narrower. You should be able to do this at any time without affecting the contents of any of the cells in the column adjusted. For example, if a column is twelve characters wide and you want it to contain numbers that will be at most three digits, e.g. age in years, then you can reduce the width of the column.

Copying and moving cells

You may find that you want to **move** cells to a different position in the spreadsheet or **copy** cells so that they contain the same data as other cells.

A spreadsheet will allow you to move a single cell or a range of cells. You can copy a single cell to another cell, or a range of cells to another range of cells. You can also copy a single cell to a range of cells.

Where a cell contains a formula, the formula will also be copied across. There are these possibilities:

'Relative cell references'

> ▶ The structure of the formula remains unaltered but the cells it refers to are **changed**. For example, if the formula SUM(D5:D17) in cell D20 is copied to cell E20, we might want the formula to change so that it adds up E5 to E17. The formula would be changed to SUM(E5:E17) during the move or copy. In this case, D5 and D17 have been specified as **relative cell references** so that they change when they are moved or copied.

'Absolute cell references'

> ▶ The formula will be copied with the cell references unchanged. For example, if the formula SUM(D5:D17) in cell D20 is copied to cell D23 with the formula unchanged, it would remain as SUM(D5:D17) in cell D23. In this case, D5 and D17 have been specified as **absolute cell references** so that they do not change when they are moved or copied.

Absolute cell references are often written in a different way to relative cell references. For example, if the relative cell reference was D5, an absolute cell reference for the same cell might be written as $D$5.

This may sound somewhat complicated! Unfortunately, different spreadsheets have different ways of dealing with moving and copying formula. Some spreadsheets default to absolute cell references and others default to relative cell references. You should carefully check formulae after doing a move or a copy.

Delete and insert rows and columns

You can **insert** rows and columns, that is, you can put in an additional row between existing rows or an extra column between existing columns. You can also **delete**, i.e. remove, rows and columns.

Windows

A **window** is a rectangular area of the screen that is used to display part of the spreadsheet. Most spreadsheets will allow you to open more than one window. This can be very useful if you want to view different parts of the spreadsheet on the screen at the same time.

Sorting

A spreadsheet should allow you to **sort** the rows into some order depending on the contents of the cells in a particular column. You should also be able to sort the columns depending on the contents of the cells in a particular row.

For example, suppose you were setting up a spreadsheet where each row contained details referring to a particular person. Column A might contain their name, column B, their rate of pay, and so on. Your aim is to end up with a list of personal details with the names in alphabetic order. You might find it easier to enter all the details in whatever order they occur, then sort the rows into alphabetic order on the names. A spreadsheet will allow you to do this.

Graphs

Many spreadsheets will allow you to construct a variety of graphs. Bar charts, pie diagrams and line graphs are often available.

Printing

'Printing the spreadsheets'

A spreadsheet will allow you to *print* all of the spreadsheet or only part of the spreadsheet. You should be able to print the values of the cells as displayed on the screen or the underlying formulae. You can also print graphs.

Printers used with microcomputers usually print 80 characters on a line. If your spreadsheet has more than 80 characters on a row it cannot be printed as it has been set up without some adjustment.

If condensed print is possible on your printer, you might find this facility useful, as you can print 160 characters on a line that would normally be only 80 characters wide. You may also consider using a wide carriage printer. You may be able to adjust the width of the print line from within the spreadsheet to suit the print style or printer you are using.

Import and export

Groups of cells and graphs can be exported to other software. For example, to a word-processor for including in a report.

▷ Stock-keeping in a small shop

We are now going to look at an **IT system** based on a spreadsheet. As an example, we will look at *stock control* in a small electrical appliance shop. There are many other similar applications that a spreadsheet can be used for.

A shopkeeper uses a spreadsheet to keep a record of sales from a small electrical appliance shop. The income from the shop does not yet justify the cost of full-scale computerization including on-line point of sale terminals. The spreadsheet is used to speed up calculations, providing reliable results and additional sales information.

When goods are sold, the shopkeeper gives the customer a receipt (see Fig. 10.3). The receipt is written on a two part carbonized pad so that both the customer and the shopkeeper have a record of the transaction. At the end of the day the shopkeeper works out the quantity of each item sold from the receipts. The shopkeeper uses the form in Fig. 10.4 to help accumulate the quantity of each item sold. These are entered into a spreadsheet. The spreadsheet multiplies the quantity sold by the price to work out the value of sales of the item. The total value of sales of all goods sold that day is also calculated.

'Stock control in a small shop'

At the end of the day, the shopkeeper adds up the total takings from the tills. This should be equal to the total sales value calculated by the spreadsheet. If these are not equal, there is some error in the data collection process or there has been a theft from the tills. The shopkeeper must repeat the entire process, beginning with the receipts, to be sure that the error is due to theft. This check helps identify and prevent theft from the tills.

The system also helps the shopkeeper identify which goods have a high turnover, which should be carefully managed because of their high price, and which contribute most to

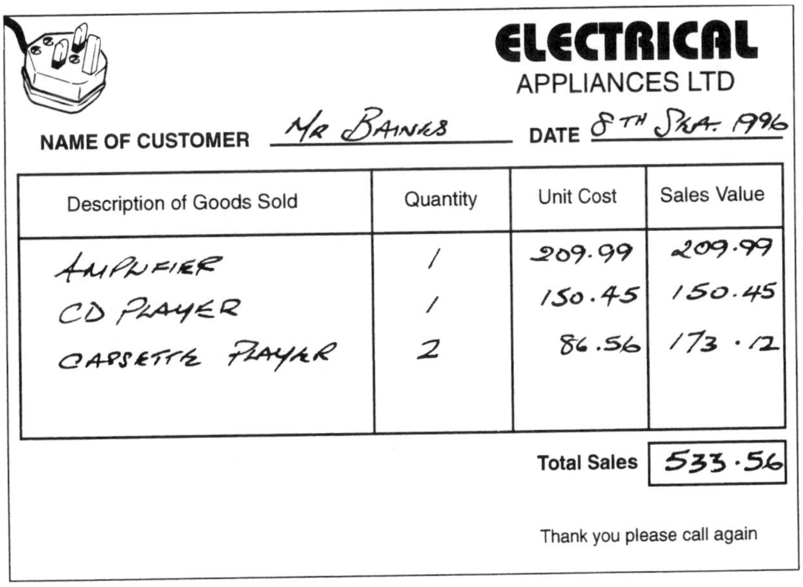

ELECTRICAL
APPLIANCES LTD

NAME OF CUSTOMER *Mr Baines*   DATE *8th Sept. 1996*

Description of Goods Sold	Quantity	Unit Cost	Sales Value
AMPLIFIER	1	209.99	209.99
CD PLAYER	1	150.45	150.45
CASSETTE PLAYER	2	86.56	173.12
		Total Sales	**533.56**

Thank you please call again

Fig. 10.3 The receipt used in data capture

profitability. Whilst the daily process of data collection is time consuming, this additional information is easily extracted.

A diagram illustrating the essentials of this simple IT system is shown in Fig. 10.5.

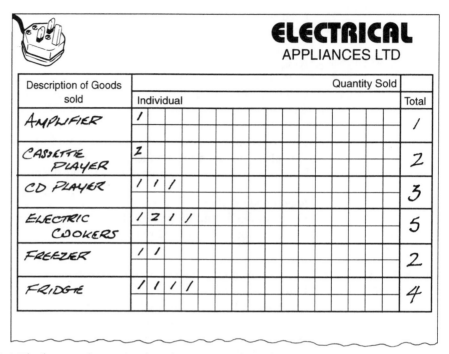

Fig. 10.4 The form used to accumulate the quantity of each item sold

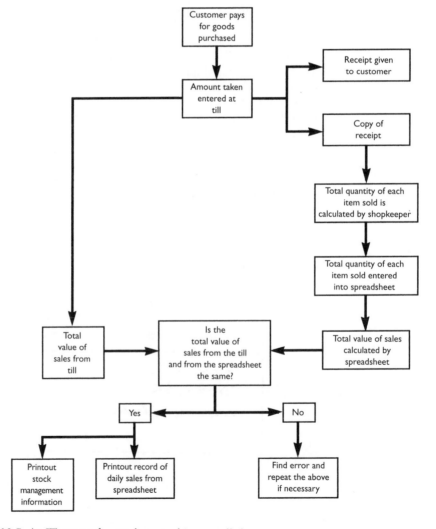

Fig. 10.5 An IT system for stock control in a small shop

The limitations of the spreadsheet example used

There are only a few items for sale listed in the example spreadsheet as there is not space in this book to include several printouts of a very large spreadsheet. In practice, a small electrical appliance shop might stock several hundred different items.

The spreadsheet that has been set up in the example uses only a small proportion of the rows and columns available. The spreadsheet could be set up to cover an entire week or a month. The quantity sold, sales values and profits could be worked out on a weekly or a monthly basis.

Setting up the spreadsheet

A spreadsheet is initially **set up** containing all the data which does not change very frequently (see Fig. 10.6). The variable data which changes each time the spreadsheet is used is not entered when the spreadsheet is first set up.

'Setting up the spreadsheet in the stock control example'

For each item sold, the spreadsheet will eventually contain its name or description, unit price, the quantity sold, the value of sales, the percentage profit and the overall contribution to profits. The data which does not change very frequently is the column headings, item names or descriptions, unit prices, percentage profit and any formulae. These must be set up before the spreadsheet can be used by the shopkeeper. The variable data that may change each time the spreadsheet is used is the quantity sold. This is not entered at all when the spreadsheet is first set up, as the shopkeeper will enter the quantity sold at the end of each day when using the spreadsheet.

The shopkeeper does not worry about the order in which the items are entered when setting up the spreadsheet. When the spreadsheet is in use, it will be most convenient for

	A	B	C	D	E	F
1	Item	Unit	Quantity	Sales	% Profit	Profit on
2	Name	Price	Sold	Value	on Sales	Sales
3						
4	Amplifier	209.99		.00	25	.00
5	Cassette player	86.56		.00	25	.00
6	CD player	150.45		.00	25	.00
7	Electric cooker	367.99		.00	30	.00
8	Freezer	199.95		.00	30	.00
9	Fridge	149.09		.00	30	.00
10	Gas cooker	287.55		.00	30	.00
11	Gas hob	101.01		.00	30	.00
12	Radio	34.67		.00	20	.00
13	Radio alarm	35.99		.00	20	.00
14	Record player	119.95		.00	25	.00
15	Tuner	149.95		.00	25	.00
16	TV	345.99		.00	25	.00
17						
18			Total		Total	
19			Sales	.00	Profit	.00
20						

Fig. 10.6a The spreadsheet as it was set up showing the values displayed

	A	B	C	D	E	F
1	Item	Unit	Quantity	Sales	% Profit	Profit on
2	Name	Price	Sold	Value	on Sales	Sales
3						
4	Amplifier	209.99		B4*C4	25	D4*E4/100
5	Cassette player	86.56		B5*C5	25	D5*E5/100
6	CD player	150.45		B6*C6	25	D6*E6/100
7	Electric cooker	367.99		B7*C7	30	D7*E7/100
8	Freezer	199.95		B8*C8	30	D8*E8/100
9	Fridge	149.09		B9*C9	30	D9*E9/100
10	Gas cooker	287.55		B10*C10	30	D10*E10/100
11	Gas hob	101.01		B11*C11	30	D11*E11/100
12	Radio	34.67		B12*C12	20	D12*E12/100
13	Radio alarm	35.99		B13*C13	20	D13*E13/100
14	Record player	119.95		B14*C14	25	D14*E14/100
15	Tuner	149.95		B15*C15	25	D15*E15/100
16	TV	345.99		B16*C16	25	D16*E16/100
17						
18			Total		Total	
19			Sales	SUM(D4:D16)	Profit	SUM(F4:F16)
20						

Fig. 10.6b The spreadsheet showing the underlying formulae

the shopkeeper to have the list of items with their names in alphabetical order, however, the items can be sorted into this order later. Similarly, when the system has been in use for some time and the shopkeeper wishes to add extra items to the spreadsheet, these can be added at the bottom and the spreadsheet sorted.

When the shopkeeper has set up the spreadsheet, the cells containing the formulae and the row and column headings are protected so that they cannot be altered accidentally. The spreadsheet is then saved on backing storage and a backup copy made. This secures the basic spreadsheet that will be used each day to calculate the total value of sales and to provide other useful sales information. The shopkeeper will always start to use the spreadsheet, at the end of the day, by loading it as it is now set up.

Data capture

Data capture takes place when the shopkeeper fills in a receipt for a customer who is buying something from the shop. The shopkeeper fills in the receipt when goods are sold. The receipt is written on a two part carbonized pad so that both the customer and the shopkeeper have copies of the receipt.

'Data capture is important'

The shopkeeper collects the copies of all the receipts written during the day. At the end of the day the shopkeeper goes through these receipts making a note of the total quantity sold of each item. These are accumulated on the form shown in Fig. 10.4.

Input and processing

Fig. 10.7 shows the spreadsheet *after* the shopkeeper has entered the quantity sold for each item at the end of a day. It is important to note that the shopkeeper has only **input** the quantity sold for each item. The value of sales of each item, the profit on sales, the total value of sales and the total profit were automatically calculated using the formulae stored in these cells when the spreadsheet was set up. The **processing** done by the spreadsheet is the automatic calculation of the actual values from formulae already programmed into the cells. This is done automatically when numeric values are input into the appropriate cells.

Output

Output from a spreadsheet is simply a screen display or printout of the whole of the spreadsheet, a part of it or a graph generated from it. The output can be sorted or ordered according to its use.

A list of goods sold in the shop and their prices

'Lists can help the shop keeper'

The shopkeeper may want a list of items sold in the shop and their prices for the shop assistants to refer to. This can be printed from the spreadsheet while it is displayed with the items sorted into alphabetic order. However, the shopkeeper does not want the assistants to see the sales information. Consequently, only part of the spreadsheet is printed (see Fig. 10.8).

	A	B	C	D	E	F
1	Item	Unit	Quantity	Sales	% Profit	Profit on
2	Name	Price	Sold	Value	on Sales	Sales
3						
4	Amplifier	209.99	1	209.99	25	52.50
5	Cassette player	86.56	2	173.12	25	43.28
6	CD player	150.45	3	451.35	25	112.84
7	Electric cooker	367.99	5	1839.95	30	551.99
8	Freezer	199.95	2	399.90	30	119.97
9	Fridge	149.09	4	596.36	30	178.91
10	Gas cooker	287.55	6	1725.30	30	517.59
11	Gas hob	101.01	6	606.06	30	181.82
12	Radio	34.67	6	208.02	20	41.60
13	Radio alarm	35.99	5	179.95	20	35.99
14	Record player	119.95	2	239.90	25	59.98
15	Tuner	149.95	1	149.95	25	37.49
16	TV	345.99	1	345.99	25	86.50
17						
18			Total		Total	
19			Sales	7125.84	Profit	2020.44
20						

Fig. 10.7 The spreadsheet after the shopkeeper has entered the quantities sold

```
         :         A      :: B  :
    1   Item            Unit
    2   Name            Price
    3   _____
    4   Amplifier        209.99
    5   Cassette player   86.56
    6   CD player        150.45
    7   Electric cooker  367.99
    8   Freezer          199.95
    9   Fridge           149.09
   10   Gas cooker       287.55
   11   Gas hob          101.01
   12   Radio             34.67
   13   Radio alarm       35.99
   14   Record player    119.95
   15   Tuner            149.95
   16   TV               345.99
   17   _____
```

Fig. 10.8 A list of items sold in the shop, and their prices

Output with the goods that sell the most first

The spreadsheet can be sorted so that those items which *sell the most* will be displayed first. This is achieved by sorting the rows in descending numeric order on the quantity sold (see Fig. 10.9). Sorting the spreadsheet into this order will be useful to the shopkeeper in finding out which are the best selling items. The shopkeeper will find this information useful when ordering goods. It will be necessary to order more of the items with high sales volumes, more frequently, than those that sell in lower quantities. It may also be necessary to keep higher stocks of the better selling items.

'The order can be important'

Output with the goods with the highest price first

The spreadsheet can be sorted so that the *highest priced items* appear first. That is, the spreadsheet is displayed after being sorted into descending numeric order on the unit price (see Fig. 10.10). A display in this order identifies those items which are highly priced. These items may need to be kept more securely.

Output with the goods that make the least profit first

A listing of the spreadsheet with the goods that *make the least profit* first (see Fig. 10.11) helps the shopkeeper identify goods that are not profitable. These may not be re-ordered. At the bottom of the list will be the most profitable goods. These should be re-ordered as stocks are sold. The shopkeeper can maximize profits by reducing the stock of goods that make low profits and increasing the stock of goods that make high profits.

	Item Name	Unit Price	Quantity Sold	Sales Value	% Profit on Sales	Profit on Sales
4	Gas cooker	287.55	6	1725.30	30	517.59
5	Gas hob	101.01	6	606.06	30	181.82
6	Radio	34.67	6	208.02	20	41.60
7	Electric cooker	367.99	5	1839.95	30	551.99
8	Radio alarm	35.99	5	179.95	20	35.99
9	Fridge	149.09	4	596.36	30	178.91
10	CD player	150.45	3	451.35	25	112.84
11	Cassette player	86.56	2	173.12	25	43.28
12	Freezer	199.95	2	399.90	30	119.97
13	Record player	119.95	2	239.90	25	59.98
14	Amplifier	209.99	1	209.99	25	52.50
15	Tuner	149.95	1	149.95	25	37.49
16	TV	345.99	1	345.99	25	86.50
18			Total Sales	7125.84	Total Profit	2020.44

Fig. 10.9 The spreadsheet rearranged in order of the quantity sold

Graphs

'A visual display can help'   A *bar chart* showing the value of sales and profits (see Fig. 10.12) will provide further help to the shop keeper in identifying which items should be stocked.

	A	B Unit Price	C Quantity Sold	D Sales Value	E % Profit on Sales	F Profit on Sales
1	Item					
2	Name					
3						
4	Electric cooker	367.99	5	1839.95	30	551.99
5	TV	345.99	1	345.99	25	86.50
6	Gas cooker	287.55	6	1725.30	30	517.59
7	Amplifier	209.99	1	209.99	25	52.50
8	Freezer	199.95	2	399.90	30	119.97
9	CD player	150.45	3	451.35	25	112.84
10	Tuner	149.95	1	149.95	25	37.49
11	Fridge	149.09	4	596.36	30	178.91
12	Record player	119.95	2	239.90	25	59.98
13	Gas hob	101.01	6	606.06	30	181.82
14	Cassette player	86.56	2	173.12	25	43.28
15	Radio alarm	35.99	5	179.95	20	35.99
16	Radio	34.67	6	208.02	20	41.60
17						
18			Total		Total	
19			Sales	7125.84	Profit	2020.44

Fig. 10.10 The spreadsheet rearranged in order of unit price

	A	B Unit Price	C Quantity Sold	D Sales Value	E % Profit on Sales	F Profit on Sales
1	Item					
2	Name					
3						
4	Radio alarm	35.99	5	179.95	20	35.99
5	Tuner	149.95	1	149.95	25	37.49
6	Radio	34.67	6	208.02	20	41.60
7	Cassette player	86.56	2	173.12	25	43.28
8	Amplifier	209.99	1	209.99	25	52.50
9	Record player	119.95	2	239.90	25	59.98
10	TV	345.99	1	345.99	25	86.50
11	CD player	150.45	3	451.35	25	112.84
12	Freezer	199.95	2	399.90	30	119.97
13	Fridge	149.09	4	596.36	30	178.91
14	Gas hob	101.01	6	606.06	30	181.82
15	Gas cooker	287.55	6	1725.30	30	517.59
16	Electric cooker	367.99	5	1839.95	30	551.99
17						
18			Total		Total	
19			Sales	7125.84	Profit	2020.44

Fig. 10.11 The spreadsheet rearranged with the least profitable goods first

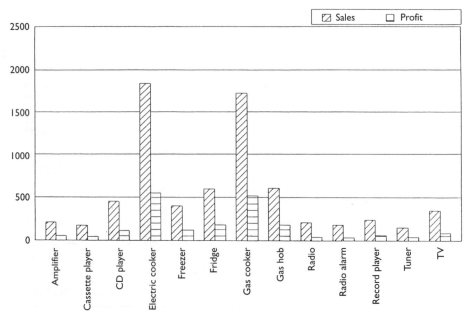

Fig. 10.12 A bar chart showing the value of sales and profits

Evaluation

Various essential items of information, such as Value Added Tax (VAT), have been left out. VAT is added to all sales of electrical goods. The VAT payable should be shown for each item and as a total for the shop.

As the number of items sold in the shop increases, confusion may arise between items with similar names. This should be avoided by giving each item stocked a *unique* item code.

This spreadsheet-based information system is of limited effectiveness. It will make useful stock control and sales data available more easily. However, the task of working out the quantity of each item sold each day will still need to be done by the shopkeeper. This is likely to be a very time consuming task. The system might not function effectively if it had to deal with a large number of customers. The need to do this task manually can be avoided by purchasing new checkout tills that print a receipt for the customer and at the same time save a record of the sale on a magnetic tape or disk connected to the till. At the end of the day the sales records for all the tills, recorded on magnetic tape or disk, can be read into the computer where the quantity sold of each item will be calculated for use in the spreadsheet.

▷ Modelling

'Models are all around us'

Models are representations of the real world. We are all familiar with some form of model. Our earliest introduction to **modelling** is likely to be moulding plasticine or clay to make representations of people or animals. You can buy toy soldiers and model cars; dolls and dolls houses. They are all models, that is, representations of the real world. Models in some form are used throughout commerce and industry. You can build a physical model of a shopping centre or other building project to demonstrate the architectural style and layout of the planned development. Models of such developments can also be built using computer software.

It is essential to remember that a model is a *representation* of the real world. It is *not* the real world. You cannot expect reality to be exactly like a model of it. The better the model, the more exactly it copies reality. The advantage of using models is that they allow us to experiment with reality. We can try out strategies and forecast what will happen. However, a forecast is based on experience of the past. The future may not mimic the past. Consequently, we must treat forecasts based on models with care.

'You can try out
strategies on models'

This ability to try out strategies is an important use of models. Models are safe. Managers do not have to bankrupt their employers when trying out new commercial strategies; farmers have no need to devastate their crops by blindly trying new methods of pest control. Whilst exploring a model is unlikely to lead us to the perfect solution to our problems, we may well improve our understanding of them and discover a range of useful strategies to tackle them.

Spreadsheet models

Spreadsheets can be used for a variety of tasks. You can use spreadsheets to record information from day-to-day and to do simple calculations.

Using a spreadsheet for storing, organizing or presenting information is not modelling. When a model is constructed using a spreadsheet, there is an intention to use it to improve understanding of a real system, for problem solving or for prediction. You are using a spreadsheet for modelling when you ask questions like 'What would happen if this input was changed? Would it solve the problem?'

The **stock control information system** described earlier in this chapter is mainly used to record what is sold and to do simple addition and multiplication. It could be used as a model, for example, to predict how sales affect profits, but its main focus is not prediction.

A spreadsheet model would be constructed with the intention to use it mainly to improve understanding of a real system, for problem solving or for prediction.

A spreadsheet-based model will:

'Aspects of a
spreadsheet-based model'

▷   Allow a range of input variables to be set.
▷   Use formulae to define the rules on which the model is based.
▷   Output information based on the input variables, the stored values, and the rules.

Typically, a spreadsheet-based model will have a limited number of input variables. These variables will be processed using the rules defined by the structure of the spreadsheet and the underlying formulae. The rules will reflect the assumptions made by the author about the relationships evident in the real world. These relationships will be built into the model. However, the author may have simplified these relationships or otherwise modified them. The rules built into a model when it is constructed do not always exactly reflect the real world.

The models described below are constructed using a spreadsheet. You may be expected to set up such models yourself. Alternatively, your teacher may set them up for you and you would be expected to explore the extent to which they represent the real world and to adjust the underlying rules so that they more closely mimic reality.

▷ **Price forecast model**

'Input variables'

'Rules'

A **price forecast model** is shown in Fig. 10.13. The model is used to predict the price of a commodity over a span of ten years.

The *input variables* are the initial price, the base year and the rate of inflation. These are changed when the model is used.

The *rules* are the formulae in the cells A13 to A22 and B13 to B22 (see Fig. 10.13(b)). For example, the effect of the formula in B13 is to increase the initial price copied into B12 by the percentage input in C5. This is done using the formula:

B12*(1+C5/100)

In Fig. 10.13(a), this gives:

£100.00*(1+7.5/100)
= £100.00*1.075
= £107.50

This increases £100.00 by 7.5% to £107.50 as shown.

'Absolute and relative cell references'

It is worth noting that $C$5 refers to the same cell as C5. $C$5 is an absolute cell reference which does not change when the cell is copied. This is an important distinction when setting up a model. In setting up the price forecast model, B13 was copied into cells B14 to B22. As this was done, the relative cell references changed. B12 changed to B13 as the formula was copied from B13 into B14; B13 changed to B14 as the formula was copied from B14 into B15; and so on. This pattern of changes was repeated as B13 was copied to cells B14 to B22. However, to prevent C5 from being changed, it was set up as an absolute cell reference by using $C$5. Although spreadsheets differ in the way they define relative and absolute cell references, they will all have some method of showing which is which. Setting up models is much easier if formulae can be copied from one cell to another with appropriate adjustment, if required.

'Output'

The *information output* from the model is the price adjusted for inflation over a ten year span. This can be used, for example, to predict the price of goods worth £100 in 1994 in up to ten years time (see Fig. 10.13(a)).

The model uses the average inflation figure over a ten-year period. This is reasonable providing you do not assume that inflation will be constant over the ten-year period. Inflation will rise and fall. The actual price each year may fluctuate considerably from the model. However, over a ten-year period, the model may adequately represents the overall trend in price inflation.

```
          |   A    ||   B   ||  C   ||  D  |
1         Price forecasting
2
3         _____
4         Initial price        Rate of inflation
5             £100.00               7.5 percent
6
7         Base year
8             1994
9         _____
10
11            Year      Price
12            1994      100.00
13            1995      107.50
14            1996      115.56
15            1997      124.23
16            1998      133.55
17            1999      143.56
18            2000      154.33
19            2001      165.90
20            2002      178.35
21            2003      191.72
22            2004      206.10
23
```

Fig. 10.13a The price forecast model with 1994 as the base year

```
              |    A     | |       B     | |  C  | |  D  |
          1  Price forecasting
          2
          3  _____
          4  Initial price              Rate of inflation
          5  74.80                           3.5 percent
          6
          7  Base year
          8  1985
          9  _____
         10
         11            Year              Price
         12  A8                           A5
         13  A12+1        B12*(1+$C$5/100)
         14  A13+1        B13*(1+$C$5/100)
         15  A14+1        B14*(1+$C$5/100)
         16  A15+1        B15*(1+$C$5/100)
         17  A16+1        B16*(1+$C$5/100)
         18  A17+1        B17*(1+$C$5/100)
         19  A18+1        B18*(1+$C$5/100)
         20  A19+1        B19*(1+$C$5/100)
         21  A20+1        B20*(1+$C$5/100)
         22  A21+1        B21*(1+$C$5/100)
```

Fig. 10.13b The formulae used in the model

> **Supermarket queue model**

A **supermarket queue model** is shown in Fig. 10.14. The model can be used to regulate the time a customer spends in the queue at a checkout.

```
              |     A      | |     B     | |     C      |
          1  Shopping queue model
          2
          3  _____ INPUTS: _____
          4
          5  Number of       Number        Time to get a
          6  people             of        person through a
          7  waiting        checkouts     checkout (mins)
          8     50              10                2.00
          9  _____
         10  OUTPUTS:
         11
         12  Average number     Last
         13  of people        person
         14  queuing per     wait time
         15  checkout         (mins)
         16     5              10.00
```

Fig. 10.14a The model of the supermarket shopping queue showing a waiting time of ten minutes

```
              |     A      | |     B     | |     C      |
          1  Shopping queue model
          2
          3  _____ INPUTS: _____
          4
          5  Number of       Number        Time to get a
          6  people             of        person through a
          7  waiting        checkouts     checkout (mins)
          8     50              20                2.00
          9  _____
         10  OUTPUTS:
         11
         12  Average number     Last
         13  of people        person
         14  queuing per     wait time
         15  checkout         (mins)
         16     3               5.00
```

Fig. 10.14b The model showing the waiting time reduced to five minutes by increasing the number of checkouts

```
!    A    !!     B    !!        C        !
 1  Shopping queue model
 2                      _____
 3       INPUTS:
 4
 5   Number of        Number      Time to get a
 6    people            of      person through a
 7    waiting        checkouts    checkout (mins)
 8       50              10                 1.00
 9                      _____
10       OUTPUTS:
11
12  Average number      Last
13    of people        person
14   queuing per     wait time
15    checkout        (mins)
16        5             5.00
```

Fig. 10.14c The waiting time reduced to five minutes by reducing the time taken to pass through a checkout

```
!    A    !!     B    !!        C        !  .
 1  Shopping queue model
 2                      _____
 3       INPUTS:
 4
 5   Number of        Number      Time to get a
 6    people            of      person through a
 7    waiting        checkouts    checkout (mins)
 8       50              10                 2.00
 9                      _____
10       OUTPUTS:
11
12  Average number      Last
13    of people        person
14   queuing per     wait time
15    checkout        (mins)
16      A8/B8          A16*C8
```

Fig. 10.14d The formulae used

'Input variables'

The input variables are the number of people waiting, the number of checkouts in use, and the time it takes to get a person through a checkout, that is, the time taken to serve a customer at a checkout. These are changed when the model is used.

The rules are the formulae in cells A16 and B16 (see Fig. 10.14(d)). The formula in A16 is:

A8/B8

This represents the relationship:

$$\text{The average number of people queuing per checkout} = \frac{\text{The number of people waiting}}{\text{The number of checkouts in use}}$$

The formula in B16 is:

A16*C8

This represents the relationship:

$$\text{The time the last person in a queue has to wait} = \left(\begin{array}{l} \text{The average number} \\ \text{of people queuing} \\ \text{per checkout} \end{array} \right) \times \left(\begin{array}{l} \text{The time to get} \\ \text{a person through} \\ \text{a checkout} \end{array} \right)$$

The information output from the model is the average number of people in a checkout queue, and the length of time the last person in the queue will have to wait. A supermarket manager could use the model to quickly see the effect of adjusting the number of checkouts and the time taken to get a person through a checkout. For example, Fig. 10.14(a) shows the last person wait time to be ten minutes. If the manager considers this unacceptable, the model can be used to explore alternatives. Suppose the manager wished to reduce the last person wait time to five minutes. The input variables could be adjusted to show how this can be done. In Fig. 10.14(b), a five minute wait time is achieved by increasing the number of checkouts to 20. This would double the costs involved, for example, the wages paid to checkout operators. In Fig. 10.14(c), a five minute wait time is achieved by reducing the time to get a person through a checkout to one minute. This might involve training staff, introducing a productivity scheme or buying more up-to-date checkout technology. Other solutions could be found by both increasing the number of checkouts and reducing the time to get a person through a checkout.

The model assumes that there will be a steady flow of customers to the checkouts, that they will distribute themselves equally across all the checkouts, that every checkout operator works at the same speed, that the overall quantity of goods bought remains the same, and that people will not get tired of waiting and simply leave. These assumptions are needed so that a simple, understandable model can be constructed.

▷ Break even model

A break even model is shown in Fig. 10.15. The model can be used to find the break even point. This is the point at which the total value of sales equals the total cost of production. Above the break even point companies can expect to make a profit; below the break even point they will make a loss.

To illustrate what is meant by the 'break even point' and to show why it is most important to find it, the example of a company making up T-shirts is used. The company buys in cloth and makes the cloth into T-shirts.

The spreadsheet in Fig. 10.15(a), shows that the T-shirts are sold for £6.50 each. The cost to the company of making up the T-shirts is made up of fixed costs and variable costs. The fixed costs are expenses such as the rent that must be paid for the buildings and equipment the company uses. These do not vary with the quantity of T-shirts sold and must be paid regularly and promptly. The variable costs are those that depend on the number of T-shirts sold, for example, the amount of cloth used.

The company needs to know when it is making a profit. The profit made depends on the number of T-shirts sold. If the company sells a large quantity of T-shirts, it can expect to make a profit. However, the company needs to know exactly how many T-shirts it has to sell to make a profit. The break even point is the sales quantity at which the value of sales equals the total cost of producing the T-shirts. When the company sells more T-shirts than the break even point, it makes a profit; when it sells less than the break even point, it makes a loss.

The input variables to be entered in the spreadsheet are the fixed costs, the variable costs, the selling price per T-shirt, the quantity base and the quantity increment. The quantity base and the quantity increment are used to adjust the range of sales quantities the spreadsheet covers. To find the break even point, you would first enter the fixed cost, the

	A	B	C	D	E
1	Break even model				
2					
3	Fixed	Quantity	Variable Cost		Selling Price
4	Cost	Base	per unit		per unit
5	£400.00	100	£5.00		£6.50
6					
7		Quantity			
8		Increment			
9		50			
10					
11	Fixed	Quantity	Variable	Total	Value of
12	Cost	Sold	Cost	Cost	Sales
13	400.00	100	500.00	900.00	650.00
14	400.00	150	750.00	1150.00	975.00
15	400.00	200	1000.00	1400.00	1300.00
16	400.00	250	1250.00	1650.00	1625.00
17	400.00	300	1500.00	1900.00	1950.00
18	400.00	350	1750.00	2150.00	2275.00
19	400.00	400	2000.00	2400.00	2600.00
20	400.00	450	2250.00	2650.00	2925.00
21	400.00	500	2500.00	2900.00	3250.00
22	400.00	550	2750.00	3150.00	3575.00
23	400.00	600	3000.00	3400.00	3900.00
24	400.00	650	3250.00	3650.00	4225.00

Fig. 10.15a The break even model: first attempt, with base 100 and increment 50

```
        |   A     ||    B    ||    C    ||    D    ||    E    |
    1   Break even model
    2
    3        Fixed   Quantity Variable Cost           Selling Price
    4        Cost      Base    per unit                  per unit
    5      £400.00     250      £5.00                      £6.50
    6
    7                Quantity
    8                Increment
    9                    5
   10
   11        Fixed   Quantity      Variable       Total        Value of
   12        Cost      Sold          Cost         Cost          Sales
   13       400.00     250         1250.00      1650.00       1625.00
   14       400.00     255         1275.00      1675.00       1657.50
   15       400.00     260         1300.00      1700.00       1690.00
   16       400.00     265         1325.00      1725.00       1722.50
   17       400.00     270         1350.00      1750.00       1755.00
   18       400.00     275         1375.00      1775.00       1787.50
   19       400.00     280         1400.00      1800.00       1820.00
   20       400.00     285         1425.00      1825.00       1852.50
   21       400.00     290         1450.00      1850.00       1885.00
   22       400.00     295         1475.00      1875.00       1917.50
   23       400.00     300         1500.00      1900.00       1950.00
   24       400.00     305         1525.00      1925.00       1982.50
```

Fig. 10.15b Second attempt, with base 250 and increment 5

```
        |   A     ||    B    ||    C    ||    D    ||    E    |
    1   Break even model
    2
    3        Fixed   Quantity Variable Cost           Selling Price
    4        Cost      Base    per unit                  per unit
    5      £400.00     265      £5.00                      £6.50
    6
    7                Quantity
    8                Increment
    9                    1
   10
   11        Fixed   Quantity      Variable       Total        Value of
   12        Cost      Sold          Cost         Cost          Sales
   13       400.00     265         1325.00      1725.00       1722.50
   14       400.00     266         1330.00      1730.00       1729.00
   15       400.00     267         1335.00      1735.00       1735.50
   16       400.00     268         1340.00      1740.00       1742.00
   17       400.00     269         1345.00      1745.00       1748.50
   18       400.00     270         1350.00      1750.00       1755.00
   19       400.00     271         1355.00      1755.00       1761.50
   20       400.00     272         1360.00      1760.00       1768.00
   21       400.00     273         1365.00      1765.00       1774.50
   22       400.00     274         1370.00      1770.00       1781.00
   23       400.00     275         1375.00      1775.00       1787.50
   24       400.00     276         1380.00      1780.00       1794.00
```

Fig. 10.15c Third attempt, with base 265 and increment 1

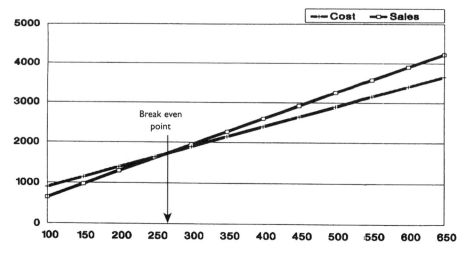

Fig. 10.15d A line graph indicating the break even point

	A	B	C	D	E
1	Break even model				
2					
3	Fixed	Quantity	Variable Cost		Selling Price
4	Cost	Base	per unit		per unit
5	£400.00	100	£5.00		£6.50
6					
7		Quantity			
8		Increment			
9		50			
10					
11	Fixed	Quantity	Variable	Total	Value of
12	Cost	Sold	Cost	Cost	Sales
13	A5	B5	B13*$C$5	A13+C13	B13*$E$5
14	A13	B13+$B$9	B14*$C$5	A14+C14	B14*$E$5
15	A14	B14+$B$9	B15*$C$5	A15+C15	B15*$E$5
16	A15	B15+$B$9	B16*$C$5	A16+C16	B16*$E$5
17	A16	B16+$B$9	B17*$C$5	A17+C17	B17*$E$5
18	A17	B17+$B$9	B18*$C$5	A18+C18	B18*$E$5
19	A18	B18+$B$9	B19*$C$5	A19+C19	B19*$E$5
20	A19	B19+$B$9	B20*$C$5	A20+C20	B20*$E$5
21	A20	B20+$B$9	B21*$C$5	A21+C21	B21*$E$5
22	A21	B21+$B$9	B22*$C$5	A22+C22	B22*$E$5
23	A22	B22+$B$9	B23*$C$5	A23+C23	B23*$E$5
24	A23	B23+$B$9	B24*$C$5	A24+C24	B24*$E$5

Fig. 10.15e The formulae used

variable cost and the selling price. You would then adjust the quantity base and the quantity increment to help you find the break even point.

The formulae used are shown in Fig. 10.15(e).

The formulae in cells A13 to A24 copy the value of fixed costs entered in A5.

In cell B13, the value entered for the quantity base is copied. The formulae in cells B14 to B24 add the quantity increment in C5 to the contents of the cell immediately above them. This ensures that the quantity sold increases by the quantity increment starting at the quantity base. For example, in Fig. 10.15(a), the quantity base is 100 and the quantity increment is 50. This ensures the quantities sold start at 100 and go up 50 at a time to give 100, 150, 200, 250, etc.

The formulae in C13 to C24 calculate the variable costs for the relevant quantity sold, using the formula:

variable cost = quantity sold * variable cost per unit

The total cost is calculated in D13 to D24 by adding the corresponding fixed and variable costs.

The value of sales in E13 to E24, is worked out using this formula:

value of sales = selling price per unit * quantity sold

'Finding the break even point'

The model can be used to find the break even point by adjusting the quantity base and the quantity increment. Suppose the T-shirts are selling for £6.50 each, fixed costs are £400 and variable costs per unit sold are £5.00.(see Fig. 10.15(a)). Setting the quantity base at 100 and the increment at 50 generates a table of total costs and the corresponding value of sales. The break even point is where the total cost is equal to the value of sales. Fig. 10.15(a) shows that the break even point must lie between the sales quantities of 250 and 300 because between these quantities the value of sales moves from being less than total cost to being more than total cost. Using 250 as the quantity base and an increment of 5 (see Fig. 10.15(b)), indicates that the break even point lies between 265 and 270. This suggests a quantity base of 265 and an increment of 1 (see Fig. 10.15(c)). At a quantity sold of 267 the total cost equals the value of sales. This is the break even point.

The break even model can be used to explore the options available to the company as it seeks to remain profitable in a competitive market. For example, it can be used to find solutions to operating problems such as those that arise due to price competition. If it is necessary to lower prices due to competition, what can be done and what are the likely effects? The company could seek to reduce fixed and variable costs or try to sell more. The break even model can be used to indicate the different impact of these strategies.

The model assumes that fixed costs do not increase as sales quantities increase. This is reasonable for relatively small changes in sales quantities. However, if sales quantities increase significantly so that, for example, larger premises are required, fixed costs may well go up. This consideration could be built into a more complex model.

It is also assumed that variable costs remain the same per T-shirt. This is unlikely to be the case. For example, as sales quantities increase, the company will use more cloth in making the T-shirts. Purchasing larger quantities will usually attract more discount than buying smaller quantities. This reduces the variable cost per T-shirt. The company can either make more profit or pass on the discount in price reductions in the hope of attracting even more sales. Again, a more complex model might have this consideration built into it so that it more exactly represents the company's operating environment.

The company is unlikely to make only one product, that is, a T-shirt selling for a single price. It is likely to sell a range of differently priced T-shirts or other similar products such as shirts, skirts, etc. These affect the overall break even point for the company. It will need to look at all its products and their cost of production when trying to find the overall break even point. The break even model shown here could be adapted to include more than one product.

Despite its limitations, an understanding of the break even model is essential in predicting when profits will be made and forecasting the effect of changes in costs and market price on the profitability of a company.

▷ Predator/prey model

Predator/prey models can be used to explore the relationship between predators and their prey. The particular example used here looks at the relationship between birds and the grubs they eat. Understanding these relationships is increasingly important as farming becomes more organic and less dependant on the use of pesticides, etc.

Imagine that a crop of cabbages is being attacked by grubs. These will destroy the whole crop if they are not controlled. The farmer uses pesticides to control the grubs. When pesticides are used, the whole population of grubs is killed. The birds that eat the grubs die too. The following year, the crop attracts more grubs. The grubs breed rapidly un-checked by the birds. The farmer now has no choice but to use pesticides as the birds that ate the grubs have died. Having once used pesticides, the farmer must use them every year.

The farmer could use the birds to control the grubs, instead of using pesticides. In this case the farmer would not wipe out the grubs but would try to regulate them. The ideal is an equilibrium state where the bird population and the grub population are both stable. The equilibrium should be established at a level where the grub population is a minimum so that little damage is done to the crop.

The spreadsheet in Fig. 10.16, illustrates this predator/prey relationship. The numbers have been kept small for simplicity. It is assumed that the birds breed in May and die in October; the grub population increases every month; the grubs breed at a different rate from April to September than during the rest of the year; the birds eat a fixed number of grubs each month and die if they do not get them.

The input variables to be entered in the spreadsheet are the number of birds and their breeding rate and death rate; the number of grubs the birds eat each month; the number of grubs and their breeding rate from October to March and from April to September. The number of birds and the number of grubs at the start of the year are also entered.

The formulae used are shown in Fig. 10.16(d).

The formula in cell C17 copies the number of grubs at the start from A12 and that in B17 copies the number of birds at the start from A7.

The formulae in C18 to C29 can be expressed in pseudo code, as follows:

IF the number of grubs that remain IS MORE THAN zero
THEN the value of the cell is the number of grubs that remain
ELSE the value of the cell is zero

The number of grubs that remain is calculated using the formula:

$$\begin{pmatrix} \text{The number} \\ \text{of grubs} \\ \text{that} \\ \text{remain} \end{pmatrix} = \begin{pmatrix} \text{The number} \\ \text{of grubs in} \\ \text{the previous} \\ \text{month} \end{pmatrix} \times \begin{pmatrix} \text{The} \\ \text{breeding rate} \end{pmatrix} - \begin{pmatrix} \text{The number} \\ \text{of birds} \end{pmatrix} \times \begin{pmatrix} \text{The number} \\ \text{of grubs} \\ \text{one bird} \\ \text{eats} \end{pmatrix}$$

```
        ¦    A    ¦¦    B    ¦¦    C    ¦¦    D    ¦¦    E    ¦
   1    Predator/prey model: birds vs grubs
   2                                        _____
   3    BIRDS:
   4                 breeding      death                   Birds
   5    Number         rate         rate                    eat
   6    at start      in May       in Oct                    4
   7           10         2           .5                  grubs
   8
   9    GRUBS:        breeding     breeding
  10                  rate in      rate in
  11    at start      Oct-Mar      Apr-Sept
  12         40          2            3
  13
  14                                        _____
  15                Number of    Number of
  16    Start of      birds        grubs
  17    Jan            10           40
  18    Feb            10           40
  19    March          10           40
  20    April          20           40
  21    May            20           40
  22    June           20           40
  23    July           20           40
  24    Aug            20           40
  25    Sept           20           40
  26    Oct            10           40
  27    Nov            10           40
  28    Dec            10           40
  29    Jan            10           40
```

Fig. 10.16a The predator/prey model: birds vs grubs, the equilibrium state

```
        ¦    A    ¦¦    B    ¦¦    C    ¦¦    D    ¦¦    E    ¦
   1    Predator/prey model: birds vs grubs
   2                                        _____
   3    BIRDS:
   4                 breeding      death                   Birds
   5    Number         rate         rate                    eat
   6    at start      in May       in Oct                    4
   7           10         2           .75                 grubs
   8
   9    GRUBS:        breeding     breeding
  10                  rate in      rate in
  11    at start      Oct-Mar      Apr-Sept
  12         40          2            3
  13
  14                                        _____
  15                Number of    Number of
  16    Start of      birds        grubs
  17    Jan            10           40
  18    Feb            10           40
  19    March          10           40
  20    April          20           40
  21    May            20           40
  22    June           20           40
  23    July           20           40
  24    Aug            20           40
  25    Sept           20           40
  26    Oct             5           60
  27    Nov             5          100
  28    Dec             5          180
  29    Jan             5          340
```

Fig. 10.16b More birds die in October: the grub population increases out of control

The formulae in B18 to B29 can be expressed in pseudo code as follows:

IF there are sufficient grubs to eat
THEN all the birds survive
ELSE only those birds that can be fed survive

The formula in B20, C20, B26 and C26 take into account the birds' breeding rate in May and their death rate in April.

Fig. 10.16(a) shows the equilibrium state for the model. This shows a situation where there are sufficient grubs to feed a stable bird population. The bird population in turn sta-

	A	B	C	D	E
1	Predator/prey model: birds vs grubs				
2					
3	BIRDS:				
4		breeding	death		Birds
5	Number	rate	rate		eat
6	at start	in May	in Oct		4
7	10	2	.25		grubs
8					
9	GRUBS:	breeding	breeding		
10		rate in	rate in		
11	at start	Oct-Mar	Apr-Sept		
12	40	2	3		
13					
14					
15		Number of	Number of		
16	Start of	birds	grubs		
17	Jan	10	40		
18	Feb	10	40		
19	March	10	40		
20	April	20	40		
21	May	20	40		
22	June	20	40		
23	July	20	40		
24	Aug	20	40		
25	Sept	20	40		
26	Oct	15	20		
27	Nov	10	0		
28	Dec	0	0		
29	Jan	0	0		

Fig. 10.16c Fewer birds die in October: all grubs and birds die

	A	B	C
1	Predator/prey model: birds vs grubs		
14			
15		Number of	Number of
16	Start of	birds	grubs
17	Jan	A7	A12
18	Feb	IF(C18>0,B17,INT(C17/4))	IF(C17*$B$12-B17*$E$6>0,C17*$B$12-B17*$E$6,0)
19	March	IF(C19>0,B18,INT(C18/4))	IF(C18*$B$12-B18*$E$6>0,C18*$B$12-B18*$E$6,0)
20	April	IF(C20>0,B19*$B$7,INT(C19/4))	IF(C19*$C$12-B19*$E$6*B7>0,C19*$C$12-B19*$E$6*B7,0)
21	May	IF(C21>0,B20,INT(C20/4))	IF(C20*$C$12-B20*$E$6>0,C20*$C$12-B20*$E$6,0)
22	June	IF(C22>0,B21,INT(C21/4))	IF(C21*$C$12-B21*$E$6>0,C21*$C$12-B21*$E$6,0)
23	July	IF(C23>0,B22,INT(C22/4))	IF(C22*$C$12-B22*$E$6>0,C22*$C$12-B22*$E$6,0)
24	Aug	IF(C24>0,B23,INT(C23/4))	IF(C23*$C$12-B23*$E$6>0,C23*$C$12-B23*$E$6,0)
25	Sept	IF(C25>0,B24,INT(C24/4))	IF(C24*$C$12-B24*$E$6>0,C24*$C$12-B24*$E$6,0)
26	Oct	IF(C26>0,B25*(1-$C$7),INT(C25/4))	IF(C25*$B$12-B25*$E$6*(1-$C$7)>0,C25*$B$12-B25*$E$6*(1-
27	Nov	IF(C27>0,B26,INT(C25/4))	IF(C26*$B$12-B26*$E$6>0,C26*$B$12-B26*$E$6,0)
28	Dec	IF(C28>0,B27,INT(C27/4))	IF(C27*$B$12-B27*$E$6>0,C27*$B$12-B27*$E$6,0)
29	Jan	IF(C29>0,B28,INT(C28/4))	IF(C28*$B$12-B28*$E$6>0,C28*$B$12-B28*$E$6,0)
30			

Fig. 10.16d The formulae used in the predator/prey model

bilizes the size of the grub population. The equilibrium state can be recognized by comparing the figures for the first January with the following January. These should be the same, i.e. we should have B17 = B29 and C17 = C29 for equilibrium. If the same rules hold every year, then if we end the year as we start it, we must once again start and end with the same values. This equilibrium state is not unique. There will a large number of different settings of the input variables that will lead to an equilibrium state.

Models such as this can be used to find a suitable equilibrium state. The farmer would start with the input variables set to the values estimated by observation. By changing these variables the farmer would try to control the grub population. This might suggest a suitable equilibrium state could be established by increasing the 'breeding rate' for the birds in May by releasing more birds. Other possibilities are to increase the 'death rate' by culling the birds in October (see Fig. 10.16(b)) or to decrease the 'death rate' by feeding the birds alternative foods (see Fig. 10.16(c)). A range of possible actions can be explored and their outcomes investigated without taking risks with the actual crop.

This predator/prey model is not a very good representation of the real world. It assumes that there is a self-contained environment in which the populations of birds and grubs change according to fixed rules. This is unlikely to be the case. There are likely to be other influences on the size of the populations, such as; the weather, the availability of alternative food for the birds, etc. However, despite its limitations, this model is useful in helping us understand the relationships between the bird population and the grub population.

EXAMINATION QUESTIONS

▷ **Question 1** EWE AND WOOL is a small business making woollen items of clothing. The owner has created a spreadsheet to help calculate the cost of making each item. The spreadsheet display is shown below:

	A	B	C	D	E	F
1	Type	Cost of wool	Time taken to	Pay per hour	Total Pay	Total Cost
2		(£)	make 1 (hrs)	(£)	(£)	for 1 (£)
3	Cardigan	5.00	3	3.00	9.00	14.00
4	Sweater	5.00	2	2.50	5.00	10.00
5	Gloves	1.50	2	3.00	6.00	7.50
6	Scarf	3.00	1	2.00	2.00	5.00
7	Hat	2.00	1	2.00	2.00	4.00
8						
9						

(a) How is the Total Pay calculated by the spreadsheet?
   A Cost of wool × Pay per hour
   B Cost of wool × Time taken to make 1
   C Time taken to make 1 × Total Cost for 1
   D Time taken to make 1 × Pay per hour
(b) Which other values does the spreadsheet work out for you?
(c) The workers who knit the sweaters are unhappy about their pay and you decide to increase their pay to £2.75. You need to see the effect on the Total Cost.
   Which cell or box on the spreadsheet would you have to change?
(d) (i) The design of the cardigan changes and it will now take longer to make one.
       Which cell or box would you have to change?
   (ii) Which other cells would change as a result?

(NEAB/WJEC)

▷ **Question 2** The spreadsheet below shows data on agriculture in the British Isles.

	A	B	C	D	E
1	Country	Agriculture	%	%	%
2	Name	Area	Grass	Arable	Fruit & Veg
3	England				
4	Wales				
5	Scotland				
6	Ireland				
7					
8					

(a) Which cell would you use to put the Total Agriculture Area?
(b) What formula would you put in that cell?
(c) The spreadsheet has the ability to produce the following types of graph:

   Bar   Line   Pie   Scatter

   Which one would be the most suitable for showing:
   (i) The proportions of Grass, Arable and Fruit & Veg for England?
   (ii) To compare the Agricultural Areas for the four countries?

(SEG, 1993)

▷ **Question 3**   The spreadsheet shown below is designed to give the price of a number of items in three different currencies.

	A	B	C	D
1				
2	Item	British	Australian	French
3		pounds	dollars	francs
4				
5	Litre of Milk	0.40	0.20	
6				
7	Bar of Soap	0.36	0.18	
8				
9	Kilo of Sugar	0.48	0.24	
10				
11	Litre of Petrol	0.44	0.22	
12				
13	Newspaper	0.26	0.13	
14		‾‾‾	‾‾‾	
15	Total Cost	1.94	0.97	

(a) How many Australian dollars made one British pound when the spreadsheet was created?

(b) When cell B11 is altered to 0.40 it is noticed that the display of cell B15 immediately changes to 1.90.

  (i) Describe the contents of cell B15.

  (ii) If the spreadsheet was well designed state what other cells should have changed and give their value.

(c) If there are nine French francs to one British pound describe what must be put in the cells in column D so that the prices in French francs will be displayed automatically.

(d) Assume that you have set up the spreadsheet using a microcomputer system.

  (i) If you want to use the same spreadsheet tomorrow, describe in detail what you should do before you switch off the computer.

  (ii) When you come back to the computer tomorrow and want to use the same spreadsheet, describe in detail what you will do to get the spreadsheet back on to the screen.

(London)

▷ **Question 4**   Below is the information which was given to you to enter into a spreadsheet.

Monday	28.60	Shopping
Tuesday	5.60	Went to cinema
Tuesday	10.20	Received cheque to pay into bank
Wednesday	2.50	Bread and cakes
Thursday	108.00	Wages paid into bank
Friday	18.50	Went out with friends
Saturday	11.99	Bought CD
Sunday	6.25	Paid for newspapers

You enter this data into a spreadsheet as follows:

Items	Mon	Tue	Wed	Thu	Fri	Sat	Sun	Total
Income								
Wages				108				
Sub-total				108				108
Expenditure								
Shopping	2.86							
Cinema		5.60						
Bread and Cake			2.50					
Cheque		10.20						
Out – friends					18.50			
Bought CD						11.99		
Newspapers							6.25	
Sub-total	2.86	15.80	2.50		18.50	11.99	6.25	57.90

(a) Circle the errors on the spreadsheet, and explain what difference this makes to the final total.
Explain what this could mean to the family.
(b) Give an example of an organization which uses spreadsheets in real life, and state the advantages of using them.

(NDTEF)

▷ **Question 5** You use a spreadsheet package to analyse the cost of a holiday in Australia.
(a) Write down ONE item of information which you want output.
(b) Write down TWO items of data you enter on the spreadsheet.
(c) Give TWO items of data which you should use to test if the results are reasonable.

(MEG)

▷ **Question 6** The owner of a cafe has decided to offer customers a new range of vegetarian dishes. She needs to work out the price to charge for the dishes. She knows how many she expects to sell each week, and is going to make 20 of each at once. She knows the cost of the ingredients, how long it takes to make a batch, and what the cost of cooking them is.
(a) State what software she would use to help her decide what to charge. Give a reason for your answer.
(b) Explain why this method is better than using a simple calculator.
(c) State another advantage for the IT method compared with setting out her plans on paper and calculating manually.

(RSA)

▷ **Question 7** Describe, using the diagram, how a model of a pupil's weekly finances could be constructed.

(MEG)

▷ **Question 8** A milkman orders milk of various types (e.g. full cream, skimmed, semi-skimmed) and other produce from a dairy and delivers to many customers. The milkman wishes to use a spreadsheet to manage the ordering and billing system for the daily deliveries to customers' homes.
Use the grid below to show the main elements of a suitable spreadsheet design. Indicate the formulae that would allow you to show each customer's weekly bill and the total weekly ordering requirements for each type of milk and other dairy products to be obtained from the dairy.

(NEAB/WJEC)

▷ **Question 9** (a) Give one advantage of using a computer model to study the relationship between hunting animals and their prey.

(b) Give two reasons why your teacher may prefer to use a simulation rather than a school trip to an African jungle.

(c) What software package would you use to display the data collected.

(City and Guilds)

▷ **Question 10** You can use spreadsheet software to make a computer model.

(a) Give an example of an investigation for which you would use a spreadsheet package to make a computer model.

(b) Describe how you would set up the model on the spreadsheet.

(c) Explain why you would use the computer model instead of creating the real thing.

(MEG)

EXAMINATION ANSWERS

▷ **Answer 1** (a) D
(b) total cost
(c) D4
(d) C3
(e) E3 and F3

▷ **Answer 2** (a) B7 or B8
(b) SUM(B3 to B6)
(c) (i) pie chart
    (ii) bar chart

▷ **Answer 3** (a) 1 Australian dollar = 2 British pounds
(b) (i) Cell B15 contains a formula that adds up cells B5, B7, B9, B11 and B13.
    (ii) C11 = 0.20
          C15 = 0.95
          (D11 and D15 would also change in the completed spreadsheet).
(c) D5 = B5*9
    D7 = B7*9
    D9 = B9*9
    D11 = B11*9
    D13 = B13*9
(d) (i) Give the spreadsheet a file name. Save the file on backing storage, e.g. floppy disk.
    (ii) Load and run the spreadsheet software. Load the spreadsheet file from backing storage, e.g. floppy disk.

▷ **Answer 4** (a) 2.86 entered instead of 28.60 for Monday, shopping. The cheque paid into the bank has been entered as 'Expenditure'.
    The family is worse off than they think. They could overspend by mistake.
(b) Shops use spreadsheets.
    Some of the advantages are:

    ▷ No human error in the calculations.
    ▷ You can set up a spreadsheet once and use it repeatedly for similar tasks.
    ▷ Easy to edit.
    ▷ Multiple printed copies can be made.

▷ **Answer 5** (a) One of:
    The cost of the holiday for different numbers of people.
    The cost of the holiday for different seasons.

(b) Two from:
Number of people going on holiday.
Cost of one person going on holiday.
Different prices for different times of year.
Different lengths of time.
(c) Produce zero cost if the number of people is zero.
Enter simple numbers (e.g. 1 person) and calculate by hand.

(MEG)

▷ **Answer 6**   (a) She should use a spreadsheet. The spreadsheet will help her do the original calculations. Once it is set up, she can use it again for different dishes or to re-assess the cost of the same dish.
(b) A calculator does not store the structure of the model or the formulae used. If you change one value in a spreadsheet, the whole spreadsheet recalculates automatically. With a calculator you would have to do all the calculations again yourself.
(c) A spreadsheet is more effective because:

▶   A spreadsheet recalculates automatically.
▶   The results are always accurate.
▶   The results are produced much quicker.
▶   You can quickly do 'what if' calculations.

▷ **Answer 7**   Diagram or description should include:
Days of the week
Items in the left column
Values in boxes
Formulae for row totals
Formulae for column totals
Formatting in columns (in £ and justification)

(MEG)

▷ **Answer 8**

	A	B	C	D	E	F	G	H	I	J
1	Prices	Full=	0.57							
2		Semi=	0.51							
3		Skimmed=	0.48							
4										
5	NAME	TYPE	M	T	W	T	F	S	S	Total
6	Jones	Full	1	1	1	1	1	2	2	Sum(C6 to I6)
7		Semi	2	1	2	2	1	2	2	Sum (C7 to I7)
8		Skimmed	0	1	0	0	1	2	2	Sum (C8 to I8)
9			Customer's weekly bill (J6*C1)+(J7*C2)+(J8*C3)							
10	Rows 6 to 9 are repeated for every customer									
11	At the end of the spreadsheet we have:									
12	Total Sales = Sum (All the customer totals)									

The weekly total for full cream milk is obtained using the formula J6+ . . . Similarly, a weekly total for semi-skimmed uses the formula J7+ . . . and for skimmed, J8+ . . .
Note that the prices are stored only once in cells C1, C2 and C3. Elsewhere they are inserted as cell references. This means that when prices change at most 3 cells have to be changed.

▷ **Answer 9**   (a) Some advantages are:
▶   The relationship in the model can be studied without the observer travelling to the area in which the animal lives.

▶ The observer does not interfere with the relationship or the animals' habitat.

▶ The observer is not in danger from the animals.

(b) Cost, and danger to pupils are avoided.

(c) You could use a spreadsheet or a dedicated, pre-programmed model.

▷ **Answer 10**   (a) One from:

▶ Capacitor decay

▶ Radioactive decay

▶ Economic model

▶ Any suitable answer

(b) Description of model given in part (a) should include:

▶ The data input

▶ The rules expressed as formulae

▶ The information output and how it is displayed

(c) One from:

▶ Too costly to build a physical model

▶ Too time consuming to build a physical model

▶ Variables can be changed easily to see the effects of any change in input

▶ Any suitable answer

(MEG)

▶ **EXAMINATION QUESTION WITH STUDENT ANSWER**

A ferry that sails from Calais to Dover has a duty free shop.

The duty free shop has five checkouts. A computer based model works out the longest time a customer has to queue at a checkout.

These are screen displays from the model.

Total number of customers waiting	8	
Number of checkouts being used	2	
Average number of customers at each checkout	4	
Average time to process one customer at a checkout	3	minutes
The longest time a customer has to queue	12	minutes

Total number of customers waiting	20	
Number of checkouts being used	4	
Average number of customers at each checkout	5	
Average time to process one customer at a checkout	4	minutes
The longest time a customer has to queue	20	minutes

(a) Fill in the values that the model should produce.

Total number of customers waiting	20	
Number of checkouts being used	5	
Average number of customers at each checkout	4	
Average time to process one customer at a checkout	2	minutes
The longest time a customer has to queue	8	minutes

(b) The shop manager wants to reduce the longest time customers have to queue.
Tick TWO boxes to show what the manager can do to reduce the longest time customers have to queue.

	Tick TWO boxes
Advertise the duty free shop to increase the number of customers	
Increase the number of checkouts being used	✓
Ask all the customers to queue at one checkout	
Introduce bar code readers to speed up the time taken to process a customer at a checkout	✓
Make one checkout for customers wanting to pay cash	

(c) The model can be constructed using a spreadsheet

	A	B	C
1	Total number of customers waiting	20	
2	Number of checkouts being used	5	
3	Average number of customers at each checkout		
4	Average time to process one customer at a checkout	2	minutes
5	The longest time a customer has to queue		minutes

(i) Write down the **formula** that would be in cell B3.

$B2 \div B1$

(ii) Write down the **formula** that would be in cell B5

$B3 \times B4$

(iii) Describe ONE advantage in using formulae in a spreadsheet.

You can copy them easily

(d) Tick THREE boxes to show why the model may **not** be accurate.

	Tick THREE boxes
Customers can pay in French Francs or Pounds Sterling	
The average time to process a customer was worked out when some checkout operators were working slowly	✓
The checkouts process customers at different speeds	✓
The duty free shop is very busy	
Customers do not distribute themselves evenly between the checkouts	
One of the checkouts cannot be used as it is being repaired	✓

(e) (i) Using a term from the list, complete the sentence.

constant
resource
variable

The total number of customers waiting is a ....*constant*...

    (ii) Using a term from the list, complete the sentence.

eradicate

input

output

The model will ....*input*.........the longest time a customer has to queue.

(SEG, 1996)

▷ **Examiner's comment**

(a) *Correct*

(b) *Correct*

(c) (i) *Incorrect. B1 and B2 are the wrong way round. The correct answer is B1 ÷ B2. It would be better to write B1/B2 as this is the way the formula would be entered in a spread sheet.*

     (ii) *Correct. However, it would be better to write B3 * B4 as this is the way the formula would be entered in a spreadsheet.*

     (iii) *This is an advantage of using a* **spreadsheet** *not of* **using formula** *in a spreadsheet. A better answer would be: 'They recalculate automatically when the values they refer to are changed.'*

(d) *The sixth answer is incorrect as the model takes into account only checkouts that are working. All others are ignored. The second, third and fifth answers are correct.*

(e) (i) *The total number of customers is a* **variable** *as it can be expected to change. The answer given is incorrect.*

     (ii) *Incorrect. The inputs to this model are the total number of customers waiting and the number of checkouts being used. The longest time a customer has to queue is an* **output**.

SUMMARY

This chapter looks at what spreadsheets can do, and their use in modelling.

▷   A **spreadsheet** is divided into horizontal rows and vertical columns.

▷   A **cell** is the intersection of a row and a column.

▷   Cells can contain text, number, formulae, dates and times.

▷   Cells can be referred to individually (e.g. E5) or in groups (e.g. E5:G7).

▷   Cells can be moved or copied from one part of the spreadsheet to another.

▷   **Relative cell references** change when formulae are copied from one cell to another.

▷   **Absolute cell references** do not change when formulae are copied from one cell to another.

▷   **Formulae** may **recalculate automatically** when the numbers in the cells they refer to change.

▷   You can **sort** groups of cells. For example, the rows may be sorted so that names in column A are in alphabetic order.

▷   **Graphs** can be generated that illustrate the numerical information stored in the spreadsheet.

▷   You can **export** groups of cells, graphs, etc. to a wordprocessor for including in a report.

▷   A **model** is a representation of the real world. It is not the real world.

▷   Models are used so that you can learn about an unfamiliar situation and experiment without danger or expense.

▷   You can use a spreadsheet to record and store information, or you can use it for modelling.

▷   When a spreadsheet is used for modelling, there is an intention to use it to:

      ▷   improve understanding of a real system;

      ▷   for problem solving;

      ▷   to predict what will happen.

▷   A spreadsheet model will:

      ▷   allow a range of input variables to be set;

      ▷   use formulae to define the rules on which the model is based;

      ▷   output information using the input variables, stored values, and the rules.

Monitoring and control

This chapter should be read if you are preparing for GCSE IT assessment with the following examining boards:

C & G	MEG	NEAB	SEG
London	NDTEF	RSA	WJEC

 GETTING STARTED

Data logging is the automatic collection and storage of the information provided by sensors. This may take place over long distances. A common data logging application is the collection and storage of the information from weather stations.

Control systems may use sensors to measure environmental conditions, and actuators to adjust them. Control systems often involve feedback. **AND, OR and NOT logic** is used in designing control systems. **Dedicated control systems** are built into machinery and other equipment. An example is a fault detection system for an industrial machine. **Computer control systems** are computer based, and communicate with sensors and actuators through a control interface. For example, a greenhouse control system.

Computers themselves are controlled by programs. Different types of program structure are described. These are **conditional statements**, **loops** and **procedures**. There are examples of programs in Logo, BASIC, Pascal and COBOL.

 GLOSSARY

Sensors	Sensors are used to measure environmental conditions. Sensors can monitor heat, light, humidity, sound, pressure, wind speed, wind direction, tilt, etc.
Actuators	Actuators are used to adjust environmental conditions. Actuators are heaters, motors, pumps, etc.
Feedback	Feedback is a cycle of sensing, processing and reaction.
Computer program	A computer program is a list of instructions to a computer written in a computer language such as Logo.

C & G	LONDON	MEG	NDTEF	NEAB	RSA	SEG	WJEC	TOPIC	STUDY	REVISION I	REVISION 2
✓	✓	✓	✓	✓	✓	✓	✓	Data logging			
✓	✓	✓	✓	✓	✓	✓	✓	Dedicated control systems			
✓	✓	✓	✓	✓	✓	✓	✓	Computer control systems			
✓	✓	✓	✓	✓	✓	✓	✓	Computer programs and languages			

WHAT YOU NEED TO KNOW

Data logging involves the automatic collection and storage of the information provided by sensors. This may be over long distances or from widely dispersed locations. It may be processed immediately or at a later date.

Control systems may be dedicated or computer controlled. *Dedicated systems* are designed using electronic components, including logic gates. AND, OR, and NOT logic gates are explained and their use in some dedicated control systems is illustrated.

Computer control systems have sensors so that they can measure environmental variables, such as temperature. The computer will look at the environmental variables and try to adjust them using actuators such as heaters and motors.

Measurement and control systems often involve *feedback*. This is a cycle of sensing, processing and reaction. For example, the cycle of finding out the room temperature, deciding if it is at the right level and taking action to get the temperature to the right level is a *feedback loop*. Feedback loops are important in constructing systems that control the environment. Some computer systems with feedback loops are described. These are a system to control the operation of a lift in a building; a system to control the temperature and humidity in a greenhouse; a flight simulator.

Programs control computers. Computer programs can be written in a variety of **languages**. Machine code is difficult for people to use and understand as it consists of a list of ones and zeros. Assembly language is easier for us to understand but it is still too similar to machine code for general use. High level languages, such as Logo, BASIC, Pascal and COBOL are much easier to use and understand. However, all computer languages must be converted to machine code so that the computer can understand them. Examples of programs written in Logo, BASIC, Pascal and COBOL are shown. You will be expected to be able to write a simple program, and understand conditional statements, loops and procedures.

'Feedback'

'computer programs'

▷ Data logging

A **sensor** is a device that responds to environmental conditions by outputting a signal. This signal is most likely to be a small voltage. It varies in proportion to the magnitude of the condition sensed. Sensors can measure many different environmental conditions. For example, heat, light, tilt, and pressure.

Data logging is the automatic collection and storage of the information provided by sensors. It may take place over long distances, and may involve the gathering of data from a number of remote sites.

The **frequency of sampling** is an important consideration. The graph in Fig. 11.1(a) shows the temperature in an unheated greenhouse. If you only took measurements at midday every day, you would collect the information shown in Fig. 11.1(b). As a result, you might assume that the greenhouse was warm enough. Consequently, you might not heat the greenhouse properly with the result that some plants would die when the temperature becomes too low. Alternatively, if you only took measurements at 6.00 a.m. each day, you might assume that the greenhouse was not warm enough. This might cause you to heat the greenhouse to too high a temperature. Clearly, a more sensible schedule for heating the greenhouse would be based on the information gathered at both midday and at 6.00 a.m. Even so, the temperature in the greenhouse could change quite dramatically between these times. Look at Wednesday in Fig. 11.1(a). The temperature was much higher just before it was recorded at midday, and much lower just before it was recorded at 6.00 a.m. You would get a clearer picture of the temperature in the greenhouse if you sampled it more frequently. In this case, sampling the information every half-hour might be satisfactory, as it is unusual for the temperature to change so rapidly that damage would be done to the plants in the greenhouse before the change was sensed.

'Frequency of sampling affects performance'

Cooling curves

One application of data logging is in generating cooling curves (see Fig. 11.2). A heat sensor is placed in a liquid that has been heated. As the liquid cools, the computer automatically collects and records its temperature. The time between sampling may be very short where the liquid is expected to cool very quickly. In contrast, it may be relatively long where the liquid is expected to take a long time to cool.

Using a computer for data logging means that the time between samples can be easily adjusted to suit the material being monitored. Once the data has been collected, it can be used to generate cooling curves or analysed in other ways. The computer may be able to display cooling curves for different materials simultaneously so that comparisons can be made.

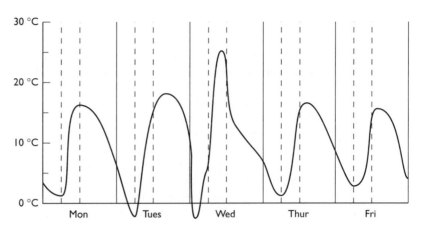

Fig. 11.1a The actual temperature in the greenhouse

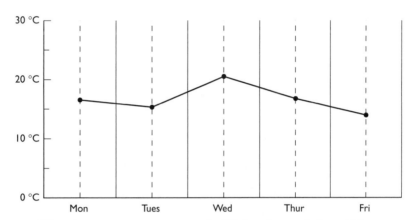

Fig. 11.1b What the temperature appears to be if it is only sampled at midday

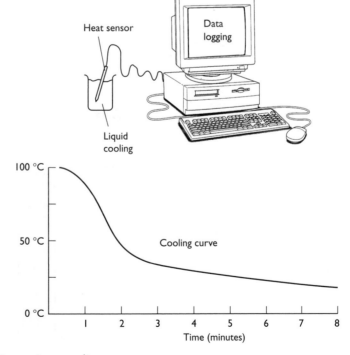

Fig. 11.2 Generating a cooling curve

Weather stations

Weather stations (see Fig. 11.3) are used to collect information about the weather. They may have sensors that measure the temperature, wind speed, wind direction, whether it is raining, how much rain has fallen, visibility, etc. This information may be collected from a weather station by a computer communicating with it using the telephone network. The computer will automatically collect the information and record it on backing storage. This is an example of data logging. The information collected can be useful in many ways. For example, for weather forecasting.

Local councils may find it useful to have weather stations. These will tell them if the temperature is likely to fall below freezing point so that they know when and where to grit the roads. Using weather stations spread throughout the district helps them save money as grit may not be needed everywhere. Having reliable records of past usage helps local councils predict future demand.

Local radio stations often provide information to car drivers commuting to work. Weather stations can give them information about driving conditions. For example, whether it is foggy; if there are high winds; whether it is raining or snowing; and if the roads are likely to be icy. Traffic can sometimes avoid these hazards if they are localized. For example, Queensbury is on the top of the hills overlooking Bradford and Halifax. It is often very foggy when surrounding areas have good visibility. Some commuters find it convenient to drive through Queensbury on their way to work. However, many would choose to take a different route if it was foggy. The local radio station could use the information from a weather station to find out if it is foggy and let drivers know if it is.

The information provided by a weather station could be obtained by a computer communicating with it over the telephone network. The computer could automatically contact a number of weather stations spread over a wide area. It might contact them in rotation, collecting the information as often as possible. Alternatively, it might contact each weather station at particular times each day. The frequency of sampling might be designed so that a good illustration of the weather conditions throughout the day was recorded but sampling was kept to a minimum. This would provide useful information while keeping costs as low as possible.

If up-to-date information was not needed immediately, details of the prevailing weather conditions could be recorded on backing storage at the weather station. The computer might communicate with the weather station very infrequently, perhaps only once or twice a year. When the weather station and the computer were in contact, the information recorded on backing storage at the weather station would be transmitted to the computer.

Weather stations are simply groups of sensors that provide useful information about the weather. They are only one of many data logging applications where information is col-

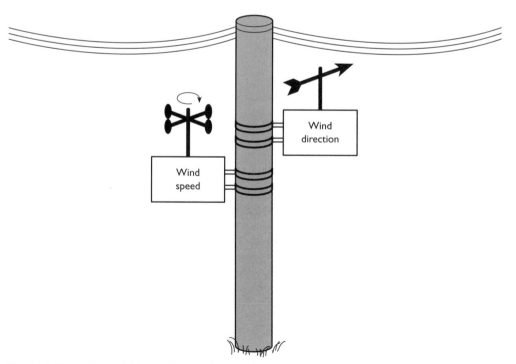

Fig. 11.3 Part of a roadside weather station

lected and recorded automatically from remote, widely dispersed or dangerous locations. Other groupings of sensors can provide information about different environmental conditions. For example:

▶ sensors on icebergs can provide scientists with information that helps them understand how they formed and what becomes of them;
▶ sensors underground can record information about earthquakes;
▶ sensors on space vehicles can provide information about the atmosphere on different planets.

Dedicated control systems

Although the electronic components used in dedicated control systems can be very complex, they are made up of simple basic elements. The complexity lies in the ways in which these basic elements are combined together.

This section looks at the logic operations AND, OR and NOT, and how these can be used to build dedicated control systems.

Truth tables

Truth tables are used to describe how logic operations work. They are a convenient way of expressing the possible inputs to a decision based on well defined rules, and the results.

Look at Fig. 11.4. There are two inputs, 'On holiday' and 'A weekday' that are combined to give four different input conditions. 'False' means Paul is *not* 'On holiday' and 'true' means he *is* 'On holiday'. Each input condition has a result defined by the rule given.

Rule:
Paul has decided that he will go fishing if he is on holiday OR if it is NOT a weekday.

Inputs		Outputs
A weekday	On holiday	Goes fishing
FALSE	FALSE	TRUE
FALSE	TRUE	TRUE
TRUE	FALSE	FALSE
TRUE	TRUE	TRUE

Fig. 11.4 A truth table

Switch circuits

Truth tables can be used to describe how electrical circuits containing switches work. Look at Fig. 11.5. This shows a **switch circuit** and the corresponding truth table. There are three switches labelled, A B and C, in the circuit. Since there are three switches, these combine to make eight different input conditions. In order for the light bulb to come on, either switch C must be on or switches A and B must both be on.

Logic

In both of the above examples we see **binary logic** being used. If we consider '1', 'true' and 'on' to be equivalent, and similarly with '0', 'false' and 'off, we get the truth tables shown in Fig. 11.6 (a) and (b).

In both of the examples, the rule expressing the relationship between the inputs and the output uses the terms AND, OR and NOT. These are the basic logic operations. They can be fully described using truth tables (see Fig. 11.7).

'Logic operations and truth tables'

These logic operations are the same whether they are applied to control systems (as in this chapter), or used in search conditions to select information from a database (as in Chapter 9).

Logic gates and circuits

Logic gates are electronic components that perform logic operations such as AND, OR and NOT (see Fig. 11.7).

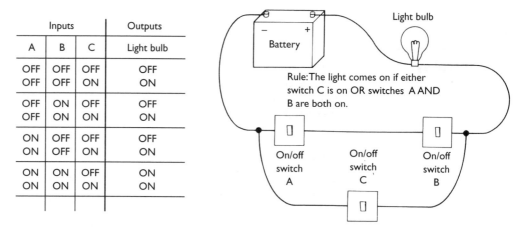

Inputs			Outputs
A	B	C	Light bulb
OFF	OFF	OFF	OFF
OFF	OFF	ON	ON
OFF	ON	OFF	OFF
OFF	ON	ON	ON
ON	OFF	OFF	OFF
ON	OFF	ON	ON
ON	ON	OFF	ON
ON	ON	ON	ON

Rule: The light comes on if either switch C is on OR switches A AND B are both on.

Fig. 11.5 A switch circuit and its truth table

(a) Paul goes fishing

Inputs		Outputs
A weekday	On holiday	Goes fishing
0	0	1
0	1	1
1	0	0
1	1	1

(b) The switch circuit

Inputs			Outputs
A	B	C	Light bulb
0	0	0	0
1	0	1	1
0	1	0	0
0	1	1	1
1	0	0	0
1	0	1	1
1	1	0	1
1	1	1	1

Fig. 11.6 Binary logic truth tables

AND gate

Inputs		Outputs
0	0	0
0	1	0
1	0	0
1	1	1

OR gate

Inputs		Outputs
0	0	0
0	1	1
1	0	1
1	1	1

NOT gate

Inputs	Outputs
0	1
1	0

The output is 1 only if both inputs are 1   The output is 1 if either input is 1

The output is 1 if the input is 0
The output is 0 if the input is 1

Fig. 11.7 AND, OR and NOT logic gates

Logic gates can be combined to make **logic circuits**. They can be built into machine tools, washing machines, etc. to perform the simple logic required for some control tasks. These are dedicated control systems.

How a logic circuit works

'Logic circuits and truth tables'

The example shown in Fig. 11.8 is not a useful circuit. It is an example to show how the output from a logic circuit can be worked out from the inputs. In the example, A, B and C are the inputs; E and F are intermediate processing states; X is the output.

The truth table is worked out by first entering all the different input conditions. Since there are three inputs, there will be eight different input conditions. These can be listed by counting in three bit binary from zero to seven. The intermediate processing state, E, is the result of A AND B; F is the result of NOT C. The output, X, is given by E OR F.

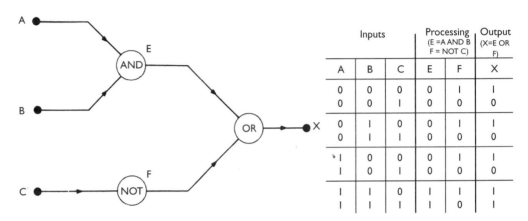

Inputs			Processing (E =A AND B F = NOT C)		Output (X=E OR F)
A	B	C	E	F	X
0	0	0	0	1	1
0	0	1	0	0	0
0	1	0	0	1	1
0	1	1	0	0	0
1	0	0	0	1	1
1	0	1	0	0	0
1	1	0	1	1	1
1	1	1	1	0	1

Fig. 11.8 A logic circuit and its truth table

A decoder

A **decoder** is used to select a single output from a range of possible outputs in response to the binary code input. A two bit decoder is shown in Figure 11.9. Notice that only one of the four outputs is selected, i.e. has a value of 1, depending on the binary code input. For example, if 01 is input then B is the only output that has a value of 1, that is, an input of 01 selects output B.

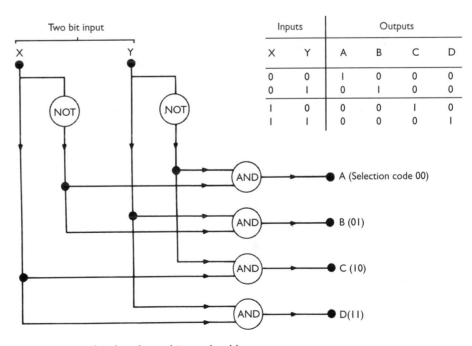

Inputs		Outputs			
X	Y	A	B	C	D
0	0	1	0	0	0
0	1	0	1	0	0
1	0	0	0	1	0
1	1	0	0	0	1

Fig. 11.9a A two bit decoder and its truth table

A two bit decoder could be built into a stereo amplifier that is connected to a CD player, a tape deck, a radio receiver and a video recorder. Pressing a button selects one of these and excludes the others, ensuring that sound from each of them is not mixed (see Fig. 11.9 (b)).

Using more than two bits for input, a decoder can be used to genuerate the appropriate character when a key is pressed on a computer's keyboard. There are many similar applications.

(button)	Pressing the button generates this code	The code selects the control switch that opens this channel	Source of sound input to amplifier
CD	00	A	CD
Tape	01	B	Tape
Radio	10	C	Radio
Video	11	D	Video

Fig. 11.9b Using a two bit decoder to select the source of the sound input to a stereo amplifier

A control switch

A control switch is an electronic switch. It can allow or prevent information passing down a wire (see Fig. 11.10).

If the switch is off, the control bit is 0 and all the output is 0. If the switch is on, the control bit is 1, and whatever is input is output. This is the principle behind the control switches referred to in Fig. 11.10.

A fault detection system

All industrial machines should have automatic systems for monitoring their performance. This is essential for good quality manufacture and safety. Logic circuits can be designed to detect breakdowns, etc. as they occur. The following describes a typical arrangement.

An industrial machine has its own monitoring system which sets a 'fault detect' signal when the machine breaks down. When a breakdown happens, a green light which is nor-

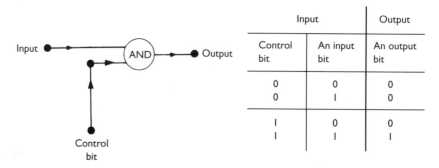

Input		Output
Control bit	An input bit	An output bit
0	0	0
0	1	0
1	0	0
1	1	1

Fig. 11.10 A control switch and its truth table, showing the effect on a single input bit

mally *on* is turned *off*, a *red light* comes on and a *bell* rings. The machine operator can use an override switch to turn the bell off but the red light stays on until the fault is cleared. This type of arrangement is a basic safety system for machine tools and other industrial machines. Figure 11.11 shows a logic circuit that could be used.

A traffic light controller

Logic circuits can be used to control traffic lights (see Fig. 11.12). The control circuit interprets the two bit output from the timer and determines which combination of lights will be turned on.

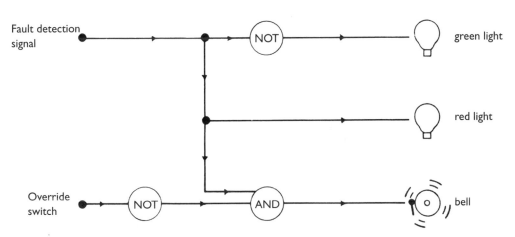

Fig. 11.11 A safety system for industrial machines

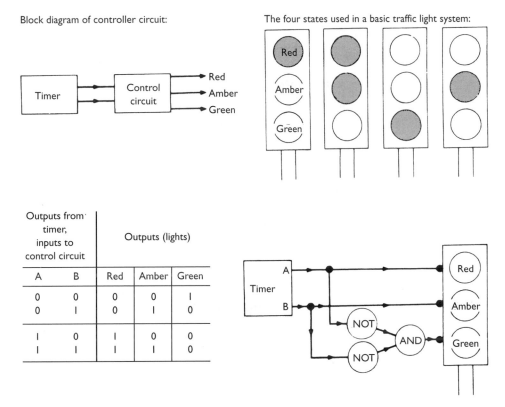

Fig. 11.12 A traffic light controller

Computer
control systems

'Uses of computer control
systems'

'Feedback'

'A lift control system'

Computers may replace dedicated control systems in larger and more complex control applications as they are more flexible. Computers can be re-programmed so that the environmental variables and the logic controlling the system can be changed. For example, at a road junction controlled by traffic lights, you might want to vary the time the lights stay on green throughout the day, on different days and for special occasions, such as, when the local football match ends. It would be easier to make adjustments if the traffic lights were computer controlled. If all the traffic lights on the same road were connected to the same computer, it could coordinate them so that you could drive through all lights, on green, without having to stop. The computer could regulate the speed of the traffic by regulating all the traffic lights. The speed would usually be the same from day-to-day, but might change if there were roadworks, etc. The computer could easily be reprogrammed to make these changes.

Computer control systems may have:

- sensors;
- a control interface;
- actuators;
- feedback loops.

The **control interface** is hardware that provides the interface between the computer and the control system. The control interface translates the signals from the sensors so that the computer can understand them. It also translates the signals from the computer that tell the **actuators** what to do. An **actuator** is a hardware device, such as a motor, that performs the actions the computer tells it to do.

A **feedback loop** is a cycle of sensing, processing and reaction. For example, a heat sensor gives information to the computer about the temperature in a room. The computer inputs the information from the heat sensor and decides if the temperature in the room is at the right level. If the room temperature is too low, the computer turns on the heating. The heat sensor tells the computer the temperature is higher. When the temperature reaches the right level, the computer turns off the heating. The feedback loop is a cycle of finding out the room temperature, deciding if it is at the right level and taking action to get the temperature to the right level.

A lift control system

Part of a **lift control system** is shown in Fig. 11.13. In this case, sensors, an actuator, a control interface and a microcomputer are used.

As the lift is moving upwards, the infra red beam attached to the bottom of the lift passes sensor B, which sends a signal to the computer. If the lift has to stop at this floor the computer will signal the control interface to stop the motor and the lift will slow down and stop. However, if sensor A is passed while the lift is slowing down, then the floor of the lift will be too far above the level of the floor of the building. In this case the computer will reverse the lift motor and the lift moves downwards. As sensor A is passed by the lift going downwards, the computer detects this and stops the lift motor so that the lift slows down and stops. However, if sensor B is passed the floor of the lift will be too far below the level of the floor of the building! The computer senses this and reverses the lift motor so that the lift is moving upwards again. This process is repeated until the floor of the lift comes to rest between sensors A and B. This is a **feedback loop**. Feedback loops are an essential part of most computer control systems.

A computer is used to control the lift because the logic is complex. This may be only a small part of a larger system that may involve selection of floors from inside or outside the lift and scheduling of several lifts. The logical decisions involved can be easily expressed in a computer program.

A computer controlled greenhouse

Figure 11.14 is an illustration of a computer control system for a greenhouse. The aim of such a system is to regulate temperature and humidity, so that optimum plant growth is achieved.

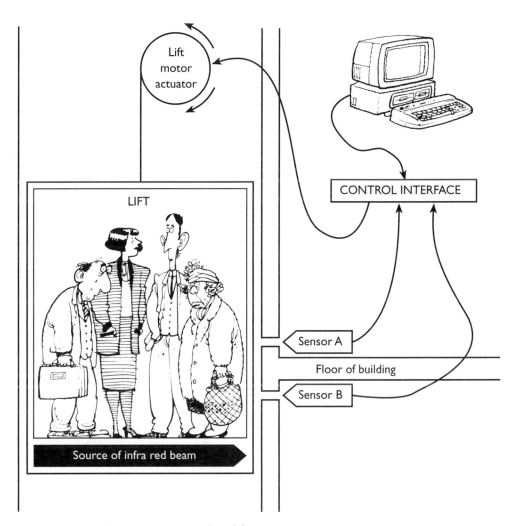

Fig. 11.13 Part of a computer system for a lift

The temperature and humidity sensors monitor the environmental conditions in the greenhouse and the heater, window motor and overhead spray actuators are used to control them.

'A computer controlled greenhouse'

The humidity sensor generates a voltage that is proportional to the amount of water vapour in the air. Voltage is an analog signal. This signal is input to the ADC which converts it to a binary number. If the humidity is low, the voltage is low and the binary number is also low. The size of the binary number output from the ADC and input to the computer is proportional to the humidity in the greenhouse.

The computer is programmed to respond to low humidity by turning on the overhead spray and closing the windows. This is done by sending control signals to the window motor actuator and the overhead spray actuator. These turn on the overhead spray and the motor to close the windows. This has the effect of increasing the humidity. As the humidity increases, the sensors sense this and the system responds until an *equilibrium state* is reached. This is another example of a **feedback loop**.

'Computer control is flexible'

A computer control system for a greenhouse is only justified if the business is large enough for the improved quality and quantity of produce grown to pay for the computer system. In practice, one computer would control several greenhouses. In a large business with several greenhouses the advantages of a computer control system lie in its ability to *precisely* control temperature and humidity in all the greenhouses at all times. Each greenhouse will have its own program of temperature and humidity settings stored in the computer. These can be set at different levels depending on the time of day. To alter the settings it is only necessary to enter new values at the keyboard. The computer will automatically change the environment in the greenhouse to these new settings. The control system constantly monitors the environment day and night. It responds immediately to any variation from the required settings. The entire system can be controlled from the com-

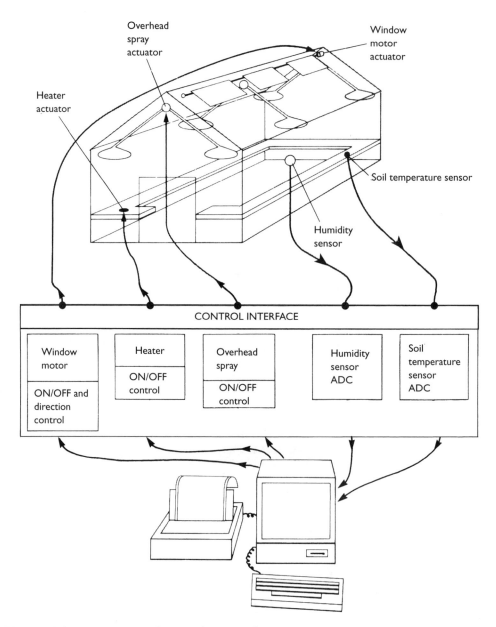

Fig. 11.14 A computer control system for a greenhouse

puter. Other sensors and activators could be fitted to control lighting, shade and other factors if needed.

If necessary, temperature and humidity data can be recorded at regular intervals so that
a record of the environmental conditions in the greenhouse is kept. This data would be
saved on backing storage, in this case floppy disks. The process of collecting and saving
environmental data is known as **data logging**. Data logging is done so that we can analyse
the recorded data at a later date.

'Data logging'

Robots

Robots are hardware devices that perform mechanical tasks. These tasks may be complex
industrial or manufacturing tasks. Robots are used for welding, paint spraying, assembling
products, packaging and handling molten metals, etc. They have many different shapes and
sizes, however, they all work in broadly similar ways.

A common example of a robot is the robotic arm (see Fig. 11.15). The robotic arm illustrated is typical of this type of robot. The arm can rotate at the waist and at the shoulder,
elbow and wrist. The gripper can turn its jaws so that the object to be lifted can be placed
between them. The grippers could be replaced with any useful tool, for example, a hook, a
scoop, a magnet, a vacuum cup, a welding torch, etc.

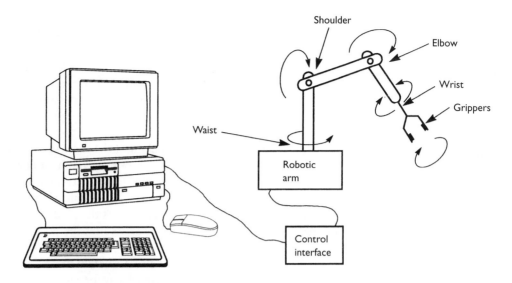

Fig. 11.15 A computer controlled robotic arm

'Control of robots'

The way robots are controlled is determined by the complexity of the task that is to be done and the purchase cost. Robots with simple control systems that do simple tasks cost less than those with more complex control systems. A simple robot may be programmed directly using a keypad built into it. More complex robots may be controlled by a computer. Such robots can be told what to do by programming the computer. The computer is programmed using a language similar to the Logo language (see later in this chapter) that is adapted to the particular robot to be controlled. For example, a simple robot may be instructed to pick up an object by a program like this:

```
START
OPEN GRIPPERS
DOWN 5
CLOSE GRIPPERS
UP 5
STOP
```

'Teach and learn methods'

Robots can also be programmed to do tasks using a variety of 'teach and learn' methods. You can program the robot under direct control of the computer, one instruction at a time. You watch what the robot does as it performs the instruction. If it is what you want the robot to do, you can save the instruction. In this way you can build up a complete program to control the robot. You can also program a robot by physically moving it through the actions you want it to do. The computer converts these actions into a program and saves it.

'It helps if the robot does have a feedback system'

Computer controlled robots may *not* have a *feedback system* built into them. In this case, it is difficult to know exactly what the robot is doing. These robots cannot respond to their environment. It may be dangerous for humans to work with this type of robot. As the robot cannot sense the presence of a person, it may continue doing its task, for example, welding, when a human is in the way or when there is no panel to weld. More intelligent robots have built-in feedback systems that tell the computer what the robot is doing. These help the robot detect and avoid humans and alert them to unusual situations, such as the absence of a panel to weld.

'Robots help with repetitive tasks'

If humans are asked to do the same task over and over again, they may become bored or lose concentration. This could affect the quality of their work. Robots can do repetitive tasks with no loss of quality. Robots can also work in dirty, hot, radioactive, dangerous environments where humans would find it difficult to work. However, it is time consuming to set up a robot to do a particular task. If this task is only going to be done once, it could take longer to set up a robot than to get a human to do the task. Humans are more flexible and creative than robots and can do a wider range and variety of tasks.

A flight simulator

Flight simulators (see Fig. 11.16) are used to train pilots to fly aircraft. They are very complex constructions involving a wide range of computer control sub-systems with highly developed and interacting feedback loops. A trainee pilot using a flight simulator experiences what it is like to fly an aircraft without actually having to fly one. While 'flying' the simulator, trainees can explore what the aircraft can do without risk to themselves or an actual aircraft. Trainees can also be given experience of unusual situations and emergencies.

'Characteristics of the flight simulator'

A flight simulator will have a cockpit of the same size and shape and with the same controls, seats, etc. as those in the real aircraft. A computer controls the view the trainee pilot sees through the cockpit windows and gives the trainee a realistic feeling of how the real aircraft would move. The view through the cockpit windows is a projected video image. It is controlled by the computer and changes as the pilot 'flies' the simulator. The simulator is mounted on mobile legs which are used to alter the position of the cockpit. The computer moves the legs when the pilot moves the simulator's controls. The trainee pilot feels the simulator move in the way the real aircraft would move.

Unusual situations and emergencies can be simulated. Fire can be simulated by the introduction of smoke into the simulator's cockpit and the programming of the pilot's displays to mimic those on a real aircraft that is on fire. Similarly, the displays and the reaction of the simulator to the pilot's controls can be modified to represent bad weather conditions, engine failure, etc.

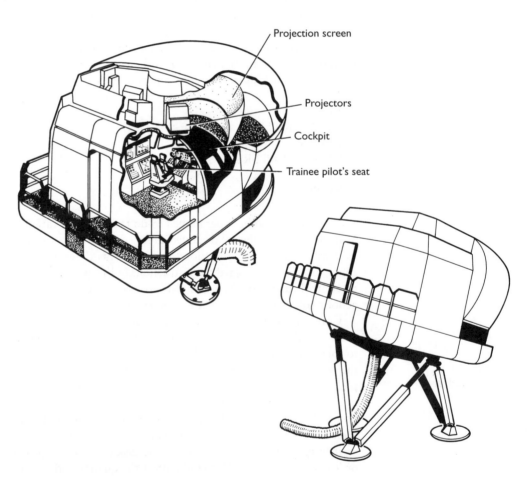

Projection screen

Projectors

Cockpit

Trainee pilot's seat

Fig. 11.16 A flight simulator

▷ Computer programs and languages

What is a program?

A **program** is a list of instructions to a computer. The computer starts at the beginning of the program, and carries out the instructions one at a time. It usually begins at the top of the list and works down the list, one instruction at a time. There are several program structures that may cause the computer not to run the program in this way. Some of them are described below.

Conditional statements

This is an example of a **conditional statement** taken from the example BASIC program given later in this chapter:

    80 IF A$ = "A" THEN GO TO 110

This conditional statement may change the order in which instructions are carried out. If the variable A$ contains only the character 'A', then the next instruction run will be that on line 110. If the variable A$ does not contain only the character 'A', then the next instuction run will be that immediately following the conditional statement.

Another example of a similar conditional statement is:

    80 IF A$ = "A" THEN PRINT "A is for Apple"

This statement does not change the order in which instructions are carried out. If A$ contains only the character 'A', then the phrase 'A is for Apple' is displayed on the screen. If A$ does not contain only 'A', then this instruction has no effect. Whatever the contents of A$, the next instruction run will be that immediately following the conditional statement.

Loops

A **loop** is a cycle of instructions. The computer repeats the instructions in the loop either for a fixed number of times or infinitely. There are various loop structures.

This is a **repeat loop** in the Logo programming language:

    REPEAT 4 [FD 40 LT 90].

The two instructions FD 40 and LT 90 are repeated 4 times. The effect of this loop is to draw a square on the screen.

This is a **while loop** in the Pascal programming language:

```
count :=0;
WHILE count < 10 DO
  BEGIN
    WRITLN(count);
    count := count + 1;
  END;
```

The instructions between BEGIN and END are repeated until count is not less than 10. The effect of this loop is to display the numbers from 0 to 9 on the screen.

Procedures

A **procedure** is a self-contained sequence of instructions that can be run from elsewhere in the same program. The following procedure is written in pseudocode. **Pseudocode** is not a real computer language. It is used to illustrate the logic or structure of a program.

'Defining a procedure'

```
Define Procedure Circumference_of_Circle(IN: radius; OUT: circumference )
BEGIN
circumference = 2*Π*radius
END
```

This procedure calculates the circumference of a circle. It can be called (i.e. run) from anywhere in a program when the programmer needs to calculate the circumference of a circle. A procedure can have **input parameters** and **output parameters**. In this case, the input parameter is the radius of the circle, and the output parameter is the circumference.

For example, this procedure call causes the circumference of a circle with a radius of 4 to be calculated and its value to be placed in the variable 'perimeter'.

'Calling a procedure'   Circumference_of_Circle(4, perimeter);

Computer programming languages

When a computer executes an instruction, it is always in machine code. Programs can be written in other languages and *converted* into machine code before running on a computer. This section looks at machine code, assembly language and high level languages, such as BASIC and LOGO.

Machine code and assembly language

Machine code is the language that computers use. Every different type of computer will have its own machine code. Machine code instructions are written as binary codes.

'A machine code instruction'

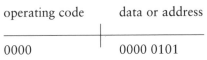

operating code	data or address
0000	0000 0101

Unless you knew that 0000 0000 0101 was a machine code instruction, you might easily mistake it for a character code or a number in binary. Even so, it is not immediately obvious what is meant! Machine code instructions are understood by computers, but are very difficult for most people to remember and use. For this reason it is very unlikely that a programmer would write a computer program in machine code.

To make programming at this level easier, **low level languages**, or **assembly languages**, have been developed. Assembly language is slightly easier to understand than machine code. Every machine code instruction has a single corresponding assembly language instruction.

This is a typical assembly language instruction:

'An assembly language instruction'

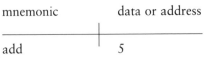

mnemonic	data or address
add	5

This is easier to understand! However, it is not clear what we are to add, or what the 5 stands for.

Assembly language and machine code programs are **machine orientated**, that is, they will not run on any computer other than the particular type they are designed for. Every computer runs a machine code, but they do not all run the *same* machine code. This means that a machine code or assembly language program cannot be run on *all* computers. When programs can be run on any computer, we say that they are **portable** from one computer to another. Assembly language and machine code programs are not portable between different types of computer.

Because machine code and assembly languages are difficult to understand and are not portable, they will not be used unless there are good reasons to do so.

Programs in assembly language or machine code are usually small compared to other languages. They will be needed if a program is likely to be too big to fit into the amount of RAM memory available. Also, machine code runs *very quickly* and is therefore used if a program must be fast.

For these reasons, games programs may be in machine code, as there is a need to write fast programs to run on computers with relatively small memories. Competition between software writers to produce more varied games encourages the introduction of more and better graphics (see Fig. 11.17) which use up more memory. Similarly, they attempt to cram programs with more and more facilities in the same amount of memory.

Some industrial machine tools, robots and modern domestic appliances, such as washing machines, are microprocessor-controlled devices. A **microprocessor** is a 'computer on a chip' (see Fig. 11.18), i.e. a computer consisting of a CPU and very small amounts of RAM and ROM memory built onto a single silicon chip. A machine code program, either stored in ROM or loaded into RAM, controls the device when it is used.

Fig. 11.17 A graphics screen from a computer game

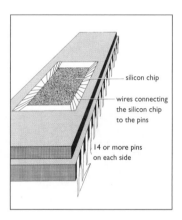

silicon chip

wires connecting
the silicon chip
to the pins

14 or more pins
on each side

Fig. 11.18 A microprocessor

High level languages

The high level programming languages most commonly used in schools and in the education system generally are Logo, BASIC and Pascal. COBOL is a high level language used in business and commerce. Brief examples of programs written in Logo, BASIC, Pascal and COBOL are illustrated in the following sections.

LOGO (from the Greek word LOGOS, which means 'word') **Logo** is a dialect of LISP, which is a language used in research into artificial intelligence. Logo is a simple, but powerful, language that can be used for a wide range of tasks.

Logo can be used to program screen graphics. For example, this logo program could be used to draw a square on the screen. You would type in the instructions at the keyboard and a 'pen' draws the square on the screen.

'A Logo program'

```
FD 40
LT 90
FD 40
LT 90
FD 40
LT 90
FD 40
LT 90
```

FD 40 means 'go forward 40 units'.
LT 90 means 'turn left, i.e. anticlockwise, 90 degrees'.
As a square has four sides of equal length, FD 40 and LT 90 are repeated four times.
Logo lets us abbreviate the program using a REPEAT **loop**. For example:

'Using a repeat loop'   REPEAT 4 [FD 40 LT 90]

If we wished to turn this instruction into a **procedure** that would allow us to draw a
square or any other regular polygon, this could be extended to:

'Defining a procedure'
TO SHAPE 'NUMBER' 'SIDE' 'ANGLE'
REPEAT:NUMBER [FD:SIDE LT:ANGLE]
END

To draw a square, as before, you would type in:

'Calling a procedure'   SHAPE 4 40 90

To draw an equilateral triangle (3 sides, all of length 50 and all angles 60 degrees), you
would type in:

SHAPE 3 50 60

'A turtle'
A small, mobile robot called a turtle can be attached to a computer running Logo (see
Fig. 11.19). The turtle can be controlled by the Logo program so that it moves in the same
way as the graphics being drawn on the screen.

Fig. 11.19 A Valiant turtle in action (photo courtesy of Valiant Technology Ltd)

Logo can also be used to manipulate text, for example:

'A Logo program'

```
TO FAN.CLUB
LOCAL "NAME
PR [HI, WHAT'S YOUR NAME?]
MAKE "NAME RL
TEST EQUALP :NAME JOE DAVIES
```

'Using a conditional statement'

```
IFTRUE [PRINT [WOW, CAN I HAVE YOUR AUTOGRAPH?]]
IFFALSE [PRINT SE [OH, HELLO,] FIRST :NAME]
END
```

BASIC (Beginners All-purpose Symbolic Instruction Code) BASIC is widely used in education and is often the first programming language learnt. BASIC is a powerful, flexible language used for a wide variety of commercial and scientific applications.

'A BASIC program'

```
10     REM ************** Sample BASIC program **************
20     REM This is a Menu driven program to calculate areas
30     PRINT "Menu"
40     PRINT "A. Area of Rectangle"
50     PRINT "B. Area of Circle"
55     PRINT "C. Finish"
60     PRINT "Please input your option choice (A, B or C)"
70     INPUT A$
80     IF A$ = "A" THEN GOTO 110
90     IF A$ = "B" THEN GOTO 180
95     IF A$ = "C" THEN GOTO 999
100    GOTO 30
110    REM ********** Calculate the area of a Rectangle **********
120    PRINT "Input the length of the rectangle"
130    INPUT L
140    PRINT "Input the breadth"
150    INPUT B
160    PRINT "The area of the rectangle is"; L*B
170    GOTO 30
180    REM ************** Calculate the area of a circle **************
190    PRINT "Input the radius of the circle"
200    INPUT R
210    PRINT "The area of the circle is"; 3.14*R*R
220    GOTO 30
999    END
```

'Using conditional statements'

Fig. 11.20 Blaise Pascal, the French mathematician

PASCAL (Named after the French mathematician Blaise Pascal (see Fig. 11.20)) Pascal is often the second language learnt by students of computing. It is used in colleges, universities, scientific computing and commerce.

Pascal is a *structured* language. It was designed as a teaching language to encourage good program design and a clear structure. Procedures are used to make programs easier to write, read and understand. There are a range of facilities that make programming easier and more convenient.

'A PASCAL program'

'Defining a procedure'

```
program swap (input, output);
(* sample pascal program: two numbers are input in order,*)
(* their order swapped and then they are printed        *)
var first, second  :  integer;
(* *************************************** *)
procedure numbersin;
begin
    write ('This program inputs two integers'  *);
    writeln ('and prints them in reverse order');
```

```
            writeln ('Input the first number');
            readln (first);
            writeln ('Input the second number');
            readln (second);
        end;
        (* *************************************** *)
        procedure switch;
        var temporary  :  integer;
        begin
            temporary :=first;
            first := second
            second := temporary;
        end;
        (* *************************************** *)
        procedure printout;
        begin
            write ('In reverse order the numbers input are');
            writeln (first, 'and', second);
        end;
        (* *************************************** *)
        (* the main program which calls the procedures      *)
        begin
            numbersin;
            switch;
            printout;
        end.
```

'Calling procedures'

COBOL COmmon Business Orientated Language   COBOL is used in business and commerce. It is particularly useful because files, records and fields are easily defined and manipulated. COBOL instructions read very like English in comparison with other languages.

COBOL has been a popular commercial language for at least thirty years. It has been regularly updated with extra features, so that it can cope with the changes in computer technology that have taken place during that time.

'A COBOL program'

```
INDENTIFICATION DIVISION.
PROGRAM–ID. RESULTS.
PURPOSE. PRINTS OUT GCSE RESULTS.
PROGRAMMER. A. HOULBROOKE.


ENVIRONMENT DIVISION.
INPUT–OUTPUT SECTION.
FILE–CONTROL.
SELECT RESULT–FILE
ASSIGN DK ACCESS DYNAMIC ORGANIZATION INDEXED.
SELECT PRINT–FILE
ASSIGN PROUT.


DATA DIVISION.
FILE SECTION.
FD   RESULT–FILE
        BLOCK 12 RECORDS
        DATA RECORD RESULT-DETAILS
        LABEL RECORD STANDARD.
```

'Defining a file'

```
01   RESULT–DETAILS.
        03 ID–NO                    PIC  X(5).
        03 NAME                     PIC  X(50).
        03 SYLLABUS–CODE            PIC  999.
        03 EXAM–GRADE               PIC  X.
```

'Defining records and fields'

```
FD   PRINT–FILE
     DATA RECORD PRINT–LINE
     LABEL RECORD OMITTED
     LINAGE 60 FOOTAGE 60 TOP 3 BOTTOM 3.


01   PRINT–LINE      X(132).


WORKING STORAGE SECTION.
01   PRINT–IMAGE.
     03 DUMMY–1                PIC  X(28)
        VALUE " RESULT FOR CANDIDATE, NAME ".
     03 PRINT NAME             PIC  X(50).
     03 DUMMY–2                PIC  X(12)
        VALUE ", SYLLABUS CODE".
     03 PRINT–CODE             PIX  999.
     03 DUMMY–3                PIC  X(4)
        VALUE " IS ".
     03 PRINT–GRADE            PIC  X.
```

'The program instructions'

```
PROCEDURE DIVISION.
OPEN INPUT RESULT–FILE.
OPEN OUTPUT PRINT–FILE.
READ–LOOP.
    READ RESULT–FILE NEXT END GO TO END–ROUTINE.
    MOVE NAME TO PRINT–NAME.
    MOVE SYLLABUS–CODE TO PRINT–CODE.
    MOVE EXAM–GRADE TO PRINT–GRADE.
    MOVE PRINT–IMAGE TO PRINT–LINE.
    WRITE PRINT–FILE BEFORE ADVANCING 1 LINE.
END–ROUTINE.
    CLOSE RESULT–FILE.
    CLOSE PRINT–FILE.
    EXIT.
```

Important features of high level languages

High level languages are easier to understand than machine code or assembly language. You can design and write a program in a high level language more easily than in machine code or assembly language.

High level languages have features that make programming in them easier. They allow the programmer to use expressions very much like the algebra and arithmetic used in maths, e.g. $A = 3*B + C$. **Key words**, that is words that define an operation, e.g. PRINT (in BASIC), are used. **Labels** are used for branching to other parts of the program. Sometimes the labels will be words or simply line numbers as in BASIC. Structures such as procedures, conditional statements, functions and loops are available.

However, before a high level language program can be run, it must be converted to machine code. Each high level language instruction will be translated to several machine code instructions.

Errors

'Types of program errors'

Before a program is used, it is checked for errors. **Syntax errors** are errors resulting from incorrect use of the rules governing the structure of the language, e.g. using PRONT instead of PRINT in BASIC. An **execution error** is an error that occurs while the program is running, e.g. division by zero.

Logic errors are errors in the logic of the program. The syntax may well be correct and the program may run and produce output but because the program logic is incorrect, the required processing will not be done. Consequently the output will be faulty.

EXAMINATION QUESTIONS

▷ **Question 1**   Tick the TWO examples of computer control:

Automatic pilot	
Flight-booking system	
Producing a price list	
Robots making a car	
A model of traffic flow	

(SEG, 1993)

▷ **Question 2**   Many computer controlled devices are activated by sensors. Write down what type of sensor might be used to:

(a) Switch on street lights automatically when it is dusk.
(b) Activate traffic lights when cars approach a junction.
(c) Switch on a heater when the temperature falls below 50°C.

(City and Guilds)

▷ **Question 3**   Sort the statements listed below into the right order, so you can record a programme from TV onto a video recorder.

    Select time on
    Turn timer on
    Load tape into machine
    Select time off
    Turn recorder on
    Select day
    Select TV channel

(NDTEF)

▷ **Question 4**   When Dominic leaves his office at the end of the day he has to set the office burglar alarm.
    The burglar alarm has two types of **sensor** which can send inputs to the control box. These are:

    door contact points
    window contact points

Inputs to the control box are in the form of binary digits representing 0 for *off* and 1 for *on*.
    The bell will sound if the alarm power is turned on and any of the inputs is also on.

(i)   State what is meant by *sensor*.
(ii) Fill in a pattern of four binary digits below which will sound the alarm.

ALARM POWER	DOOR 1	DOOR 2	WINDOW

(iii) Fill in a pattern of four binary digits below which will not sound the alarm.

ALARM POWER	DOOR 1	DOOR 2	WINDOW

(London)

▷ **Question 5**   The heating of water in a tank is under the control of a microprocessor. Cold water enters the tank via Valve 1. It is heated to a set temperature and leaves the tank via Valve 2.

(a) Describe how feedback could be used in the system.
(b) (i)   Where should an analog-to-digital converter be placed in the system?
     (ii) Why is the analog-to-digital converter necessary?

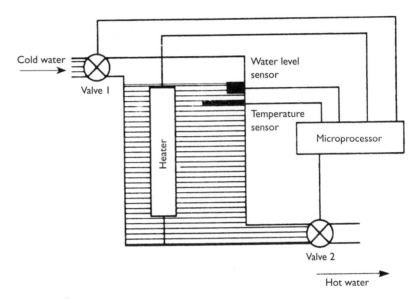

Fig. 11.21 Water heater

(MEG)

▷ **Question 6**   A floor turtle contains a pen and faces east. The turtle follows these instructions:

PEN UP	Lift the pen off the floor
PEN DOWN	Place the tip of the pen on the floor
FORWARD n	Move n steps forward
BACKWARD n	Move n steps backward
LEFT b	Turn left b degrees
RIGHT b	Turn right b degrees

Write instructions for the turtle to draw this triangle.

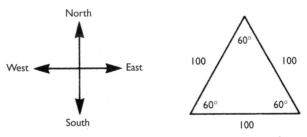

Fig. 11.22 Floor turtle

(MEG)

▷ **Question 7**   A robot is used to retrieve fuel rods from a nuclear reactor. To get the rod from the position labelled 'X', the following instructions could be given:

FORWARD 3
TURN RIGHT
FORWARD 1
TAKE

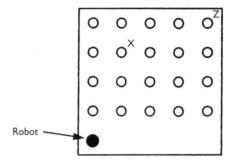

Fig. 11.23 Robot

(a) Write sensible instructions to get this rod placed into position Z and bring the robot back to its starting place.
(b) Why would a robot be used for this job?

(SEG, 1993)

▷ **Question 8**   (a) A computer program is used to control a robot which is moving and stacking boxes in a warehouse. The program uses commands to control its movements.

FORWARD steps
BACK steps
RIGHT angle
LEFT angle
UP steps
DOWN steps

For example, FORWARD 50 moves the robot forward 50 steps in a straight line.
RIGHT 45 turns the robot 45° to the right.
UP 2 raises the forks 2 steps.
It is found to be dropping the boxes in the wrong place.

Give two different mistakes in the program that could be making this.
(b) Following a nasty accident, the robot has to be adapted to stop if it meets an unexpected obstacle in its path. What changes would need to be made to the robot design?

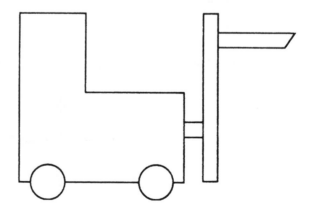

Fig. 11.24 Robot

(NEAB/WJEC)

▷ **Question 9**   Tilda Shower is a geography teacher.

Tilda wants the school weather station to provide her class with very detailed weather data over a period of a week.

The instructions below are part of a computer program which, every 30 minutes, stores the temperature that the weather station detects.

WAIT 30
DETECT TEMP
STORE TEMP

Tilda now wants the temperature to be stored every 15 minutes.
(a) Show how one of the instructions will have to be changed.
(b) (i) Explain why these three instructions by themselves would not keep on storing the temperature.
(ii) Show the extra instructions that would be needed so that the computer will store the temperature 'forever'. (You may invent your own instructions.)
(c) 50 °C is very very hot.
   –50 °C is very very cold.
      Sometimes the weather station does not work properly so silly values of tempera-ture are stored.
      Explain how the program could be improved to prevent the computer storing silly values for temperature.
(d) Tilda wants the rainfall data to be recorded every hour for a whole year.
      She also wants the results to be printed in the form of a booklet.
   (i) Describe how this amount of data could have been collected without the aid of a computer.
   (ii) Explain why, in a school, it would not be practical to collect this amount of data without a computer.
   (iii) State one advantage to Tilda's pupils of having this amount of data.

(London)

▷ **Question 10**   An automatic weather station on the roof of a house is connected to a home computer and suitable software.
(a) Describe how such an information system might be used to collect and store weather data.
(b) Give TWO reasons why it may be better to use a computer to help record the weather rather than a manual method.
(c) A choice of two weather stations is available.
      A – one which needs to be connected to the computer at all times
      B – one which collects the data inside the station for transmission at a later date.
      Discuss the relative merits of these two systems.

(MEG)

   EXAMINATION ANSWERS

▷ **Answer 1**   Automatic pilot
Robots making a car

▷ **Answer 2**   (a) light sensor
(b) pressure sensor
(c) temperature sensor

▷ **Answer 3**   (a) Turn recorder on
Load tape into machine
Turn timer on
Select time on
Select time off

Select day
Select TV channel

▷ **Answer 4**   (i)   A sensor is an input device used to sense environmental conditions. Sensors for door and window contact points could be expected to return two different voltages. For example:

5V ≡ 1 = ON
0V ≡ 0 = OFF

(ii) All these patterns would sound the alarm:

1001   1101   1111
1010   1011
1100   1110

(iii) These patterns will not sound the alarm:

0000   0011   0110
0001   0100   0111
0010   0101   1000

▷ **Answer 5**   (a)   The sensor reads the temperature.
If it is too cold the microprocessor turns on the heater.
If it is too hot the microprocessor turns off the heater.
The tap can only be opened when the water is in the correct temperature range.
(b)   (i)   Between the temperature sensor and the microprocessor.
(ii) The temperature sensor outputs an analog signal. This must be converted to a digital signal which the computer can interpret.

(MEG)

▷ **Answer 6**

PEN DOWN		PEN DOWN		PD
FORWARD 100		FORWARD 100		B100
LEFT 120	OR	RIGHT 60	OR	R60
FORWARD 100		FORWARD 100		B100
LEFT 120		RIGHT 60		R60
FORWARD 100		FORWARD 100		B100
PEN UP		PEN UP		PU

(MEG)

▷ **Answer 7**   (a)   FORWARD 3
TURN LEFT
FORWARD 1
PLACE
TURN LEFT
FORWARD 4
TURN LEFT
FORWARD 4
(b)   Because the inside of a nuclear reactor is not a safe place for a human.

▷ **Answer 8**   (a)   The commands in the program could be in the wrong order or missing. Incorrect values could have been given for the number of steps or the angle.
(b)   There would have to be sensors on the front of the robot. The program would stop the robot if there was an object in its way.

▷ **Answer 9**   (a)   WAIT 30 becomes WAIT 15.
(b)   (i)   Because there are no instructions to repeat the three instructions given.
(ii) For example:

REPEAT
        WAIT 30
        DETECT TEMP
        STORE TEMP
UNTIL THE PROGRAM IS INTERRUPTED

(c) You would validate the temperature detected and ignore it if it was not realistic. For example, if this instruction:

IF –5°C>TEMP OR 35°C<TEMP
THEN go to the DETECT TEMP instruction

was inserted after DETECT TEMP, the program would loop until a realistic temperature was detected.

(d) (i)   If you don't use a computer, you would have to use a thermometer, read it yourself and write down the results.

(ii) You could not expect school pupils or teachers to record the temperature every hour, without fail, especially at night.

(iii) Whatever you are studying, you should collect as much data as you can. You can always discard the data you don't need. The more data you have, the more accurately you can describe what is happening.

▷ **Answer 10** (a) Weather data is recorded using sensors for temperature, wind speed, wind direction, rainfall, pressure and humidity. The computer stores the data in memory or on disk. Data is displayed when the user needs to see it.

(b) Two from:
Computer can automatically record the weather whereas humans have to remember to collect the data.
Computer readings are usually more accurate than readings taken by humans.
Computers can store historical data.
Computers can retrieve and display data in a variety of forms quickly.

(c) A will require the computer to be connected at all times. It would be tricky to use the computer for other functions whilst it is collecting data whereas with B data can be viewed at the convenience of the user. With A the computer must never be switched off which could cause a problem. If it was switched off by accident, data would be lost from the weather station.

(MEG)

▶ **EXAMINATION QUESTION WITH STUDENT ANSWER**

▷ **Question data**

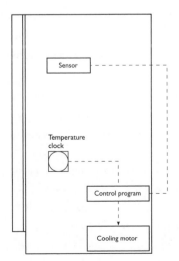

Fig. 11.25 Fridge diagram

This is a diagram of a fridge. The fridge has a sensor, a control program and a cooling system motor which takes the heat out of the refrigerator.

(a)   What does the sensor in the fridge do?

It senses the temperature in the fridge.

(b)   The fridge uses feedback. What is feedback?

Feedback occurs when a sensor detects a situation that causes the computer to indicate action that alters the data collected by the sensor.

(c)   Write down instructions to show how the control program operates the cooling system.

If the temperature is too high the cooling system is switched on.

(City and Guilds)

▷ **Examiner's comment**

(a) *Correct.*

(b) *This is a text book definition of feedback. It is not incorrect but it does not relate to the context of the question. A better answer would be:*

'If the temperature is too high, the sensor detects this and the control program turns on the cooling motor. The temperature in the fridge falls. When the temperature is too low, the sensor detects this and the control program turns the cooling motor off. This cycle of sensing and re-action is called feedback.'

You should always relate what you have learnt to the context of the question.

(c) *This answer is correct but incomplete. The student has forgotten that the cooling motor should be turned off when the temperature is too low.*

SUMMARY

This chapter looks at monitoring and control systems, and computer languages.

▷ **Data logging** is the automatic collection and storage of the information provided by sensors. This may take place over long distances. For example, collecting information from remote weather stations.

▷ **Control systems** use sensors to measure environmental conditions, and actuators to adjust them.

▷ **Sensors** are used to measure environmental conditions. Sensors can monitor heat, light, humidity, sound, pressure, wind speed, wind direction, tilt, etc.

▷ **Actuators** are used to adjust environmental conditions. Actuators are heaters, motors, pumps, etc.

▷ Control systems involve **feedback**. Feedback is a cycle of sensing, processing and reaction.

▷ **AND**, **OR** and **NOT logic** is used in designing control systems.

▷ **Dedicated control systems** are built into equipment. For example, a fault detection system for an industrial machine.

▷ **Computer control systems** are computer based. For example, a greenhouse control system.

▷ Computers themselves are controlled by programs.

▷ A **computer program** is a list of instructions to a computer written in a computer language. Logo and BASIC are computer programming languages.

▷ Different types of **program structure** are used in computer programs:

   ▷ **Conditional statements** may change what the program does depending on whether a condition has been satisfied or otherwise. For example, IF INPUT="YES" THEN AffirmativeAction ELSE NegativeAction

   ▷ A **loop** is a series of instructions that is repeated.

   ▷ A **procedure** is a self-contained sequence of instructions that can be run from elsewhere in the same program.

IT systems at work

This chapter should be read if you are preparing for GCSE IT assessment with the following examining boards:

C & G	MEG	NEAB	SEG
London	NDTEF	RSA	WJEC

▶ ## GETTING STARTED

This chapter reviews the IT systems used in several commercial applications. For example, in booking airline tickets, and doing stock control in a supermarket. The IT systems are chosen to illustrate batch, real time, and on-line, interactive processing.

All IT systems go through the stages of the system's life cycle. That is, system investigation; feasibility study; system analysis and design; program design, coding and testing; implementation; system documentation; evaluation; and maintenance. These are described in this chapter. Jobs in IT are briefly described.

C & G	LONDON	MEG	NDTEF	NEAB	RSA	SEG	WJEC	TOPIC	STUDY	REVISION I	REVISION 2
✓	✓	✓	✓	✓	✓	✓	✓	Payroll			
✓	✓	✓	✓	✓	✓	✓	✓	Airline booking system			
✓	✓	✓	✓	✓	✓	✓	✓	Supermarket stock control			
✓	✓	✓	✓	✓	✓	✓	✓	Geographic information systems			
✓	✓	✓	✓	✓	✓	✓	✓	The system life cycle			
✓	✓	✓	✓	✓	✓	✓	✓	Systems investigation			
✓	✓	✓	✓	✓	✓	✓	✓	Feasibility study			
✓	✓	✓	✓	✓	✓	✓	✓	Systems analysis and design			
✓	✓	✓	✓	✓	✓	✓	✓	Program development			
✓	✓	✓	✓	✓	✓	✓	✓	Implementation			
✓	✓	✓	✓	✓	✓	✓	✓	System documentation			
✓	✓	✓	✓	✓	✓	✓	✓	Evaluation			
✓	✓	✓	✓	✓	✓	✓	✓	Maintenance			
✓	✓	✓	✓	✓	✓		✓	Jobs in IT			

GLOSSARY

IT system   The whole system of hardware, software and human activities that are used in an application.

Batch processing   In an IT system that uses batch processing, all the data to be processed is available before processing starts. Data is processed in batches. Batch processing is not interactive. For example, a payroll system.

Real time processing   In a real time IT system, data is processed as it is input, before any other data is input. Data may be input at any time from a variety of sources. The results of processing can influence further input. Real time systems are fast and interactive. For example, an airline booking system.

On-line, interactive processing   On-line, interactive systems are typically multiaccess systems that are slower than real time systems. For example, stock control in a supermarket.

WHAT YOU NEED TO KNOW

Large companies and businesses need to access high volumes of data every day. They need to be able to do this quickly, accurately and inexpensively. Because of the large scale of their information needs they invest in IT systems that are designed to meet their own requirements. They are likely to employ their own staff to design and implement IT systems that will provide solutions to their own information needs.

The applications described in this chapter have been chosen to illustrate the variety of demands met by IT systems. The systems have been characterized as **batch**, **real time**, and **on-line interactive**. These types of IT systems are commonly found in commerce and industry.

Only simple outlines of the payroll, airline booking, supermarket stock control and geographical information systems described have been given. In reality, these IT systems are much more complex than described. The data structures will be more extensive and detailed and the volumes of data processed much greater than can reasonably be described in a GCSE text.

It is also most likely that, in practice, an IT system will be a *hybrid*, involving some batch and on-line interactive processing with links to a real time system where one is in use. For example, both payroll and stock control could be run by a supermarket on the same mainframe computer.

The organization of an IT department in a large company and the life cycle of an IT systems are inextricably linked. This is perhaps not surprising since the role of the IT department is to meet the needs of the company by providing appropriate IT systems, and staff with the skills to run these systems.

▷ Payroll

Every company or business has to pay its employees. Although this is a fairly straightforward task, it has to be done frequently and accurately. Employees will be annoyed if they are not paid the correct amount at the appropriate time. However, it is not a task which needs to be done instantaneously. The data to be input is readily available when required and it might be possible to do the data processing needed over a few days or longer. Provided the system is well organized and the payroll software works to our satisfaction, all should be well! In following through the description of the payroll system given below, it would be useful to refer to the systems flowchart (see Fig. 12.1).

Data capture

'Data capture using clock-cards'

In a warehouse, workers each have their own 'clock-card'. When they arrive at work they 'clock-in', that is they put the clock-card in a slot in a machine which prints the time onto the clock-card. When they leave work, they 'clock-out' by putting the clock-card in the slot again, so that the time they finished work is printed on the clock-card. Workers find their own clock-card by using their name which is printed on the card but there is also an 'employee number' printed on the clock-card that uniquely identifies each worker. The clock-card is used to *capture* the data needed for processing so that a wages slip can be printed for each employee.

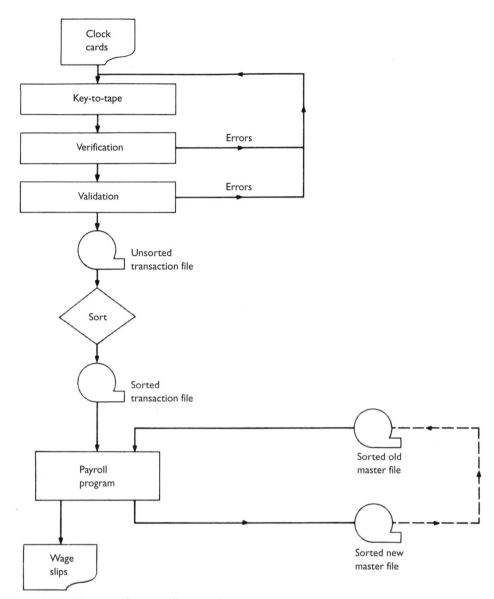

Fig. 12.1 An IT system for payroll processing

The information about an employee on each clock-card is:

▶ name
▶ employee number
▶ clock-in time and clock-out time for every day worked

Workers are paid a week in arrears, that is they are paid for the week *before* the one they have just worked. If the clock-cards are collected at the end of the week there is one week to process the payroll data.

When the clock-cards have been *collected*, as there are a very large number of them, they are divided into *batches*, i.e. bundles, of 50. A hash total is calculated for each batch by adding up the employee numbers. This total is a meaningless number, but each time it is calculated it should be the same. To check that all the cards are in the correct batch and that none have been lost or misplaced, all we have to do is re-calculate the hash total. If it is unaltered, the batch is complete; if it is different, there is something wrong and we will have to carefully check the batch. This will be done by data control staff after each step in the processing.

'Collecting and batching'

'Key-to-tape'

Now that the data has been collected and batched, it must be *recorded* on a computer-readable medium. The computer cannot read the printing on the clock-cards, so this data must be prepared in a form the computer *can* use. This is done using a key-to-tape machine. The data is *entered* at the keyboard and recorded on magnetic tape. During data preparation, the data entered from each clock-card is:

▶ employee number
▶ clock-in time and clock-out time, for every day worked

Note that names of employees are not entered. This is not necessary, as each employee is identified by their unique employee number.

Verification and validation

'Verification'

To check that the data on each clock-card has been entered accurately, it is *verified* by keying in the entire batch again and checking the newly entered data against the original. If any errors arise they must be corrected before the batch of clock-cards can proceed any further. Batches of clock-cards that have been successfully transferred to tape and verified can now be *validated*. There will be one record for each clock-card in the file on magnetic tape containing the data entered.

'Validation'

Validation checks on each field in the record can be performed. Employee numbers can be checked against a table of known employee numbers; the clock-in time and clock-out times can be checked to see if they are in the range between 0.00 hours and 23.59 hours; the clock-out time should be later than the clock-in time; the hours worked each day should usually not exceed 16 hours; the total hours worked should usually be less than 60. Data that is successfully validated is written to the unsorted transaction file; invalid data must be corrected before further processing.

The unsorted transaction file contains only the data transferred to it from the clock-cards. This is the data about employees that changes from week to week. The data that does not change so frequently is saved on the old master file. There is one record on the old master file for each employee. The records are stored in employee number order.

A record on the old master file would contain the following:

▶ employee number
▶ name
▶ address
▶ hourly rate of pay
▶ tax and national insurance details
▶ total tax paid this year
▶ total national insurance paid this year
▶ total pay this year

Sorting

'Sorting'

For each employee the record on the transaction file and the record on the old master file must be matched, so that all the data for an employee is available when the payroll program is run. For this reason the unsorted transaction file is next *sorted* into the same order as the old master file. Both files are sorted into ascending order on the employee number. It is important to have both files in the same order because they are recorded on magnetic tape. Magnetic tape only allows serial or sequential access to files recorded on it, that is, records are read in order from the beginning of the file to the end. If the sorted transaction file and the master file were not in the same order, matching the corresponding records for an employee would be very slow.

Now that the data to be processed has been captured, entered, verified, validated and sorted, it can be *input* to the payroll program. In the payroll program each sorted transaction file record will be matched with the corresponding old master file record. The *hours worked*

'Processing'

will be calculated from the clock-in and clock-out times on the sorted transaction file. The *hourly rate of pay* is found on the old master file so that *gross pay* can be calculated. Gross pay is the amount earned before deductions. Tax and national insurance details on the old master file are used to calculate deductions from the gross pay to arrive at *net pay*. Net pay is the actual amount paid to employees after deductions from the amount earned. The *tax paid* will be added to the total tax paid this year and the *National Insurance contribution paid* will be added to the total National Insurance paid this year. These totals are changed each week, so a new master file record is created containing the updated totals.

'Printing wage slips'

A *wage slip* is printed for each employee, giving all the pay details necessary (see Fig. 12.2) and including the name of the employee, taken from the old master file. The wage slips will be printed on continuous computer stationery with perforations between each one. The stationery must be trimmed to remove the sprocket holes and separated at the perforations before distributing the wage slips to employees.

RADIO U.K. LTD. ✟

Name: A. Jones	Employee number: 86502	Date: 10/07/92
Hours worked: 45	Hourly rate of pay: £3.50	

Gross pay:	£157.50		
Tax:	£26.25	Tax paid this year:	£240.75
National insurance:	£17.40	National insurance paid this year:	£136.14
Net pay:	£113.85		

Fig. 12.2 A wage slip printed by the payroll system

It will also be necessary to *add* records for new employees to the new master file and *remove* the records of those who have left the company. This is done by adding extra records to the transaction file to indicate which records are to be inserted and deleted. When the payroll program is run, an extra record is created on the new master file for each new employee. The records of those employees that have left are not copied across from the old master file to the new master file.

File backup

Backups of files for security purposes are generated as a consequence of the need to create a new master file each time the payroll program is run. Using the ancestral backup system, the new master file is the son, while the old master file (which was the previous son) becomes the father. The previous old master file (which was the father) now becomes the grandfather. Copies of the sorted transaction file must also be kept. Such a system allows recovery from the loss of current files by regenerating them from the historical data contained in the backup files.

This payroll processing system would run effectively using either magnetic tape or magnetic disk. Provided the files are sorted into the same order before input to the payroll program, magnetic tape is unlikely to be significantly slower than magnetic disk relative to the time available to do the job. Consequently, magnetic tape may be used in preference to disk, as it is a cheaper medium for storage of high volumes of data.

Batch processing

The system described above is known as a **batch processing** system because the data captured is divided into batches before processing. It is characteristic of batch processing that *all* the data to be processed is available *before* processing begins and that there is no need to process the data immediately. The system is not interactive. The user sends the batches of data to be processed to data control who pass it on to data preparation for input. Computer operators supervise the processing, then the final output is returned to the user. There is no interactive input to the system while the payroll program is running.

▷ **Airline booking system**

'An example of an airline booking system'

A large airline keeps details of flight schedules and passenger bookings (see Fig. 12.3).

Finding a seat

Customers may make enquiries at travel agents anywhere in the world to find if a seat is available on any of the flights operated by the airline. Customers require immediate up-to-date information. The travel agent can make on-line contact with the main computer using a microcomputer and a modem connected via the telephone network. This gives access to the flight information and booking file held on magnetic disk on the main computer.

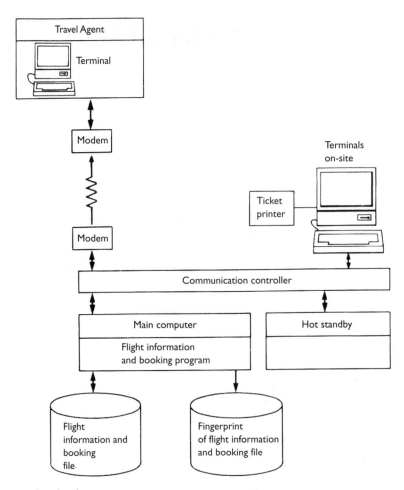

Fig. 12.3 An airline booking system

The main computer should support multiaccess, as there may be a large number of travel agents wanting to make enquiries at the same time. The flight information and booking file must be held on magnetic disk as data held on disk can be read by direct access. Access to the flight information and booking file must be made using direct access for high speed data retrieval. The information requested can be displayed instantaneously and will be kept up-to-date while displayed on the screen.

Booking a seat

The customer may decide to book a seat on a flight. The travel agent books the seat using the terminal. Once a seat has been booked the flight information and booking file must be updated immediately so that further enquiries, perhaps by other agents, show the seat as already booked. When the flight information and booking file is being accessed to book a flight, to avoid double booking, all other attempts to book the seat must be locked out.

Tickets may be printed out on-the-spot or may be sent to customers at a later date. Payment may also be made via the on-line link using a credit card, or customers may be sent the bill by mail some days later. If a customer pays the travel agent in cash this will be charged to the travel agent in due course. There should also be a facility for cancellation and refund of payments using the on-line link.

'Security'   Security of access to the system is maintained by giving agents a unique user identification number and password.

'Fault tolerance'   Since the system may be on-line twenty-four hours a day, it is very important that the computer is not out of action for any time due to mechanical breakdown. This is avoided by having two identical computers, the main one in use and an additional computer available as a **hot standby** to be used if the main computer breaks down.

'Backups'   As the system is in constant use, file backups cannot be done in the usual way by copying all the files on disk to tape. This would mean halting the flight information and booking program while the backups are done. Instead, two disks are used, both having copies of the flight information and booking file on them. Any changes that are made to the file are made on both disks at the same time. This technique is known as **finger printing**. It also ensures that if one disk becomes faulty there is an exact copy of the file immediately available on the other disk.

The computer hardware and software involved are only used for running the airline booking system. This is a dedicated IT system and any other processing required must be done on other computers.

Real time

An on-line booking system such as the one described above is an example of a **real time** processing system. It is so called because processing is in real time, i.e. as data is input it is processed, before any further input can be processed. A real time computer system must be fast enough to ensure that input data is processed immediately because the results can influence any further input. Typically, data can be input to a real time system at any time, from a variety of sources. Even so, processing must be instantaneous and immediate.

'Example of process control'

Real time systems are also used in industry for **process control**. A manufacturer of a chemical product may use electronic sensors at various points in the production process to monitor the progress of dangerous reactions. For example, a heat sensor may be used to record the temperature. If the reaction becomes too hot, an explosion may occur. To avoid this the process must be cooled or shut down immediately if it overheats. If the heat sensor is connected to a computer control system the computer can be used to monitor the heat of the reaction. When the reaction overheats, the computer will take immediate action to lower the temperature or shut down the reaction if necessary. A computer control system must be a real time system as a slow or delayed response could lead to an explosion or some other disaster.

The need for the immediate response of a real time computer system is also important when computers are used to control the movements of robots. A slow reaction to a touch sensor indicating an obstruction could mean loss of life to workers or damage to the robot.

▷ **Supermarket stock control**

'An example of a supermarket stock control system'

A large modern supermarket will have a computer system situated within the store. At the checkout, the Point of Sale (POS) terminal has attached to it a laser scanner. This is used to read the bar code printed on items sold in the supermarket (see Fig. 12.4). The POS terminal also has a keyboard for entering the product details of items that do not have bar codes printed on them. A small screen is used to display messages sent from the central computer to the POS terminal and a small dot matrix printer built into the terminal is used to print

Fig. 12.4 A supermarket checkout

receipts. There will be several checkouts in the supermarket, each with a POS terminal. All of these are connected to the computer located in the store. This computer also has network stations in the warehouse and elsewhere. There are disk drives, a printer and a modem link to other computers via the telephone network.

The computer system is a general purpose system and is used for all the data processing done by the supermarket, including payroll, etc. However, we are only going to look at its use for stock control (see Fig. 12.5).

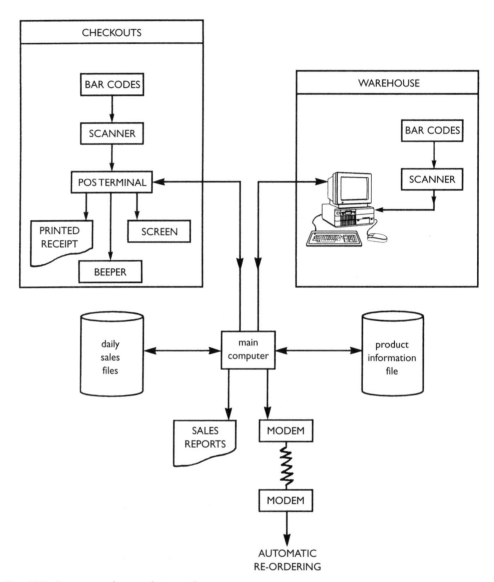

Fig. 12.5 A supermarket stock control system

Using bar codes

Most products sold by the supermarket have on them a bar code. The data held on a bar code identifies the product and includes a *product code* and a *check digit*. When an item is sold, the bar code is read by the laser scanner and the data on it is transmitted to the main computer. Here the check digit is re-calculated from the product code and checked against the check digit received from the POS terminal. If these are not the same, the bar code must be re-entered. If both check digits are the same, the product code is checked against the product information file. A record on the file contains the following fields for each product:

▶   product code, e.g. 152907
▶   name of product, e.g. baked beans 570 g
▶   price

If the bar code received from the POS terminal is *not* on the product information file, the bar code may have been entered incorrectly. In this case the bar code must be re-entered. The entry of valid bar codes is indicated by a loud beep.

The product code is used to find the corresponding record in the product information file. The name of the product and the price contained in this record are sent to the POS terminal from the main computer. These are printed on the customer's receipt by the small dot matrix printer built into the POS terminal.

'The price is not in the bar code'

It is a very common belief that the bar code contains the name of the product and its price. This not so. These are kept in the product information file stored on the main computer. They are transferred to the POS terminal when required.

For every item sold, the price is added to the total for the customer. This is printed on the receipt when the bar codes on all the items purchased by the customer have been read by the laser scanner. Access to the product information file must be fast enough so that customers are not kept waiting and, in consequence, it is a direct or random access file on disk.

Stock control

The sales made at each checkout are recorded in the daily sales file as the goods are sold. It is sufficient to record the product code of each item sold. At the end of every day the individual product codes are read from this file. The quantity of each item sold is calculated and a *report printed* showing the product code, name of product and the total number of each product sold. An extract from this report follows:

Wed 23rd March

product code	name of product	total number sold
152907	baked beans 570 g	500
923673	pea soup 300 g	258
025993	peaches 420 g	367
300609	pasta 500 g	124
007085	tomato puree 50 g	356

This information is also used to update the stock control file. The stock control file contains a record for each product with fields as follows:

▶ product code, e.g. 152907
▶ number in stock, e.g. 1200
▶ re-order level, e.g. 1000

For each product, the total number sold that day is *subtracted* from the number in stock, which is updated. In the above example the total number of baked beans 570 g sold on Wed 23rd March is 500. The number in stock is 1200 so the updated number in stock is 1200 *less* 500, i.e. 700.

'Occasional stock report'

The supermarket has to be careful that it does not run out of stock as this will annoy customers, and sales and profits will be lost. Periodically a *stock report* will be printed showing existing stock levels as recorded on the stock control file. Those products that have a lower number in stock than their re-order level will be emphasized in the report. The supermarket manager will go through the report and re-order those products that are needed, using the information contained in the report. In this case, the manager should re-order baked beans 570 g, as 700 is less than 1000.

'Re-ordering'

Automatic ordering

If the manager wishes, items can be ordered automatically when the stock control file is updated. For those products that have a lower number in stock than their re-order level, the manufacturer is contacted and asked to send more of the product. This is done automatically using electronic mail sent by the supermarket's computer to the manufacturer's computer using a modem and the telephone system.

When items that have been ordered arrive at the supermarket they are sent to the warehouse. At the warehouse the goods are checked as they arrive and stored until they are moved into the supermarket to be sold. As they arrive, the warehouse manager enters the quantity of each product delivered at the network station in the warehouse. This data is used to update the stock control file, e.g. if 800 cans of baked beans 570 g are delivered then the number in stock is updated to 700 plus 800, i.e. 1500, bringing the number in stock above the re-order level. Using this system the manager can control the flow of stock into the supermarket in response to sales of stock to customers.

Extra information

The above description focuses on one basic aspect of a stock control system. In practice, the same system would be used to do a range of *additional* tasks:

▶ the *number of items* sold and the *takings at each till* could be recorded and used to monitor the performance of checkout operators;

▶ the *rate of sales of each product* could be calculated and used to increase the choice of popular goods or to reduce stocks of unpopular items;

▶ the *pattern of sales* of every product could be recorded so that stocks are not held at times of the year when goods are unlikely to sell;

▶ the *effectiveness of sales promotions* can be monitored;

▶ goods that have *high profit margins* can be stocked in preference to those with lower profit margins.

'Low stock = low costs'

To keep business expenses to a minimum, stocks of goods should be kept as low as possible. If a *maximum stock level* is recorded for each product on the stock control file, then the quantity re-ordered can be adjusted so that this level is *not exceeded* when new supplies arrive at the warehouse. This maximum stock level can be adjusted so that the extra costs involved in frequent re-ordering are balanced against the expense of storing larger quantities of a product in the warehouse.

Security

'Reducing the loss of stock'

The system can also be used to determine the extent of theft from the supermarket and improve security. If the actual number of each product in stock is counted and found to be less than the number in stock on the stock control file, then this difference is due to loss of stock. Loss of stock can be due to damage or theft. If damages are recorded as they occur then loss due to theft can be calculated.

'Advantages of a computer-based stock control system'

Computer-based stock control systems allow managers to monitor stock levels very closely and to exercise greater control over the business. This allows the manager to increase the profitability of the business and improve customer service. Prices can be kept lower and customer service is quicker due to the speed of the POS terminals. The customer's receipt is itemized and fewer mistakes occur at the checkout. However, the purchase cost of the system is high and it will be necessary to train employees to use it. Because the productivity of checkout employees is increased there will be a reduced number of employees at the supermarket or improved customer services.

On-line interactive processing

The stock control system described above is an **on-line interactive processing** system. On-line systems use terminals connected to a computer. These terminals interact with the computer system, sending data to it and receiving data from it. A real time system is an on-line interactive system but not all such systems are real time. The stock control system described here is not real time.

Sales data is captured using the POS terminals, which must be permanently connected on-line to the computer. In order to print an itemized receipt showing the description and price of every item sold, this data must be found in the product information file, using the product code contained in the bar code input by laser scanner, i.e. interactive processing is necessary as an interchange of data takes place. However, there is no need to immediately update the stock control file as goods are sold. Stock control data does not need to be updated immediately. It is quite acceptable for recorded stock levels to be a day or two out of date, as this is unlikely to significantly affect the business. The expense of a specialized real time system cannot be justified in these circumstances.

Geographic information systems (GIS)

The most important feature of **Geographic Information Systems** (GIS) is that they can display maps (see Fig. 12.6). These maps are often based on aerial photographs that have been recorded in a form that computers can manipulate. The GIS can zoom in and out to display the maps at various levels of detail. For example, a local map showing the houses in a street or a district map showing only the towns could be displayed.

The maps could have various layers. Layers might show the location of all the schools, all the hospitals, all the roadworks, all the night clubs, etc. You could alter the map so that it displayed only the layers with the motorways and A roads. You could display only one layer on the map or several layers at the same time.

A GIS uses maps to display information in relation to its geographic location. It has a built-in database to store information. The information in the database can be provided with the GIS, for example, census data. Alternatively, users can input their own data.

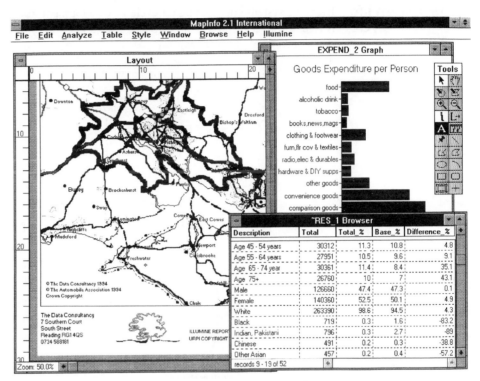

Fig. 12.6 A screen map in a GIS (courtesy of the Data Consultancy)

Examples of the use of GIS
The following are a few of the tasks you can do using a GIS.

'Route planning'
> Transport companies can plan the route that each truck in a fleet will take to deliver its load throughout the country. The actual location of the trucks can be shown on the map as they move around the country. The position of roadworks and accidents can be shown so that the trucks can be re-routed to avoid them.

'Marketing'
> Manufacturing companies can use GIS to market their products more effectively. The location of actual and potential customers can be shown on a map. Only those customers with particular needs can be shown. This helps companies target their advertising and other marketing activities more effectively. For example: from census data you can find out which areas have most young people living there. Young people buy computer games but tend not to buy office furniture. An area with a large number of young people would be a good place to sell a new range of computer games but might not be such a good place to sell filing cabinets. Sales can be mapped so that the impact of sales promotions can be seen.

'Crime fighting'
> The police can record and analyse crime, pinpointing areas of high criminal activity. Patterns of crime can be displayed on a map. You can look at the pattern for burglaries, compare it with patterns for other crimes and with other layers of the map, to identify likely suspects. You can compare census data with a crime pattern to see if lifestyle and criminal behaviour are connected. You can use the GIS to generate bar

charts showing the percentage of different crimes committed each hour, from day-to-day. GIS make crime patterns more visible and more understandable. They can also predict when, where, how much and what type of crime will happen in the future. When used to model crime in this way, the predicted results should be used with care, however, GIS do help the police record, analyse and predict crime more effectively.

GIS display data in a way which is more meaningful. Instead of lists of numbers, you can look at a map which shows you what is happening and where it is happening. GIS are essentially visual map-based displays of data extracted from a database. They are interactive systems and, in some instances on-line or, more rarely, real time systems. It is likely that the use of GIS will be increasingly important in the future.

▷ **The system life cycle**

Every IT system goes through a cycle of development and use until it becomes obsolete or is replaced by a better system (see Fig. 12.7). The stages in this cycle are described below in the sequence in which they occur.

'Stages in the system life cycle'

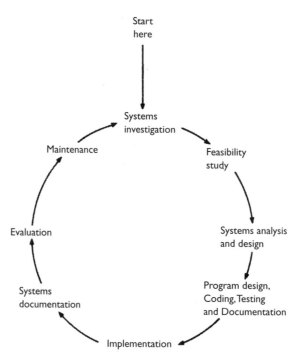

Fig. 12.7 The system life cycle

▷ **Systems investigation**

The realization that it would be useful to have an IT system to do a particular task may arise due to a new and completely novel idea, or to a new technological invention. However, many new IT systems are created because the system currently in use is unable to handle increased volumes of data, or new demands on it.

For example, a manual system for processing orders might work quite well until the rapid growth of the company and product diversification leads to many more customer orders, with a wider variety of terms and conditions of sale. Because of the increased complexity of the task, mistakes are made and there is a general confusion over what processing is required in some cases. Customers want their orders to arrive on time, to contain the items ordered and to be charged the right price! They become angry and frustrated when this does not happen. This in turn leads to a decline in orders. Having worked hard to increase production and sales, it is disappointing to find that confusion within the department dealing with order processing is responsible for lost sales. To improve this situation a computer-based system to help process customers' orders is suggested.

'An order processing system'

The **systems investigation** outlines the organizational problems identified, and recognises the *need* for improvements. A brief outline of a proposed system is made. This will identify the desired objectives, in this case the processing and delivery of the correct order, within a stated period, and charging customers the right price. A system will be described in broad outline and a rough estimate of costs will be made.

▷ Feasibility study

'Conducting a feasibility study'

If the systems investigation has uncovered a development that will be of use to the company, then a **feasibility study** is undertaken. This is a rather more detailed investigation of the proposed IT system.

Firstly, the *present* system is examined in greater detail.

▶ The order processing manager is asked what is done, and how it is done.
▶ The staff who do the job are asked to describe what they actually do.
▶ The records kept by the department, the forms they receive from customers, those filled in within the department and all correspondence are looked at.
▶ Customers are asked to provide details of letters and forms received from the department and are encouraged to explain how the service might be improved.

The new system is now developed in greater detail in a written report. Where possible, the new system is based on existing practice, to minimize the eventual disruption and retraining of staff when it is introduced. It must be shown that the new system will achieve the original objectives of improved performance, faster delivery of orders, and the accurate charging of customers.

Additional benefits of the new system will also be described, for example, improved working conditions for staff.

The software required to run the new system will be specified and the costs to develop it calculated. The extra cost of additional hardware should be given and the extent to which this will help with other processing tasks estimated. Savings due to increased staff productivity can be taken into account and the cost of necessary re-training shown. The time taken to develop and introduce the system is also estimated. In the case of large, complex or expensive systems, several different designs might be developed and outlined in the report.

The report on the feasibility study is passed to senior management within the company for approval. They will allocate the resources necessary if the new system is to proceed.

▷ Systems analysis and design

If the feasibility study has shown that the proposed IT system is worthwhile, and will meet stated objectives at an economic cost, then it is likely to be approved by senior management. Further development will then proceed.

The next stage in the system life cycle is **systems analysis and design**, i.e. the in-depth analysis of the requirements of the system and the preparation of a detailed design of a final system. The design outlined in the feasibility study will be further enlarged to provide a precise description of what the new system will do. At every stage in this process the systems analyst will refer back to the eventual users of the system, i.e. the order processing department and senior management, to ensure that the detailed system design meets their needs.

Output

'Output from the system'

The **output** required from the system will be specified. In the case of the order processing system this will include the following items.

▶ **Invoices** to be sent to the warehouse and to customers. An invoice is a printed confirmation of a customer's order. It lists what the customer has ordered, with the price of each item and the total cost. The invoice is first sent to the warehouse where it is used to select the items the customer has ordered. The invoice is then sent with the order to the customer. The customer uses the invoice to check that the order is correct and that the company has delivered everything that was ordered. The company will need to store the information shown on the invoice so that it knows what has been sold and how much is owed by the customer.

▶ **Internal reports and statistics.** Reports and statistical summaries of performance will be needed by senior management to help them improve the performance of the company. The total sales of every item stocked can be summarized either for all items stocked, in a printed report, or for a selection of items, on a monitor screen.

The layout of all printed reports and screen displays will be shown in detail. They must be presented in a way which is clear and easy to understand. An example of what each looks like will be drawn in sufficient detail to allow a programmer to write a computer program to produce the required output exactly.

The demand for specific data displays implies a need for the corresponding output peripherals. These could be simply monitor screens and printers but may also be more specialized output devices, for example, graph plotters.

The way in which output is obtained from the system will also need to be examined. For example, the systems analyst must consider whether reports need to be printed immediately, on request, or not at all. These considerations may lead us to equip the order processing department with network stations connected to local printers, so that reports can first be displayed on screen and only output if required. For reports that will always and only be printed the system line printer may be satisfactory.

Input

'Input to the system'

The **input** to the system is now looked at in greater detail. All the output from the system is produced from the input. It is important to be sure at an early stage that all the data needed will be *captured*. If this does not already occur in the existing system, then arrangements will have to be made to get the required data. The way in which data is input to the system should be designed in order to help data preparation staff and others to work quickly and easily.

In the case of the order processing system, it is likely that most of the input needed for the new system is already being generated by the old. It is possible that a manual system could manage without customer numbers if the orders are filed using the customer's name. However, a computer based system must have customer numbers, to be used as a key field to identify customers. If the existing order processing system does not use customer numbers, then arrangements will have to be made to generate these and persuade customers to use them.

Similarly, in a manual system the invoice containing details of the order can be identified using the date of the order. In the case of two or more orders on the same day the actual items ordered could be used to identify the invoice. This is rather cumbersome and makes reference to orders difficult. Consequently each invoice is given an invoice number which the customer and the order processing department can refer to in case of enquiries, etc. concerning the order.

The *way* in which the data is input must also be considered. Key-to-tape or key-to-disk may be satisfactory, but other methods should be considered. Customers could be sent mark sense documents, i.e. specially designed order forms that can be read directly into the computer by a mark sense reader. All useful possible means of input should be looked at and the benefits of each evaluated.

File structures

'The file structures used'

The **file structures** used within the system are decided on by examining the permanency of the data and whether it relates more closely to an invoice, or to a customer. Some of the data to be input could be recorded on backing storage and used several times, whereas some data will change from order to order. For example, an order from a customer will generate the following data:

name
address
customer number (identifies customer)
invoice number (identifies order)
date of order

for each item ordered: item code (identifies item)
                                description
                                quantity
                                price per item

The customer number (to identify the customer) and the invoice number (to identify the order) are both generated by the order processing department.

Invoice files

The customer's name, address and customer number do not change from order to order, whereas the other data relating to the items ordered will almost certainly change. The transient data relating to the order rather than to the customer will be kept on the **invoice file**. The invoice file contains a record for each invoice as follows:

'An invoice file record'

invoice number (identifies order)
customer number (identifies customer)
date of order
for each item ordered: item code (identifies item)
                                description
                                quantity
                                price per item

When an invoice is paid it is deleted from the invoice file. This file contains only those invoices that have not yet been completely processed.

Customer files

The name, address and customer number are kept on the **customer file**. This file has a record for each customer containing information that relates more directly to the customer rather than to an actual order. Customer file records include the following fields:

'A customer file record'

▶ customer number (identifies customer)
▶ name
▶ address
▶ credit limit
▶ discount rate

Records on the invoice file can be matched with the corresponding record on the customer file, using the customer number. Invoices can be printed and sent to the warehouse. The warehouse packs the items ordered and sends them to the customer with the invoice. The total amount owed by each customer can be calculated by adding up the amounts owed on individual invoices still to be paid.

Following through the above discussion we can see that the output requirements of the system suggest what input is needed. The file structure is decided upon by analysing the input data and the processing needed to be done to produce the necessary output. Inevitably, the file structures, the processing to be done and the style of output chosen, influence the choice of backing storage. Sequential access files on magnetic tape will be used for economy if only printed output is needed and the slower turnaround time is acceptable. Otherwise, direct access files on magnetic disk will be used to give immediate access to up-to-date information for screen displays and printed reports. An order processing system could be designed using either batch processing or on-line interactive processing.

'Choice of backing storage'

Telephone enquiry service

In the example order processing system, a telephone enquiry service may be offered (see Fig. 9.10). In this case, immediate access to customer and invoice files would be needed in order to answer enquiries on-the-spot. This would necessitate the use of direct access files on disk. Customer records would be accessed using either the customer number or name to find the record and the address would be used to confirm that the correct record has been located. The telephone operator would also have particular hardware needs if a large volume of enquiries is anticipated. A headset and microphone to replace the standard telephone might be useful. This would free the hands to enable the keyboard to be used more easily.

Data security

'Choice of data security arrangements'

Arrangements for data security should also be carefully thought out. The *ancestral* file system for file backup will be used and the times and frequency of backups should be stated. Arrangements for the physical security of files should be made. Each generation of backup should be kept in a different place. Fireproof safes, etc. may need to be purchased. Storage facilities at remote sites may be necessary in some cases.

Program specification

Systems analysis and design is a searching, in-depth look at the proposed system. It results in an exact statement of the input, processing and output needed and the hardware, software and data required to meet these needs. The system design details what will be done, how it will be done, the purpose in doing it and the cost. This will be described using system flowcharts, tables, diagrams, screen layouts, etc.

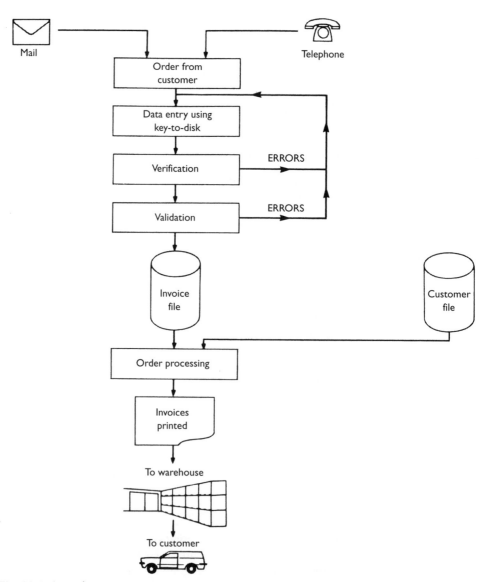

Fig. 12.8 An order processing system

The system may be designed as one or more inter-related programs. A **program specification** will be written for each computer program. This specifies in detail the input, processing and output to be done, the file structure, and any other details needed. The program specification gives sufficient detail to allow the programmer to write the program.

At this point it is perhaps worth noting that an order processing system is unlikely to be designed in isolation. It is likely to be integrated with, at least, a stock control system and possibly with wider financial reporting and control systems. The system described in the example is the basis of the more complex systems that are used in practice (see Fig. 12.8).

▷ **Program development**

'The design, coding, testing and documentation of a program'

The program specification written during the analysis and design of the system is handed over to a *computer programmer*. It contains enough information about the program to enable the programmer to design a program to do the required processing. The structure of any data input or output will be specified and also the type of file access used. The program to be written may be part of a large system involving many programs. It should not be necessary for the programmer to know how the whole system, or any other program in the system, functions in order to design the program. The programmer will read the specification carefully, then design the program.

Program design

The **program design** can be illustrated in various ways. A flowchart may be drawn, or alternatively it may be written in pseudo-code. The design is often **dry run** to test if it works. In a dry run the programmer uses examples of the input data and processes it according to the program design to see if the expected output results.

Coding

When the program has been designed, it is **coded**, i.e. written in a computer language. There are a variety of computer languages and the programmer may be free to choose which one to use. However, it is more likely that all the programs in the system will be written in the same language. An appropriate language to use for the order processing system would be COBOL. COBOL is a very good language for file handling as it is easy to define and manipulate records and fields. Commercial applications are often dominated by file handling making COBOL particularly appropriate. In the order processing system used as an example there are no complex calculations to be done, but there will be considerable file handling.

Testing

Next, the program is **tested** to see if it works. The programmer inputs test data to see if the program produces the expected output. Test data may be typical data likely to be generated when the system is running under normal conditions. It should also include extreme or rare data unlikely to occur in practice. The aim is to write a robust program that can deal with any input data, either processing it or reporting errors. If the test data causes unexpected output or crashes the program (i.e. stops it running) then the programmer will have to amend the program and do another test run. The cycle of testing, amending and re-testing continues until the programmer is satisfied that the program works.

Documentation

Program documentation is done throughout the design, coding and testing of a program. It is based on the original program specification and will cover the program design, including flowcharts. There will also be a listing of the source code of the final version of the program with details of test data and the resulting output. File structures for all input and output files and samples of printed output and screen displays will be included. The purpose of the documentation is to provide enough detail for a different programmer to understand what has been done in case the program unexpectedly crashes and the original programmer is not available to put it right.

▷ **Implementation**

'System testing'

'Training users'

If the extra hardware needed to run the new system has not been bought at an earlier stage, it will have to be purchased and installed before proceeding further. Consumables, such as printer stationery and disks, may need to be purchased. Extra electric wiring may be needed in the user department for powering terminals, etc. and a room with special features, such as air conditioning, may be required. Additional specialist computer staff may be employed to run the computer equipment and maintain the system.

When the *individual programs* that make up the system have been tested separately then the *entire system* is tested as a whole. Test data is used and the output checked against that expected. If errors are found they must be corrected and the system re-tested.

When it appears that the system is working correctly, it is implemented, i.e. it is put to work. However, there will still be a possibility that the system does not work as intended. To avoid costly mistakes a *parallel run* may takes place (see Fig. 12.9).

Both the new system and the old system are run on real input data and the results from the manual and the computer-based system are checked against each other. It is not unusual when looking for the reasons for differences in the output between the old and the new systems to discover that the new system is correct. Frequently, manual systems that have evolved piecemeal are found to be inferior to properly designed IT systems.

When the new system can be relied on to work correctly it 'goes live' and the old system is no longer used. This does not always happen overnight. It may be a gradual process, as parts of the old system are discontinued and replaced by the new system. Eventually, the only system in use is the new system.

System implementation also involves training users in the new system. There may be changes in practice which staff in the user departments, e.g. the order processing department, have to understand and follow. If the change is from an entirely manual system to a computerized system, staff will need to gain confidence in using the new technology.

System implementation involves the installation of both hardware and software, and the employment and training of staff. It is extremely complex and requires adequate planning and finance if it is to be successful. Even so, mistakes *will* occur and it is important that these are seen simply as problems to be overcome rather than personal faults of particular employees. The implementation of a computer based system demands personal change and adjustment of all employees. This must be recognized in a considerate way if the new system is to be implemented smoothly.

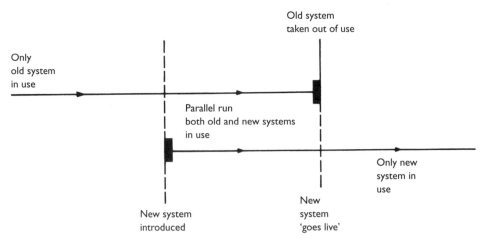

Fig. 12.9 A parallel run

▷ **System documentation**

System documentation consists of technical documentation and user documentation.

Technical documentation

The **technical documentation** includes all the system design, and program documentation. The purpose of the technical documentation is to provide all the detail needed to understand *what* the system does, and *how* it does it. If the system goes wrong, the technical documenta-

Jobs in IT   221

tion will be helpful to the maintenance programmers who will attempt to make the system work again. Similarly, if there is a need to *extend* the system, so that it can do extra tasks, the technical documentation will make it easier to build in additional processing capability.

User documentation

User manuals or **user documentation** are written to help employees use the system. They are needed when staff are trained, and so that staff can refer to them for help in using the system. User documentation should include a general review of the job done by the system, instructions on how to load and run the system, and a description of the input required, the processing done and the output produced.

The technical documentation is written to help the computer department in running and maintaining the system. The user manuals are written for the user departments to help them make use of the system. The technical documentation will be kept in the computer department, so that it can be referred to when necessary. The user manuals are kept in the user departments and are likely to be referred to fairly frequently. Technical problems beyond the scope of user departments will be passed on to the computer department.

▷ Evaluation

'Anticipating the need for change'

When the system was first thought of, it was hoped that it would solve certain difficulties in running the business. In the case of the order processing department, the system was expected to ensure the processing and delivery of the correct order, within a stated period, and charging customers the right price. On implementation, the new system should achieve these objectives. However, in due course the same problems could arise again as the volume of orders increases once more.

Evaluation of the system aims to check that it is still effective in doing the job it was designed to do.

It is easier to deal with problems if they are anticipated. Instead of waiting for angry customers to draw the attention of management to the breakdown of the system as it becomes overloaded again, constant evaluation of its effectiveness will identify problems before they result in customer dissatisfaction and lost business. If problems are known to exist, they can be avoided by either increasing the effectiveness of the existing system or developing a new system.

At some point in their life cycle all systems become obsolete and are replaced by new systems. Even reliable, well designed, systems will become obsolete at some time, if only because the technology used is superseded.

▷ Maintenance

'Correcting errors and extending the system'

Any system, however well designed and tested, is likely to go wrong at some time. There may be an error in the logic of one of the programs, or a condition or circumstance may arise which was not anticipated. **Maintenance** of the system involves the correction of errors in existing programs, or the extension of the system to cope with different tasks. Maintenance of the system may involve changes to any of the components of the system. It may be necessary to re-program existing software; design and write new programs to extend the capability of the system; and repair existing hardware or buy new. The system documentation and user manuals will need to be updated as the system changes.

▷ Jobs in IT

'Roles in the IT department'

The organization of an IT department in a large company is shown in Figure 12.10. It is not the case that *every* IT department is organized in this way, but many are organized in a very similar way.

The IT department organizes the highly skilled workers who develop and use IT systems for the maximum benefit of the company that employs them. As companies vary in terms of size and organization, so do IT departments. In some cases jobs done by individuals are broader, and in other instances narrower, than will be suggested, but the tasks to be done are the same whether they are done by one person in a small company or several in a larger company.

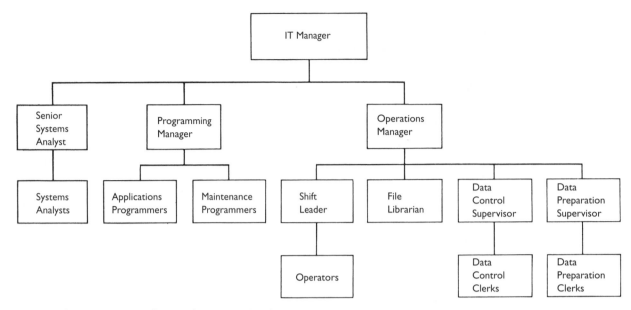

Fig. 12.10 The organization of an IT department in a large company

The systems analyst

A **systems analyst** is responsible for the development of an IT system through all the stages of the system life cycle (see Fig. 12.11). The systems analyst responsible for a system often works on it alone, but frequently acts as a team leader, organizing others in their work on the system.

'Responsibilities of a systems analyst'

For example, during the stage of system analysis and design the analyst responsible may lead a team of analysts who will develop the system design as directed. Similarly, during the stage of program design, coding, testing and documentation the analyst responsible for the system will direct the team of programmers who are working on the programs that make up the system.

Computer systems are developed as a result of *teamwork* by employees with different skills and specialisms. The systems analyst is the person responsible for developing the computer system and leading the various teams working on the system at different times. A good systems analyst must have a thorough knowledge of computers, commerce and people.

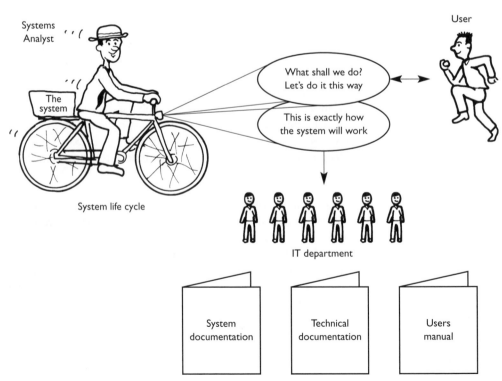

Fig. 12.11 The job of a Systems Analyst

Systems analysts must be good communicators, creative, logical, persistent and work well as part of a team. This knowledge can only be acquired through hard work, training and experience. Systems analysis is intellectually demanding, but interesting and varied.

'Becoming a systems analyst'

To become a systems analyst you will need to find a company to employ you, since *experience* and *ability* are worth more than qualifications. To convince a company you are a good prospect to take on as a trainee, useful qualifications to acquire are a degree or HND in IT or a related subject.

Many systems analysts start as humbler employees and through hard work and perseverance work their way up. Frequently, firms encourage study for membership of professional organizations. The British Computer Society (BCS) entry exams are popular. They not only improve professional skills and knowledge, but also lead to membership of the BCS. System analysts are important employees and a prudent company will pay them well and invest in their training.

Systems analysts are employed wherever there are IT systems in development or use. They are employed by large companies, software houses, local government, the Civil Service, universities, etc. Good systems analysts will get to know the companies they work for very well indeed. They will probably change jobs from time to time to gain yet further experience. This overall view of business organization can be a useful stepping stone to higher management positions or consultancy work. Salaries tend to be high for those with proven ability and experience.

Computer programmer

Computer programmers write programs in a computer language that tell a computer to do the tasks described in the program specification provided by the systems analyst (see Fig. 12.12).

'Responsibilities of a computer programmer'

Programmers may specialize in the development of new programs or the maintenance of existing systems. Applications programmers design, code, test and document new programs using the program specification given to them by the systems analyst. Maintenance programmers put right programs in systems that are already in use, but have been identified as having errors in them. They rely on the program documentation written by the applications programmer to help find these errors.

'Becoming a computer programmer'

Programmers need to think logically and be good at solving problems. Programming is an interesting, high pressure job, not really suitable for those wanting a quiet life. Working hours can often be extended at short notice when an urgent job has to be done. Programmers must work well with others, as teamwork is usual. They need to be flexible and not too worried about having a routine lifestyle. A measure of enthusiasm and an obsession with the job are also useful!

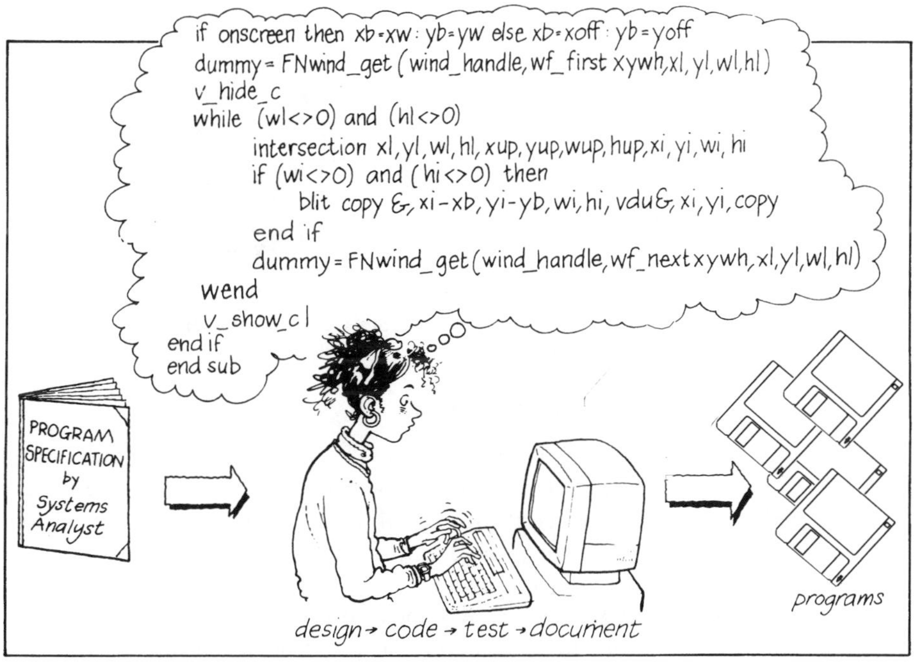

Fig. 12.12 The job of a Computer Programmer

Programmers are valued for their skill and experience. However, qualifications are useful in finding a job. Most employers would expect A-levels or equivalents, preferably including IT or a related subject. GCSEs in Maths and English are almost essential.

Most companies would provide training in the computer language needed where a programmer was not fluent in that particular language.

Programmers are generally found in employment where systems analysts are also employed, i.e. companies, local government, etc. Skilled programmers are highly paid and there are opportunities for foreign travel. Programming skills are in short supply in most industrialised countries.

Data preparation clerk

'Responsibilities of a data preparation clerk'

When data has been captured or collected for input, it may not be in a form the computer can read. For example, an order from a customer may be written on a piece of paper. The computer cannot read the writing on the paper so the information is transferred to magnetic disk or tape. Data preparation is the entering of data at the keyboard of a key-to-tape or key-to-disk machine. This is the job of a **data preparation clerk** (see Fig. 12.13).

'Becoming a data preparation clerk'

Good keyboard skills are important. Qualifications at GCSE level in English, Office Practice or Typing might be useful in getting a job, but again, it is the *ability to do the job* that is important. Touch typing skills and familiarity with wordprocessing are almost essential.

Payment is often related to the number of key depressions per hour when entering the data on the keyboard. A fast keyboard operator can earn high wages in comparison to similar work, as the wage paid may relate to the volume of work done rather than the time spent.

A skilled data preparation clerk can progress to a supervisory position or move into computer operations. It is possible for a determined and capable employee to be promoted from data preparation, through operations, to programming and beyond.

Fig. 12.13 The job of a Data Preparation Clerk

Data control clerks

'Responsibilities of a data control clerk'

When a system is in use, the input, processing and output are carefully controlled. **Data control clerks** monitor the flow of data through the system as it moves from data preparation, to verification, validation and processing on the computer (see Fig. 12.14). They collect any printed output and send it to the appropriate person. Data control clerks make sure that no data gets lost and that it is processed as required. The Data Preparation department receives most of its work through the Data Control department as data to be input to working systems will be sent to Data Control initially. Enquiries from other departments about the progress of data being processed are dealt with by Data Control.

'Becoming a data control clerk'

Data control clerks need to be thorough and reliable, with a good understanding of the computer systems used by the company they work for.

A data control clerk works in a modern office environment, at times using a network station to monitor the progress of the data being processed. Data control is a good training for operations work and a period in data control is often part of the training schedule for newly employed operators.

Fig. 12.14 The job of a Data Control Clerk

Computer operators

'Responsibilities of computer operators'

Computer operators look after the computer while it is running (see Fig. 12.15). They start up the computer and close it down. Computer operators monitor the status of programs running on the computer and provide tapes and disks as requested. They change the paper in the printer and keep all other peripherals in the computer room supplied with media.

Operators are employed at mainframe computer installations. Mainframe computers need a carefully controlled environment in which to run. They need air-conditioning to disperse the heat generated by the computer, and air filtering to keep the air clean so that

Fig. 12.15 The job of a Computer Operator

disks, tapes and machinery are not damaged. A computer operator works in the computer room. These are possibly the best working conditions experienced in any job!

Operators need to be alert and react calmly in a crisis. They will need to respond in a sensible way if problems such as machine failure do arise. Attention to detail and care in doing routine tasks are very important. They must work reliably on their own, without supervision.

Most companies train their own operators. Operators need to know *what* the computer does, *who* uses it and *for what purpose*. This is best learnt through a combination of on-the-job training and day-release courses. However, GCSEs in Maths and English could help in getting a job as an operator. Experience and ability rate more highly than qualifications once basic skills have been learnt.

Most operators will work shifts as large computers are kept running twenty-four hours a day.

Career opportunities are good. Operating is a skill that is transferable from one company to another. Operators may become Shift Leaders and go into Operations Management. Operating provides a good opening to higher level work with computers.

Other jobs in IT

Computer manufacturers employ sales staff to *sell* computers. They may also employ staff to provide *technical advice* and *equipment maintenance* as part of their after-sales service. Research and development staff may be needed to develop new products, and there will be engineering jobs available in production and quality control.

There are also jobs available in teaching and training. These may be in training departments in large companies, or as part of customer services. Most schools, colleges and universities now employ teachers of Information Technology and related subjects.

Looking for a job in IT?

If you want to work with IT and you are looking for your first job, the best thing you can do is get some experience and qualifications. There are several possibilities:

▶   Buy or borrow a personal computer and learn how to use it.
▶   Talk to someone who works in IT. Discuss where they work and what they do.
▶   Learn the basics of a programming language.
▶   Learn to use a wordprocessor, desk top publishing and graphics software, a spreadsheet, a database and communications software.
▶   Study for a specialist qualification in IT at as high a level as possible.

You may not be able to find the time to do *all* these, but make sure you have done enough so that an employer will recognize you as a sound prospect for employment and further training. Remember, employers want *value for money*. If you can show them that you have done as much as you possibly can, short of getting a job, then you will have a much better chance in the employment market.

The next step is getting a job. Don't expect to start at the top. Do look for a job that offers *training*. However, any job is better than none and you can always use the experience gained when looking for better employment.

▶   Look in the local papers for jobs. Buy computer magazines. In particular, try and get hold of *Computer Weekly* and *Computing*. Most trade papers in computing are crammed with job adverts.
▶   Write to companies and agencies advertising for IT staff and ask if there is any possibility of being taken on as a trainee.
▶   Visit local agencies specializing in IT staff.

There is a national shortage of IT specialists but this varies from place to place. You would probably find a job more easily in a city such as London, Birmingham, Manchester or Leeds. Don't be put off because your first applications are unsuccessful. The next job could be yours. Good luck!

EXAMINATION QUESTIONS

▷ **Question 1**

When a cheque is paid into a bank, a magnetic ink encoder prints one of the following on the cheque.

(a) the bank's name   [   ]
(b) the payer's name   [   ]
(c) the value of the cheque [   ]
(d) the date   [   ]

(City and Guilds)

▷ **Question 2**

> Sue Saddler buys a microcomputer from Vision Computing for £800 and pays for it by cheque.
>
> Sue has an account with Barston Bank and Vision Computing has an account with Llyndell's Bank.

Question data

Put the following statements into the correct order to show how Sue's cheque is processed.

(a) The clearing bank sorts the cheques into bank and branch order.   [   ]
(b) £800 is added to Vision Computing's account.   [   ]
(c) Llyndell's Bank sends the cheque to the clearing bank.   [   ]
(d) Vision Computing pay the cheque in to Llyndell's Bank.   [   ]

(City and Guilds)

▷ **Question 3**

(a) Write down TWO applications which must use on-line processing.
(b) Write down TWO applications which must use computer control.

(MEG)

▷ **Question 4**

Payroll	
Monitoring a patient's temperature	
Controlling a lift	
Robotics	
Producing electricity bills	
Controlling traffic lights	

Tick TWO applications which can use batch processing.

▷ **Question 5**

Refer to the stock control IT system.

(a) The computer system cannot be described as 'dedicated'. Why not? Explain your answer.
(b) Describe the information stored on a bar code.
(c) Where is the price and description of a product stored?
(d) After a bar code is read, the price of the product and its description are printed on the receipt. Describe the process that makes this possible.
(e) The bar codes of products delivered and the quantity delivered are input in the warehouse. The bar codes of products sold are input at the checkout. How does the computer know what quantity of each product is in stock? Describe the algorithm in detail.

▷ **Question 6**

Many supermarkets now use computerized systems to add up sales, produce till receipts and check stock levels.

State two effects that such systems have on:

(a) Shoppers
(b) Management
(c) Employees

(NEAB/WJEC)

▷ **Question 7**

A company wants all administration centralized. The consultant, therefore, recommends a mainframe computer is installed in the company headquarters, and networked to the other sites.

(a) Explain the main parts of the mainframe computer, and what they are used for.

The finance department first looks at transferring the payroll onto the mainframe, from all the sites.

(b) Explain what sort of information they would need to transfer to the mainframe.

(NDTEF)

▷ **Question 8**

A group of estate agents have joined together to give the customer greater access to the properties on the market. They are considering having a computer system installed to help them manage this information transfer and also to manage more effectively their own businesses and work schedules. Obviously the system will need to ensure confidentiality of individual business activities but share other data.

(a) Discuss the various ways in which a computer system could be of use to the partnership and the types of facilities which would need to be included.
    You should also discuss the hardware and software requirements. You should refer to data protection, data security and the input and output requirements.
(b) Discuss the effects the introduction of the system might have on:
    (i) the owners
    (ii) the community
    (iii) the manufacturing/installation companies

(NDTEF)

▷ **Question 9**

Describe the following stages involved in producing an IT system:

(a) Designing
(b) Testing

(NEAB/WJEC)

▷ **Question 10**

Chris has had his office computer for 6 years. It has a 20Mb hard drive and two $3\frac{1}{2}$ inch double density floppy drives. He has a 9-pin dot matrix printer that does not produce good quality printouts but does enable him to use pre-printed paper for invoices. He has decided to upgrade the system.

(a) Chris understands that a Feasibility Study Report should be undertaken covering hardware and software, staffing, operating costs and expected benefits. Explain how such a study would help Chris to choose what he needs.
(b) Explain the steps he has to go through to produce a specification that could be sent to prospective suppliers of the new system. What information should the specification contain?
(c) What equipment, hardware, software and peripherals would you recommend that Chris purchase? Give reasons for your choice.
(d) Explain how Chris might go about choosing the correct supplier after he has received a number of quotations.
(e) Once Chris has chosen a system, how should he get it up and running in his firm?

(RSA)

▷ EXAMINATION ANSWERS

▷ **Answer 1**   (c)

▷ **Answer 2**   The correct sequence is:
(d), (c), (a), (b)

▷ **Answer 3**   (a) Two from: (b) Two from:
    Database interrogation   Building cars
    Viewdata   Building any product using robots
    Electronic mail   Flight simulators
    Any suitable answer   Railway points control systems
                                              Any suitable answer

(MEG)

▷ **Answer 4**   Payroll
Producing electricity bills

▷ **Answer 5**   (a) Because it can do tasks other than stock control. For example, payroll.
    (b) Country of origin code
        Manufacturer code
        Product code
        Check digit
    (c) In the product information file.
    (d) The information on the bar code is sent to the main computer. The check digit is used
        to check that the bar code has been read and transmitted accurately. The computer
        checks that there is a record with the same product code as the bar code on the prod-
        uct information file. The name of the product and its price are read from the product
        information file and sent to the checkout. These are printed on the itemized receipt.
    (e) Quantity in stock

$$= \left(\begin{array}{c} \text{Quantity at} \\ \text{last stock} \\ \text{check} \end{array} \right) + \left(\begin{array}{c} \text{Quantity} \\ \text{delivered} \end{array} \right) - \left(\begin{array}{c} \text{Quantity} \\ \text{sold} \end{array} \right)$$

▷ **Answer 6**   (a) Shoppers:
        ▷ receive itemized bills. This reassures them that they have been charged correctly;
        ▷ cannot easily do price comparisons within the supermarket as the price of the
           product is marked on the shelves not on the product.
    (b) Management:
        ▷ receive up-to-date accurate information on sales;
        ▷ can direct the computer system to order stock automatically. This relieves man-
           agers of unnecessary work.
    (c) Employees:
        ▷ the job of a checkout operator is simplified;
        ▷ management can use the IT system to see which checkout operators handle the
           most sales. This puts the jobs of some operators at risk.

▷ **Answer 7**   (a) CPU: Central Processing Unit – this does all the processing.
        Memory: stores programs and data that are in use.
        Backing storage: disks and tapes; used to store programs and data not in use.
        Printer: for printed output.
        Communications hardware: to handle communications with terminals via LANs
        and WANs.

(b) They would need an 'employee' file with a record for each employee containing fields, such as, name, address, rate of pay, tax code, etc. They may need other files with current information, such as, the number of hours each employee has worked in the current week. A file containing tax and national insurance details may also be needed.

▷ **Answer 8** (a) A networked system, possibly based on a mainframe computer, should be used. There will need to be separate terminals for customers and employees. Employees will use the computer system for payroll, accounts and other administrative tasks. They will also set up and maintain a database of all the houses being sold by the group. Only the information needed for the task will be collected and this will be organized so that only those who need access to it have access to it. For example, customers will not have access to the names and telephone numbers of vendors. Input will almost always be using a keyboard and output will usually be on screen with print facilities available when needed.

(b) (i) The system will allow sharing of information and access to it wherever and whenever it is needed. Customers can be given details of all houses for sale at all estate agents within the group.

(ii) The community benefits through improved access. Customers can find out details of houses in districts a long way from their homes. This is useful if they have to move.

(iii) The job of manufacturing/installation companies becomes more complex and must be organized over a wider area. However, they can expect increased sales of products used with networks, such as modems, etc.

▷ **Answer 9** (a) The design of an IT system involves:
▶ Designing the data capture form (if any).
▶ Specifying the input needed.
▶ Specifying the output needed.
▶ Designing the format of the output.
▶ Designing the file structures.
▶ Specifying the backup and security features to be used.

(b) The testing of an IT system should involve:
▶ Designing test data for extreme, standard and unusual input data.
▶ Working out the results expected from the test data.
▶ Comparing the output from the IT system when using test data with the output expected.

▷ **Answer 10** (a) A Feasibility Study would evaluate the possible options available to Chris. It should indicate the costs involved in acquiring additional hardware and software and the match between existing staff capabilities and the new skills needed. The type and extent of training needed would be identified and costed. All aspects of the development and operation of the system would be identified and costed. The expected benefits should be clarified and evaluated.

(b) Chris should decide exactly what the new system should do. The specification should clearly show prospective suppliers what is required and when it is required. A specification should contain:
▶ An explanation of the need for the IT system placed in the context of the business.
▶ The expected volume of data to be handled.
▶ An exact statement of the performance requirements of the system that have been developed as a result of the feasibility study.
▶ Timescales for development.

(c) Hardware and peripherals:
▶ Pentium processor.
▶ SVGA monitor.
▶ High density floppy disks drive (1.44 Mbyte).
▶ 12 Gbyte hard disk.
▶ Keyboard.

▶ Mouse.
▶ Laser printer.
▶ A scanner.
▶ CD-ROM drive.
▶ MODEM.

Software:

▶ A GUI, probably Microsoft Windows.
▶ Wordprocessor, Database, Spreadsheet, DTP, Graphics software.
▶ Applications software such as accounting packages.

Some reasons for these choices are:

▶ The faster processor will speed up the operation of Chris's software.
▶ The monitor is of a high resolution suitable for DTP, etc.
▶ High density floppy disks store more data than double density floppy disks (720 Kbytes) so fewer disks are required.
▶ A larger hard disk enables more or larger programs and data to be stored on it. The more powerful, easy to use, modern programs are also larger.
▶ The mouse is helpful with all software but especially graphics and DTP.
▶ A scanner can be used to scan photos and printed text etc. into the computer.
▶ A MODEM would allow Chris to communicate with on-line databases and acquire useful business information.
▶ A CD-ROM drive would allow Chris to access a wide range of useful information, clip art, etc. stored on CD-ROM.

(d) Chris will have to judge which proposal best suits his needs. The availability of after sales support could be important.

(e) Chris could pay the company supplying the system to set it up and test it. He will need to test it himself and ensure his staff are trained to use it.

▶ EXAMINATION QUESTION WITH STUDENT ANSWER

Members of a library are given a membership card when they join the library. The membership card has a bar code on it.

Fig. 12.16

(a) Tick TWO boxes to show which of these statements are true.

	Tick TWO boxes
The number printed under the bar code is also stored in the bar code.	✓
Different members have the same number on their membership cards.	
Every member has a different number on their membership card.	
The member's address is stored in the bar code.	✓
The library computer would understand the bar code on a can of baked beans.	

(b) When a member borrows a book, either the bar code on their membership card is read into the computer using a bar code reader, or, the librarian types the number on the card into the computer.

Explain why a bar code reader is used.

The bar code is read faster.

(c) The bar code has a check digit in it.
   (i) Tick TWO boxes to show which of these statements is true.

	Tick TWO boxes
When you work out the check digit on a bar code, you should always get the same answer.	✓
The number under the bar code does not contain the check digit.	
If you know the check digit, you can find out the information stored in the bar code.	
Different bar codes will have the same check digit.	
Every bar code has a different check digit.	✓

   (ii) Check digits can be used to detect errors when a bar code is read. Explain how check digits can be used to detect errors.

They are worked out when the bar code is read. They should be the same all the time.

(d) Every book in the library has a different bar code in it.

Fig. 12.17

When a member borrows a book from the library, the bar code on their membership card and the bar code on the book are read into the computer. When a member returns a book, only the bar code in the book is read into the computer. Explain why only the bar code in the book is read.

The computer remembers who has the book.

(SEG, 1996)

▷ **Examiner's comment**

(a) The first answer is correct.

The second answer is incorrect. This information might be obtainable using the membership number which is stored in the bar code. However, the address itself would not be stored in the bar code.

The third option is correct.

(b) This is partially correct. The information in the bar code will be input to the computer much faster. Input is also likely to be much more accurate.

(c) (i) The first answer is correct.

The second answer is incorrect. As check digits are 0 to 9 and X, some bar codes must have the same check digit as there are more than 11 different bar codes.

The fourth option is correct.

(ii) Correct, though lacking some detail.

(d) Correct, though lacking some detail.

The book number in the book's bar code is likely to be saved in an 'Issues file'. The Issues file has a record for each book issued. It will have a book number field and a member number field. The book number identifies the record. This is deleted, releasing the member number.

SUMMARY

This chapter looks at the IT systems used in several commercial applications and the stages of the system's life cycle. The jobs in IT of a systems analyst, computer programmer, data preparation clerk, computer operator and data control clerk are briefly described.

▷   An **IT system** is the whole system of hardware, software and human activities that are used in an application.

▷   In an IT system that uses **batch processing**, all the data to be processed is available before processing starts. Data is processed in batches. Batch processing is not interactive. For example, a payroll system.

▷   In a **real time** IT system, data is processed as it is input, before any other data is input. Data may be input at any time from a variety of sources. The results of processing can influence further input. Real time systems are fast and interactive. For example, an airline booking system.

▷   **On-line, interactive** systems are typically multiaccess systems that are slower than real time systems. For example, stock control in a supermarket.

▷   The **system's life cycle** is the stages in a system's development:

   ▷   a **system investigation** outlines the problems and briefly describes how they can be solved using an IT system;

   ▷   a **feasibility study** investigates the proposed IT system in more detail, including the likely costs and advantages;

   ▷   **system analysis and design** describes in detail the requirements of the IT system and its design;

   ▷   **program design, coding and testing** is the writing (or modification) and testing of the software;

   ▷   **implementation** is setting up and testing the IT system, perhaps involving a parallel run. Users will be trained;

   ▷   **system documentation** is both user and technical documentation;

   ▷   **evaluation** is checking that the system is effectively doing the job it was intended to do;

   ▷   **maintenance** is correcting errors in the system and extending it to meet new requirements.

Chapter 13

The social impact of IT systems

This chapter should be read if you are preparing for GCSE IT assessment with the following examining boards:

C & G	MEG	NEAB	SEG
London	NDTEF	RSA	WJEC

GETTING STARTED

This chapter looks at the impact IT has on our lives. As IT is introduced into the workplace, some other skills are no longer needed, and there is more demand for workers with up-to-date IT skills. Some jobs disappear while others are done in new ways, and new jobs are created. Workers must re-train or be made redundant. Young people starting work will need to know how and when to use IT.

IT systems can store very large volumes of information and give fast access to it. Information about you and your family may be stored by doctors, the DHSS, local authorities, schools, the police, banks, employers and others. These systems can be used to improve services but your privacy may suffer. Data Protection laws give you rights to know what information is kept and what it is used for.

Lifestyle and leisure are also affected by IT systems. Domestic work has been made easier. For example, automatic washing machines have replaced manual washers. TV, microcomputers and video technology have affected how we spend our leisure time. Banks and similar institutions use computers for financial management and control. The increasing use of cash cards has led to a dramatic reduction in the use of cash in notes and coins.

The pace of change is rapid and will continue. It is important to keep up-to-date with new developments to ensure that we use IT effectively.

GLOSSARY

Objective data Objective data is information that is measurable. For example, your height in metres.

Subjective data Subjective data is a personal assessment. For example, your singing ability.

Teleworking Teleworking is working from home, using IT to do the job and to communicate with other workers.

C & G	LONDON	MEG	NDTEF	NEAB	RSA	SEG	WJEC	TOPIC	STUDY	REVISION I	REVISION 2
✓	✓	✓	✓	✓	✓	✓	✓	IT at work			
✓	✓	✓	✓	✓	✓	✓	✓	The information explosion			
✓	✓	✓	✓	✓	✓	✓	✓	Individual privacy			
✓	✓	✓	✓	✓	✓	✓	✓	Lifestyle and leisure			
✓	✓	✓	✓	✓	✓	✓	✓	The pace of change			

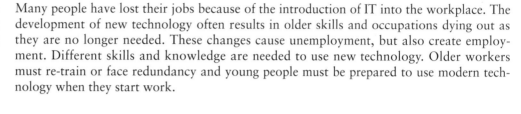

WHAT YOU NEED TO KNOW

New technology has an effect on the lives of individuals and changes the way society is organized. These changes affect us at home, at school and at work. The way we do domestic chores and spend our leisure is affected. Technology has an immediate and lasting impact. It is important to understand what changes have taken place and to ensure that these changes are used to make the world a better place to live in. This chapter looks at some of the most important changes that have taken place as information technology has been introduced throughout society.

▷ **Information technology at work**

'New technology requires new skills'

Many people have lost their jobs because of the introduction of IT into the workplace. The development of new technology often results in older skills and occupations dying out as they are no longer needed. These changes cause unemployment, but also create employment. Different skills and knowledge are needed to use new technology. Older workers must re-train or face redundancy and young people must be prepared to use modern technology when they start work.

The new technologies

There are many examples of this process of change from old technologies to the use of microprocessor and computer technology. Mechanical Swiss watches were once highly prized for their accuracy and were consequently very expensive. In 1979, a cheap mechanical watch costing around £10 might be accurate to within five minutes per day. Modern digital watches (see Fig. 13.1) based on microprocessor technology cost less and are accurate to within one hundredth of a second per month. As a result, digital watches dominate the market. The skills of the mechanical watchmaker are much less in demand. Digital watches are manufactured and assembled in highly automated factories.

Fig. 13.1 A digital watch

Robots

Cars were once completely assembled by a team of mechanics. As production techniques changed, cars were built on assembly lines where each worker repeatedly performed one highly specialized task, such as welding. Now, microprocessor controlled robot welders (see Fig. 13.2) have taken over from these workers. The robot welder is programmed to do the required task by an expert human welder. This human expert does not do the repetitive welding but programs the robot to do the task. Once programmed, the robot can do the required task indefinitely.

Petrol pumps

Self service petrol pumps are now almost universally used at garages. These are controlled by one or two employees who also collect payments from customers. Before the introduction of computer and microprocessor technology, several petrol pump attendants were needed to supervise the sale of petrol from mechanical pumps and collect the money. These attendants worked outside in all weathers. Their job is now done by fewer employees from the comfort of the garage reception area.

Telephones

Telephone exchanges were once staffed by large numbers of operators who connected callers to the line they required. Now, computer controlled exchanges automatically switch callers, giving access to the national and international telephone systems.

Offices

In commerce, large numbers of clerks were once employed to do payroll, stock keeping, etc. These tasks involved careful written recording of all transactions. They are now done using IT. The clerk's job has changed and now involves control of data as it passes through the IT system.

'Typists replaced by word processor operators'

Companies once employed large numbers of typists. It was not uncommon for fifty or more typists to work in the typing 'pool'. Much of the work was routine copy typing and

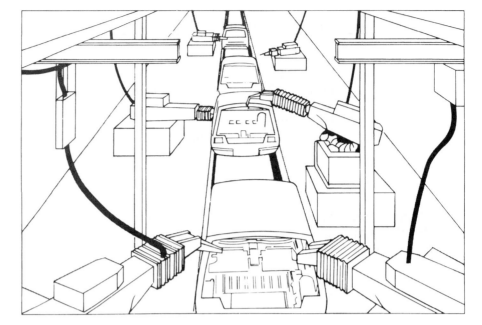

'Microprocessor-based
technologies in car
production . . .'

Fig. 13.2 Robots used on a car assembly line

production of standard business letters. This work is now done by a few wordprocessor operators. The skills required to operate a wordprocessor are quite different from those needed to use a mechanical typewriter.

In the above examples, fewer workers were required, if any, when the new technology was introduced. Where there was a continuing need for workers, the skills involved were quite different from those used previously. However, the examples are all of changes to *established* industrial products and commercial practices. Information technology has significantly extended the way some jobs are done and created *entirely new* products and employment opportunities that did not exist previously.

Jobs in IT

'New employment
opportunities'

IT obviously creates jobs in the industrial and commercial sectors concerned with its own design, manufacture, sales, maintenance and use. Many people now work in jobs in these areas. There are designers, assembly line workers, sales staff, installation and maintenance engineers, data control clerks, data preparation staff, operators, programmers, systems analysts, etc. There are journalists who write about IT and technical authors who write manuals for computer software and hardware.

New jobs

The jobs created are not only replacements for old jobs, in the sense that exactly the same job is done in a different way. IT may be originally used to do the same job more efficiently, but, once the potential is understood, it is then used to dramatically extend the scope of the job or for entirely new tasks that were once impossible or impractical. For example, stock control has always been an essential routine task for a shopkeeper, but many supermarkets have taken advantage of IT to install POS terminals with laser scanners for on-line stock control.

New products

Many new products have been designed and manufactured that are based on microprocessor technology and improvements have been made to old machines. Electronic calculators (see Fig. 13.3) are an entirely new product made possible only through the use of microprocessor technology. Washing machines have changed from mechanical, manual washers to single programme machines to multiple programme machines. These programmes are stored in a microprocessor which controls the washer. The heating and lighting in buildings may now be monitored by a microprocessor programmed to main-

Fig. 13.3 An electronic calculator

tain different temperatures in different rooms and to switch lights on and off at certain times. The work involved in the manufacture, installation and maintenance of such devices has created jobs.

New technologies

There have been radical changes in telecommunications technology. Metal core lines are being replaced by optic fibre cables; long distance cables laid under the ocean or overland are replaced by satellites; automatic exchanges have been installed in place of manually operated ones. IT is used to control the operation of these systems. These changes have improved local, national and international communications. This process of improvement and innovation has created entirely new jobs.

▷ The information explosion

The use of IT has created *demand*. Information is more readily available, which has created the demand for more information. This is known as the **information explosion**. Cheaper, more reliable microprocessor-based products have broadened the market, making these products available to more people. This has increased consumer demand. Increased demand for more information and more goods has led to new jobs in factories and offices.

IT is increasingly used for creative work. Artists, cartoonists, graphic designers, authors, journalists, etc. are now making use of IT in their work. Computers can be used to control synthesizers playing music and for musical design. On television, computer graphics are now common. IT has opened up many possibilities for the expression of human creativity.

'Jobs have been lost and gained'

It is not clear whether the introduction of computer and microprocessor technology has led to overall job losses or gains. Jobs have been lost, but jobs have also been created. There have been other effects of the increased use of computers at work which are also important.

Job skills

The skills required in many jobs, where IT is now used, have changed. For example, a wordprocessor operator uses different skills than a typist. Many repetitive tasks have been automated so that fewer people now have boring, routine factory jobs. Some complex tasks have been made easier, for example, the use of CAD/CAM has speeded up the design to manufacturing cycle, allowing more flexibility in changing the design, so that better products are made sooner. Improved production control has also contributed towards a better quality product. Productivity per employee is high and the finished product is better designed and manufactured.

Working conditions in computer related jobs tend to be pleasant, perhaps because most computers require a clean, dust-free environment at about the same temperature that people find comfortable. Salaries tend to be above average, perhaps because of the general lack of understanding of IT and the high demand for staff with these skills.

Working from home

It is increasingly common for employees who use IT to work at home, using a computer to communicate with the central workplace via a modem and the telephone network. This is called **teleworking**. There have been a small number of disabled workers working with IT for many years, particularly blind people. Teleworking has allowed more house-bound or disabled workers to find jobs. Other employees often prefer teleworking, because there is no commuting and working hours are flexible. From the employer's perspective, teleworking reduces the need to provide expensive office accommodation. Teleworking is expected to increase. Some estimates have suggested that over half the working population will work from home within a few years.

IT is now essential to most businesses and is widely used in most jobs. The introduction of computer and microprocessor technology has taken place at the same time as many other remarkable changes, such as the development of new synthetic materials for use in manufacture. These changes have not taken place in isolation, so their direct consequences are impossible to determine. It is certain that IT has had a dramatic effect on employment and it is here to stay.

▷ **Individual privacy**   Information about individuals is kept on computers (see Fig. 13.4). Because IT systems can store large volumes of data and access it very quickly, they are a more useful way of storing data than in a filing cabinet. The information can be accessed from a large number of widely spread out locations so that it is available immediately where it is needed. Usually there will be a large, central mainframe computer system which is accessed using terminals. Access will often be via the telephone network using a modem and may be possible from a moving car or van. The DHSS, the police, the DVLC, the Inland Revenue, credit card companies, mail order firms and many other organizations keep information about individuals in this way.

Personal data

'Uses of personal data'   Keeping **personal** data about individuals on IT systems has advantages and disadvantages. For example, it is important that the police have access to information to help them arrest criminals and to enforce the law. If my car was stolen I would be very pleased if this information was available to police forces throughout the country, so that the car could be returned to me as soon as possible. I would be less enthusiastic if other organizations had access to the files linking my name, address and the type of car I own. This personal data could be useful to companies selling car insurance, new cars, or specializing in spare parts for my car. These organizations might use this personal data to send me unwanted advertising literature by mail. The same information could be used for individual surveillance. This may or may not be acceptable, depending on the situation. It is reasonable to track a criminal or terrorist in a free society, but the same computer system could be used by dictators to enforce unreasonable levels of social control.

In any society there is conflict between the rights and freedoms of individual citizens and the need of national organizations to control and limit individual freedom in the interests of society as a whole. Similarly, businesses acting in their own interests may be in conflict with the needs of individuals. How these conflicts of interest are resolved is partic-

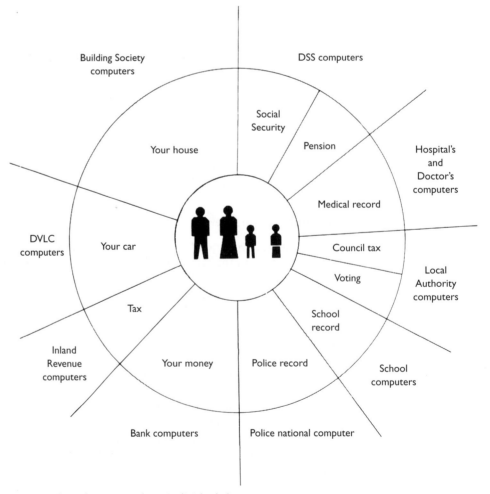

Fig. 13.4 The information about individuals kept on computers

ularly important to you, because it may be possible in the future to hold all the data about you on one national information system. Your medical, school, employment and criminal records will all be fully integrated and any information about you will be available instantaneously. You should have no need to worry if this information is used reasonably. However, events in Europe during the Second World War, for example, may suggest the need for some concern. Might not Hitler have eliminated his opponents much more efficiently with the use of computers? The major problems for individuals are concerned with privacy, accuracy, how the data is used, and security.

Privacy and accuracy

'Need for privacy and for accurate data'

Privacy is the right to control information about yourself. To do this you will need to know if anyone is keeping data about you and have some control over how they use it.

Accurate data is realistic, objective and up-to-date. Data is realistic if it describes a real situation. For example, your actual date of birth should be recorded. This could be important if you are applying for a car driver's licence, as its issue is dependent on your age. You would be upset if you were not issued with a licence because the date of birth on your record was incorrect.

If data is not kept up-to-date it may cease to be accurate. Your address will change when you move. You may change schools or leave school to get a job or go to college, or university. Old data is not accurate data. Data files must be kept up-to-date if they are to remain accurate.

Objective and subjective data

Data can be objective or subjective.

'Objective and subjective data'

Objective data is measurable. If the measurement is repeated by someone else, the same result would be obtained. Your height in metres is *objective* data. However, an assessment of your potential as a pop singer is *subjective*. **Subjective data** is a personal assessment. One person may enjoy listening to you and rate you very highly, another may not like you at all.

If your rating as a pop singer was recorded on a computer file it would be coded, perhaps on a scale from A to G. This code has the appearance of objective data, even though it is subjective. Anyone accessing your data would treat this code as a true assessment of your singing potential. People tend to believe that data kept on computers is accurate. This may be satisfactory if you were coded as A but would probably be unacceptable if your code was G! For this reason subjective data should not be recorded. If it is important to record subjective data, it must be made very clear that it is not objective data.

The use of data

The **use of data** is an important aspect of privacy. This is where the needs of individuals, organizations and society may come into conflict. For example, suppose you have invested some money in a bank. The bank will pay you interest on the money. The bank will also tell the Inland Revenue, which collects taxes, that they have paid you interest. This may lead to a demand from the Inland Revenue for payment of extra taxes. As an individual, you may not want to pay extra tax and feel it is unfair for the bank to give information about your income to the Inland Revenue. This might lead to you withdrawing your money from the bank and investing it elsewhere. The bank does not want to lose your investment, but is legally obliged to tell the Inland Revenue about interest paid to you. The Inland Revenue wants to collect all the tax that is due. This tax is used to benefit the whole of society. In this case, individuals cannot be allowed complete control of their own personal data, as this would lead to social injustice. However, it is important that you know what is being done with this information. How personal data is used by the organization that holds it could influence what you do.

Data security

If personal information is to remain private and accurate, and is to be used only in ways agreed by the individual or controlled by the law, then the data must be kept secure.

Security is the protection of data from corruption and misuse. Data is normally recorded on a backing storage medium such as disk. Data recorded on disk may be corrupted due to faulty hardware, faulty software, accidental or deliberate interference. If data is corrupted, it is important to be able to restore it to its original state as soon as possible. This is done by keeping backup copies of data files. If the current copy of the data file is corrupted, it is restored from the backup.

Deliberate interference with data is always a possibility, especially where networks are in use. To prevent unauthorized access to data files several precautions should be taken. To prevent unauthorized copying of data files saved on backing storage, disks and tapes should be kept in a safe when not in use. Physical access to terminals on the network should be restricted using security guards or electronic locks that only open when identity cards are inserted. The network cable should be inaccessible and shielded to prevent intruders connecting themselves to it. If unauthorized users do connect to the network there should be a system of user identification with passwords at all levels to prevent access to the system and to data files. A log should be kept of all users so that illegal access can be identified and traced.

The data protection act

The 1984 **Data Protection Act** establishes the principles of data protection and gives individuals some right to control personal data. Anyone who holds personal data on computer files must register with the *Data Protection Registrar*. You have a right to know if personal data is kept on you and what that data is. Personal information must be obtained fairly and lawfully. You have a right to have incorrect data changed. The data can only be used for its specified purposes. Personal data must be accurate and up-to-date. It can only be kept as long as it is in use. Security measures against unauthorized access, corruption of data files, copying of files, and loss or destruction must be taken.

Although the Act protects individual privacy to a greater extent than was the case prior to 1984, it has been criticized for not dealing with some important issues. Manual files, that is, files kept on paper in filing cabinets, are not covered. Besides being a disincentive to use IT, this allows any infringement of privacy in this area to continue.

The police and security forces are exempted from all the provisions of the act. While this is understandable, it is unfortunate. For example, there are occasions when doctors may need to cooperate with the police. Doctors are covered by the Act but the police are not. This could affect liaison between doctors and the police for the good of individuals and the community.

Another criticism of the Act is that misuse is an offence under civil law, rather than criminal law. This means that individuals must seek damages for misuse of personal data through the civil courts. Individuals are unlikely to do this because of the cost of taking court action.

▷ **Lifestyle and leisure**

Earlier in this chapter, the effects of the use of IT at work were discussed. It was noted that this leads to better working conditions and higher productivity. This in turn leads to higher wages and lower prices. Many people spend a large part of their life at work and depend on their wages to buy the goods and services they need. Better working conditions and greater purchasing power are important improvements in lifestyle. They are welcome in themselves and also because they open up other possibilities. A wider range of lifestyle and leisure options becomes available.

Information technology at home

In the *home*, domestic work has been made much easier. Programmable automatic washing machines and tumble driers allow clothes to be washed and dried with a minimum of effort. It is no longer necessary to spend a lot of time and effort on this necessary task. In the days of manual washing machines and clothes lines only, the family washing could take a day or even longer in bad weather! It is a pity the ironing has not been similarly automated!

Microprocessors are used in the manufacture of most domestic appliances, keeping prices down and quality up. Television viewing is more convenient because of remote control pads to alter the volume and contrast, change channels and switch the set on or off. Video recorders have similar facilities. TVs with a built-in teletext receiver can display pages from Ceefax or Oracle. The pages contain general information, including the times of TV programmes. These features make viewing more convenient, particularly for house-bound or disabled viewers. Computer and microprocessor technology is an essential factor in providing these services.

Home computers

Home computers are often used for leisure pursuits. Many people play computer games or use the computer for personal amusement. Software packages are available for home and financial management.

Home finances

Many people have plastic cash cards or credit cards (see Fig. 13.5). These cards can be used to access a wide range of financial services:

Fig. 13.5 A cash card

▷ money can be withdrawn from automatic teller machines throughout the World;
▷ cheques can be guaranteed;
▷ goods can be paid for in shops or by telephone.

It is easy to get a statement of payments made or received and find out how much money is left. This can be done in the bank or at an automatic teller machine. Some banks allow customers to access their accounts from home using a computer and a modem to connect to the bank's central computer. They can transfer money between different accounts, pay bills or do any other transaction while on-line. The banks and credit companies themselves rely heavily on IT to operate these systems and keep accurate records of all financial dealings.

Electronic shopping

Electronic shopping is possible using national or local viewdata systems or the WWW. The customer connects to the on-line service using the telephone network, a computer and a MODEM. A selection of goods is offered for sale. These can be ordered and paid for by credit card. Companies operating such schemes often sell goods at a lower price than in the shops. The goods ordered are delivered by mail. Some local schemes allow groceries and other consumables to be ordered. This type of service is particularly useful to the house-bound or disabled. The use of cash cards, credit cards and electronic shopping are features of the **cashless society**. Some people believe that these and other developments will eventually lead to money in notes and coins becoming obsolete. Money will then only exist as numbers recorded on the bank's computer system.

'The cashless society'

Improved transport and communications have helped families that live apart to keep in touch. They have also led to families becoming more widely dispersed. Cars are designed using IT and are built to much higher standards using microprocessor controlled robots. Motorways are planned and designed using computer aided design. The telephone network is also designed, built and controlled using IT.

The institutions of society, such as, Local Authorities, Hospitals and doctors, schools, the police, libraries, the DVLC, etc. all use IT to keep administrative records and to help improve operating efficiency. This is also true in a European and international context.

▷ The pace of change

Most of the changes that are described in this chapter have taken place during the last thirty years and are mainly due to the widespread use of computer and microprocessor technology.

▷ The range of *consumer products* has greatly increased. Their quality has improved and their price has dropped.
▷ Old skills have become redundant and knowledge of IT is now essential for all workers.
▷ Employment patterns have changed; jobs have been created and lost.
▷ Concern for individual privacy is not new, but before the introduction of national IT systems, it was not a widespread problem.
▷ The standard of living has improved greatly for those in employment.

'Author's comment'

My experience of technology as a teenager was very different from that of teenagers today. The pace of change has obviously been extremely fast. I believe this will continue. What you are learning for GCSE will be a sound basis for the future. However, I am sure that some new event will soon occur in the rapidly changing world of Information Technology. It is important to learn about these new developments. Try constantly to update your knowledge by reading magazines, visiting exhibitions and local shops that stock computers. Don't be afraid to admit things are new to you too. It is important to learn to deal with rapid, unexpected change. Try to anticipate the effect of new technology on yourself and others. This will help you to use technology effectively for your benefit and for the benefit of society as a whole.

EXAMINATION QUESTIONS

▷ **Question 1**   Ring TWO developments which make it easier for people to work from home.

Teletext   Cheap personal computers   Bank cashpoints
Electronic mail   Computerized supermarket checkouts Digital watches

(MEG)

▷ **Question 2**   A school stores dates of births of pupils. Give TWO ways in which it might sensibly use this information.

(MEG)

▷ **Question 3**   Banks store personal information about their customers on computer files.

(a)   Suggest three items of customers' personal information (other than name and address) which a bank might store.

Members of the public are often concerned that personal information stored in computer files may be misused in some way.

(b)   How might these items of information be misused?

(NEAB/WJEC)

▷ **Question 4**   Describe Electronic Funds Transfer at Point of Sale (EFTPOS) together with its benefits and drawbacks.

(City and Guilds)

▷ **Question 5**   Describe the impact the use of Information Technology at work has had on:

(a)   The number of jobs available.
(b)   The skills needed to find a job.
(c)   The exposure of employees to dirty and dangerous working conditions.
(d)   The productivity of workers.

▷ **Question 6**   It has been suggested that motorists might be charged for their use of roads by having a system which identifies each car, and when a car passes over a sensor in the road a central computer will record that car's entry into a charge zone. One of the side-effects of this is that a record could be kept for every car's movements.
    Discuss some of the social implications of such a system, giving reasons why certain groups of people may be for or against the system.

(SEG, 1993)

▷ **Question 7**   People are concerned about their personal information being held on a computer. Give three possible ways in which personal details held on computer could be misused.

(City and Guilds)

▷ **Question 8** *Question data*

> The following organizations holding personal information have direct
> computer links:
>
> ▶ The banks and the Inland Revenue
> ▶ The Police National Computer and the DVLC

Suggest possible consequences of the exchange of information, identifying the advantages
and disadvantages of these links.

(City and Guilds)

▷ **Question 9** Credit card companies use computers to calculate the monthly bills for all of their customers. This means that there is a large amount of personal data being stored. This
information is now protected but there are a number of ways that it could be used against
cardholders even without them knowing.

(a) List two other organizations that might like to use this information.
(b) State how this could affect the customer.
(c) Describe the ways that, in the period of an average week, a person could give personal
information to organizations which might keep it on a computer system.

(NDTEF)

▷ **Question 10** (a) Shane is a computer systems manager at Swish Garage. It is his responsibility to
ensure that all information about garage personnel and customers is kept confidential.
   Shane has set up the computer system so that confidentiality can be maintained. He
has made it necessary for all computer users to use a personal password to enter the
computer system.
   (i) Describe ONE other measure that Shane could have built into the computer
   system.
   (ii) Describe TWO instructions, which Shane would insist that all garage staff who
   use the computer follow, to protect confidentiality.
(b) All administration in the garage offices is now carried out using computers.
Give TWO reasons why the owners of the garage have introduced computers rather
than continuing to use manual methods.
(c) Give TWO reasons why the employees at the garage might not have been happy about
the introduction of computers.
(d) When customers ring up to book a van for hire, Jasmine uses the keyboard to enter
the enquiry. A list of possible vans available is shown on the screen. After the customer chooses a van, Jasmine gets a printed copy of the hire details and updates the
Vanhire File.
   Draw a systems flowchart for this process.

(London)

 EXAMINATION ANSWERS

▷ **Answer 1** Cheap personal computers
Electronic mail

▷ **Answer 2** Two from:
to make sure they are in correct year group/classes
to print out on school reports
any suitable answer

▷ **Answer 3** (a) Any three, for example:
    The amount of money in their accounts.
    Details of any loan they might have.
    Their credit rating.
    Their telephone numbers.
    Their employer, etc.

(b) Knowledge of the amount of money in a customer's account could be useful to people selling insurance, etc.
    A customer would be embarrassed if a credit agency knew their employer and informed the employer of their outstanding loans.
    Information given in confidence to a doctor would be misused if it were printed in a newspaper.

▷ **Answer 4** EFTPOS terminals in shops are connected via the telephone system to the bank's computer. When a customer's magnetic stripe card is read, money can be transferred directly from the customer's account to the shop's account.

Benefits
To the shopkeeper:
    ▶   No handling of cash or cheques.
    ▶   Immediate payment.
To the bank:
    ▶   No handling of cash or cheques.
    ▶   Fewer staff needed, therefore lower costs.
To the customer:
    ▶   No need to carry cash.
Drawbacks
To the shopkeeper and the bank:
    ▶   Expensive to install and maintain.
    ▶   Fraud using EFTPOS is difficult to detect.
To the customer:
    ▶   Could slow down the payment process delaying the customer. Cash payment is faster.

▷ **Answer 5** (a) It is difficult to assess the impact of IT on the total number of jobs available. In some industries IT has lead to job losses. However, IT has also stimulated demand and caused jobs to be created in IT related work.

(b) The skills needed to find a job have changed. Manual and semi-manual work is less available. IT skills are needed for many jobs.

(c) Fewer employees need be exposed to dirty or dangerous working conditions as computer controlled machines can now do this work.

(d) Workers who use IT are far more productive than those who don't use IT.

▷ **Answer 6** This system ensures that users of particular roads pay to do so. The roads charged for are likely to be motorways or in city centres.
    Charging for the use of roads in city centres encourages commuters to use public transport. Bus and railway operators would benefit as the number of passengers would increase. However, the number of people travelling into city centres might fall overall. This could result in reduced sales for city centre shops.
    Charging for motorways would discourage drivers from using them. Traffic on roads other than motorways would increase. There would be more traffic passing through villages, towns, etc. Residents would not like the increased congestion, noise and pollution. The drivers who can afford motorway charges would benefit as there would be less traffic on them.

If the computer can record every car's movements, a car could be followed wherever it went. The police could track criminals and terrorists. However, not all governments are democratic and respect individual freedoms. The ability to track the movements of a car could be used to control and restrain people for political or similar purposes. This deprives people of their human rights.

▷ **Answer 7**
- Information may be accessed by unauthorized people.
- Information may be transferred or sold to organizations which misuse it.
- Information may be incorrect or out-of-date. This may lead to authorized users taking inappropriate actions.

▷ **Answer 8**   *Banks and the Inland Revenue*:
Advantages to IR:
- Tax can be deducted directly from tax payers' accounts, e.g. tax on interest earned.
- The Inland Revenue can check up on taxpayers' finances. Fraud can be detected more easily.

Advantages to the Inland Revenue could be considered disadvantages to taxpayers.
Police and the DVLC:
Advantages to police:
- Car owners can be traced easily.
- Criminals could be prevented from legally owning cars.

Advantages to the police are often disadvantages to criminals.

▷ **Answer 9**
(a) Inland Revenue, Mail Order companies, etc. That is, any organization interested in how much money you have.
(b) Customers could be sent junk mail.
   The Inland Revenue may suspect that a customer is spending more than their declared income and investigate them for tax fraud.
(c) You could register as a patient of a doctor, dentist, etc. You could join a library or buy a bus pass. You could open an account at a bank or building society.

▷ **Answer 10**
(a) (i) Put passwords on all files. Use data encryption when confidential information is sent over the network.
   (ii) Use obscure passwords. Do not let others get hold of your password. Change your password frequently.
(b) Accurate, reliable calculations. Fast access to information. Ability to select the information needed. Fewer staff needed, so reduced costs.
(c) May have to retrain as they do not have IT skills. May fear redundancy as fewer workers are needed.
(d)

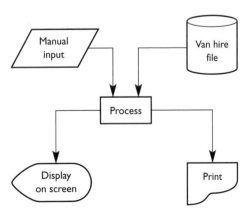

Fig. 13.6 Flowchart

EXAMINATION QUESTION WITH STUDENT ANSWER

'ABC Books' is a company that sends out books by mail order. It keeps its customer list on a computer. 'Shark Loans Ltd' asks them for a copy of their customer list so that they can send out some literature advertising their loans. What response should ABC Books make to Shark Loans? Give reasons for your answer.

ABC Books can sell its customer list to Shark Loan Ltd. This would help ABC books make more money.

(SEG, 1993)

▷ **Examiner's comment**   This answer is correct but incomplete. It is expensive to collect and keep up-to-date large data files. Selling its customer list would certainly help ABC Books with these costs. However, not all the customers of ABC Books will want to receive advertising from Shark Loans through the mail. This is widely regarded as junk mail. Many customers will stop buying from ABC Books if they know their details will be given to Shark Loans.

More importantly, the Data Protection Act only allows data to be used for the purpose it is collected. ABC Books can only give it to Shark Loans if all their customers agree.

SUMMARY

This chapter looks at the impact IT has on our lives.

▷ As IT is introduced into the workplace, some other skills are no longer needed. For example, typists have been replaced by workprocessor operators.

▷ Some jobs disappear or are done in new ways. For example, there are very few mechanical watchmakers but many electronic digital watches are made.

▷ New jobs are created. For example, manufacturing hardware and writing software.

▷ Teleworking is increasingly common. It helps the house-bound find work; improves the environment by reducing traffic congestion; and cuts employers expenses by reducing the costs of a central workplace.

▷ IT systems can store very large volumes of information and give fast access to it.

▷ Personal infomation about you and your family may be stored on IT systems by doctors, the DHSS, local authorities, schools, the police, banks, employers and others. These IT systems can be used to improve services but your privacy may suffer. For example, they help us find criminals but could be used to enforce unreasonable levels of social control.

▷ The 1984 Data Protection Act regulations the use of personal information. Users of personal information must register with the Data Protection Registrar, and they must:

  ▷ obtain personal information fairly and by lawful means;

  ▷ only use it for authorized purposes;

  ▷ only disclose it to authorized people;

  ▷ keep it accurate and up-to-date;

  ▷ only keep it as long as they need it;

  ▷ tell people what personal information is kept about them, and allow them to correct it;

  ▷ keep it secure.

▷ Lifestyle and leisure are also affected by IT systems.

  ▷ Domestic work has been made easier. For example, automatic washing machines have replaced manual washers.

  ▷ How we spend our leisure time is affected by the technology we have at home. For example, TV, home computers, video, satelite and cable technology affect what we are able to do from home.

  ▷ The increasing use of cash cards has led to a dramatic reduction in the use of cash in notes and coins.

▷ The place of change is rapid and will continue. It is important to keep up-to-date with new developments to ensure that we use IT effectively.

Index